# 5 Days IN MANILA

*A Story of
Strength and
Perseverance
through
Overwhelming Odds*

William F. Sansone

*the Peppertree Press*
www.peppertreepublishing.com

Copyright © William F. Sansone, 2024

All rights reserved. Published by the Peppertree Press, LLC. the Peppertree Press and associated logos are trademarks of the Peppertree Press, LLC. No part of this publication may be reproduced, stored in a retrieval system, transmitted in any form or by any means, electronic, mechanical, photocopying, recording, or otherwise, without prior written permission of the publisher and author/illustrator. Graphic design by Elizabeth Parry.

For information regarding permission,
call 941-922-2662 or contact us at our website:
www.peppertreepublishing.com
or write to: The Peppertree Press, LLC.
Attention: Publisher
715 N. Washington Blvd., Suite B
Sarasota, Florida 34236

ISBN: 978-1-61493-912-2
Library of Congress: 2023919032
Printed: January 2024

Manufactured in the United State of America.

# Lovingly Dedicated to:

*Julia McFetridge Sansone*
*&*
*Daniel James Cavallaro*

# Table of Contents

**Opening Statement** . . . . . . . . . . . . . . . . . . . . . . . . . . . . . . . . . . . . . . . vii

**DAY ONE:** Chapter One: And So It Begins . . . . . . . . . . . . . . . . . . . . . . 1
**DAY ONE:** Chapter Two: Steppin' Out . . . . . . . . . . . . . . . . . . . . . . . . . 19
**DAY ONE:** Chapter Three: Bayleaf Intramuros Hotel . . . . . . . . . . . . . 29
    IT IS AN ANONYMOUS PROGRAM . . . . . . . . . . . . . . . . . . . . . . . 43
    GET HONEST WITH YOURSELF . . . . . . . . . . . . . . . . . . . . . . . . . 49
**DAY ONE:** Chapter Four: Bureau of Immigration . . . . . . . . . . . . . . . . 57
**DAY ONE:** Chapter Five: Miles to Go Before I Sleep . . . . . . . . . . . . . . 71
    DON'T SWEAT THE SMALL SHIT AND IT'S ALL SMALL SHIT . . . 83

**DAY TWO:** Chapter One: United States Embassy . . . . . . . . . . . . . . . . 91
    WHO ARE YOU CREEPO? WHO ARE YOU? . . . . . . . . . . . . . . . . 117
**DAY TWO:** Chapter Two: Rizal Park . . . . . . . . . . . . . . . . . . . . . . . . . . 123
**DAY TWO:** Chapter Three: Billy and the Barber . . . . . . . . . . . . . . . . 133
**DAY TWO:** Chapter Four: National Bureau of Investigation . . . . . 141
    THERE ARE NO ATHEISTS IN FOXHOLES . . . . . . . . . . . . . . . . . 165
**DAY TWO:** Chapter Five: Into the Night . . . . . . . . . . . . . . . . . . . . . . 175

**DAY THREE:** Chapter One: Billy v. United States
                    Embassy, Part II . . . . . . . . . . . . . . . . . . . . . . . . 181
**DAY THREE:** Chapter Two: Chinatown . . . . . . . . . . . . . . . . . . . . . . 199
    BEING CONVINCED . . . . . . . . . . . . . . . . . . . . . . . . . . . . . . . . . 211
**DAY THREE:** Chapter Three: Jodieeeeee . . . . . . . . . . . . . . . . . . . . . . 217
**DAY THREE:** Chapter Four: Daddy's Little Girl . . . . . . . . . . . . . . . 229
**DAY THREE:** Chapter Five: God Have Mercy on Me . . . . . . . . . . . 239
    I'M NOT MUCH, BUT I'M ALL I THINK ABOUT . . . . . . . . . . . 243
**DAY THREE:** Chapter Six: I'm Not Judging Anybody But . . . . . . . 249

**DAY FOUR:** Chapter One: Live from Manila,
                It's Dead Air Sansone!. . . . . . . . . . . . . . . . . . . . . .257

**DAY FOUR:** Chapter Two: Camp Bagong Diwa,
                Bicutan, Taguig City . . . . . . . . . . . . . . . . . . . . . . 267

    *AS BILL SEES IT....* . . . . . . . . . . . . . . . . . . . . . . . . . . . . . . . . . . . . . . . 277

**DAY FOUR:** Chapter Three: Two Suitcases,
                Two Cabs, and One Fight. . . . . . . . . . . . . . . . . . .281

    CONTEMPT PRIOR TO INVESTIGATION . . . . . . . . . . . . . . . . . . 299

**DAY FOUR:** Chapter Four: I Came to Believe . . . . . . . . . . . . . . . . . 305

**DAY FIVE:** Chapter One: The Bags – Part Two . . . . . . . . . . . . . . . . .311

    SOMETIMES A WALK BECOMES A CRAWL . . . . . . . . . . . . . . 321

**DAY FIVE:** Chapter Two: A Walk About. . . . . . . . . . . . . . . . . . . . . . .325

    GOD DIDN'T SAVE ME FROM DROWNING
    TO KICK MY ASS ON THE BEACH. . . . . . . . . . . . . . . . . . . . . . . . 329

**DAY FIVE:** Chapter Three: The Great Escape. . . . . . . . . . . . . . . . . .339

**DAY FIVE:** Chapter Four: And Let There Be Light . . . . . . . . . . . . . 349

**Closing Statement:** Manila – Six Months Later –
                   The Blacklist . . . . . . . . . . . . . . . . . . . . . . . . . . . . . .359

*Daniel J. Cavallaro Foundation* . . . . . . . . . . . . . . . . . . . . . . . . . . . 367

**About the Author** . . . . . . . . . . . . . . . . . . . . . . . . . . . . . . . . . . . . . . . . 368

# Opening Statement

I am a criminal defense attorney, so in my world, the criminal justice system, I deal in opening statements, not prologs. An opening statement is kind of like a roadmap for the jury, a mechanism to inform the jury what is about to come and what I believe the evidence will show. In an opening statement, my goal is to get my audience to sit back in their seat, settle in, and think to themselves, "well this is going to be interesting."

This memoir has three stories interwoven into one and interconnected like vines growing up a trunk of a tree. At times, the vines may diverge, one going right and the other left. However, if they come from the same source, if the root is cut, the vines will wither and die. *5 Days in Manila* is first about a mind-bending battle to free my client from a Manila prison. This story spans two continents, two cultures, thirteen time zones, and a single desire to do what is right and just in the face of tremendous obstacles. The second story is an old-fashioned love story between Maria and me, two friends who reconnected after decades apart to join as one with a singleness of heart and an agape love that I thought only existed in the pens of novelists and authors of the Bible. A kind of love that no longer existed if it ever really existed at all.

The third story weaves through my life in everything I do, every thought I have, every breath I take. It is the story of my decision to completely humble myself and to admit that I was powerless over alcohol, my own thoughts, and my character defects, and walk into the rooms of Alcoholics Anonymous and completely surrender myself to my Higher Power. In doing so, I can awake from the terrible nightmare that had become my life. No one of these stories are complete without the other. No one can be told without the other. They exist together. The three are one.

Ladies and gentlemen of the jury, what I believe the evidence will show is that universal truths about the human condition do exist: love, loss, pain, pleasure, right and wrong, and that the highest position in life is being a humble servant to others. I want to thank anyone who picks up this book and peels back its pages for letting me share, and I hope you see something of your life amidst the tangle of vines and thorns of mine.

## 5 Days in Manila

This is a memoir. All of the events described in this book actually happened, although synthesized through the prism of my mind and memory. All quoted conversations are to the best of my recollection but are not exact. Some names have been changed to protect certain identities. If you see yourself in these pages, don't we all …

## Day 1

## Chapter One

# And So It Begins

BAM! BAM! BAM! The sound lifts me from my coma. Where am I? The room is dark. My feet hit the floor. It is cold. My head hurts. I move towards the sound, not sure where I am, or where I am going, just moving towards the sound. I open the door. A man stands in front of me in brown slacks and a collared shirt. The shirt says *Armada Hotel* on the pocket. He is a small man, young, maybe twenty-two years old, with olive skin, short dark hair swept to one side, and a smile that reveals straight white teeth.

"Room cleaning?" he asks in a high-pitched voice.

"No, thanks," I say as I close the door.

"Who was that?" Maria asks from the darkness.

"Room service."

*Why would they come so early?* I cannot remember the layout of the room and carefully make my way in the dark. We arrived at the hotel at one in the morning after three flights, and twenty-six hours of travel. Our plane landed in Manila, Philippines, at 1:00 a.m. on December 4 after traveling through thirteen times zones. We left Tampa on December 2 and while travelling at over 600 mph at 39,000 feet somewhere over the Arctic Circle on December 3, my birthday came and went.

I hit a couple of switches and then a light comes on. I walk over to my phone: 10:02 a.m.

"It's ten clock in the morning."

"No way," Maria says as she sits up from under the covers. Maria looks good in the morning. She looks good all the time. We have known each other for almost thirty years, meeting first in high school. We ran with the same crowd, going to the same parties, hanging out in the parking lot at Burger King when there was nothing else do, drinking beer and hoping the manager wouldn't come out and tell us to leave. We sat in the hall together as friends before class and talked about what high school kids in the late 1980s talked about: music videos, whose dad had a car phone, who had hooked up with whom over the weekend, and where everyone was going to go that weekend. Even though we never dated, we did kiss one night.

Two days after Halloween 1988, Ybor City in Tampa had a citywide Halloween party called Guavaween, a reason for everyone in the city to wear their costumes one more time before putting them away. Ybor City is the old cigar-making city built on the backs of Cuban immigrants in the late 1880s. It sits just north of downtown Tampa. The main street is Seventh Avenue, and is lined with old brick historic buildings. The cigar factories are gone, replaced with bars, tattoo parlors, shops, and law offices. I could go on, but this story is not about Tampa or Ybor City, but Manila and what happened in the five days Maria and I spent there, arriving and not knowing what we would do or what we *could* do.

We came to Manila to get my client out of a Filipino prison. I am a criminal defense attorney. Maria is a schoolteacher. She came to Manila to help me. Help me do *what*, we were not sure, but she came to help with whatever it was I was going to do.

But before I move on—about that kiss on Guavaween night 1988, in the backseat of someone's car. We both remember that kiss, though we never talked about it after that night. Our next kiss would be twenty-eight years later, standing in the doorway of her mother's home as we held each other up against weight of the world that had lain so heavily upon us.

Maria and I dress quickly, deciding to venture out into the foreign city for a couple of hours before I am to meet Ron's Filipino lawyer at the Bayleaf Intramuros Hotel in the old historic part of Manila. Ron is my client. He is an American lawyer from Atlanta, Georgia. He was arrested by the Filipino government at the behest of the United States and is sitting in a Filipino detention camp, waiting to be deported back to the United States. However, there is one problem: the United States is not going to pick Ron up at that camp to take him back to the United States. The arrest warrant was issued by a federal judge in Tampa, on the basis that Ron violated the terms of his supervised release by leaving the country without permission. Less than a week after Ron was arrested, I went to federal court and had the judge withdraw the arrest warrant. The judge agreed that Ron actually did have permission to leave the country, and the arrest warrant should never have been issued.

Problem solved—right? The judge withdrew the arrest warrant in August. It is now December. Ron is still in the Filipino detention facility and the Filipino government is still waiting for the United States to come pick him up on the non-existent warrant to take him back to the United States

See the problem? That is never going to happen, because the arrest warrant was withdrawn. The United States is never going to pick Ron up and take him back to the United States. So there he sat, month after month. Letter after letter that I sent to various government agencies got us nowhere. The letters were either ignored or unread.

I sent one of my many letters to the attaché at the United States Embassy in Manila. He was the one who requested that the Filipino government arrest Ron and hold him for deportation back to the United States. In my letter, I explained that the warrant had been withdrawn, and requested that he please notify the Filipino government. I faxed this letter to the United States Embassy in Manila from my office in Tampa, Florida. I attached a copy of the Court's Order withdrawing the arrest warrant, the warrant upon which the attaché based his request that the Filipino government arrest Ron.

Simple right? Certainly, the attaché would send the letter to the Filipino government and Ron would be freed. I received no response.

Not even a "Thank you for your letter, and we are looking into the issue." Not a "we will get back to you." Not a "Sorry, we cannot help." Not a "Go pound sand, you slime ball criminal defense attorney." Nothing—silence. My efforts went ignored, and so Ron sat in a filthy Manila jail waiting—waiting for me to do something.

I also made phone calls to the State Department in Washington DC. After I had the arrest warrant withdrawn, I needed to have Ron's passport reissued. At the time of his arrest, his passport was about to expire and the government seized it.

Ron told me all of this from the jail in Manila. He called me one night. When my phone rang, I saw it was a call from the Philippines. Ron told me what had happened—that he was arrested for leaving the United States without permission and was being detained in a Manila jail.

Halfway through our conversation I asked, "How are you calling me?"

"I bribed a guard 5,000 pesos to bring me a phone. Everything is for sale in Manila, but at a price." And so it went—every few days Ron would call to hear my progress. Call after call after call, he was so disappointed.

I finally contacted an actual person at the State Department on the phone to help me with Ron's passport issue. I sent him a letter explaining the entire situation, and a copy of the federal order withdrawing the warrant. Ron told me that he could not leave the prison or the country without a valid US passport.

This State Department representative told me, "Well, I have looked into this, and we can reissue your client a valid passport. I will call you in just a little while and let you know if I can get this signed off by my supervisor." He sounded young—too young, as if he was an intern who just picked up the phone and was playing US agent, but I believed him. I had to. I had no other choice.

"Thank you so much," I told him. "I look forward to hearing from you." At the time of that call, I was sitting in the public library in

Kanab, Utah. Maria and I had come to southern Utah to hike the national parks: Zion, Bryce Canyon, Canyonlands, and the northern rim of the Grand Canyon. We were celebrating Maria's birthday and our love for one another. As I sat back in the library chair, Maria walked in with her backpack on. She was wearing a red bandana on her head and carried her hiking stick, since that day we were hiking the Narrows in Zion National Park.

"How did it go?" she asked.

"Great! I think he will be out soon." That was the first week of September. It is now December. Ron is not out. He is still sitting in jail rotting, waiting for me to do something—anything—to get him out.

The State Department did reissue Ron's passport, but that was all. The Filipino government still held Ron and was waiting for the United States to come pick him up and deport him, but this was not going to happen. The arrest warrant had been withdrawn, but the Filipino government did not know that and, as the United States refused to tell them that they were never going to pick Ron up, there he sat.

Ron called me after Maria and I returned from Utah. I sat in Maria's apartment that night drinking decaf coffee and eating a green apple with peanut butter, something I do every night.

"I hired a Filipino lawyer to help us." He used the word "us" and I guess that was right. We were in this together. We had been in this together for over two years, when I first met Ron in the medical unit of the Pinellas County Florida jail. He was shopping for lawyers at that time to get him out of a federal indictment, and a friend of mine had given him my name. I went to the jail to be interviewed.

When I arrived at the medical unit of the jail, I didn't know what to expect. I knew that Ron was a lawyer from Georgia, who was sick and was in legal trouble. The medical unit is a large room, about the size of a small gymnasium. People sleep in individual cubicles, much like an office setting.

I told the deputy at the front desk that I was there to see Ron. He placed me in a small office and told me to wait. A few minutes later, he opened the door and Ron arrived using a walker and in obvious pain. As he struggled to enter, he apologized for making me wait. "I don't run so fast," he said as I helped him into a chair.

Over the next eighteen months, we would meet dozens of times in this room, going over police reports, video evidence, case law, strategy, sharing laughter, anger, frustration, and tears. Our lives would become intertwined.

One of the things I love about being a criminal defense attorney is being able to help people in times of crisis. It's not about the law, the money, or even the need to be at the top of my profession. I enjoy the personal nature of the job. In an age when most communications are electronic, criminal defense depends upon personal interaction, relationships, and old-fashioned *storytelling*.

I must connect with my clients; get to know them, as well as their spouses, children, parents, and friends. I might need all of them to weave together a story that either explains how my client is innocent of the charges or explain why the charges occurred. Mitigation is storytelling. Storytelling is not something you are taught in law school, but it is one of the most effective tools an advocate has.

That's really how I see myself—as an *advocate*. I advocate for those who have no voice. In representing a client, I need to connect with the prosecutor, that person who swore an oath to protect the citizens of the State of Florida, and convince them that my client does *not* deserve the punishment usually handed out to persons who commit this particular crime, because my client is different. My client has a story. That's my job, to tell their story.

> *Storytelling.* About three years ago, another father had called me and said he wanted to help his son. His eighteen-year-old child was charged with armed burglary and was facing a ten-year minimum mandatory sentence in Florida state prison,

and was offered three years by the State Attorney's office. The State had a full confession, with DNA evidence at the scene, and the stolen items were in the kid's room, which the father had allowed law enforcement to search. Bad facts.

I had told the father that I was not sure I could do anything more than his public defender, who was telling him to take the deal, but the father insisted that he understood and still wanted someone to fight for his son. Over the next six months, I met with the prosecutor a dozen times. I sent letters outlining my client's troubled childhood, his struggle with mental health issues, and found members of his community who were willing to come forward and speak on his behalf. However, I never once spoke with the prosecutor about the facts of the case, because the facts were terrible. My client was guilty. I only spoke to her about my client.

Professional begging is not a course in law school, but one I practice more than filing motions to suppress evidence. *Storytelling.* That's what that case was about. Tell the State a story about this kid. In the end, my client did what he had to do—he pled guilty, but he was offered a withhold of adjudication, so he would not be a convicted felon.

He would spend six months in county jail, and with a probation term of three years. His father cried at sentencing. He thanked me for saving his son's life, sharing how his son would never have made it in prison. The kid told me he would never forget me. Personal relationships. Personal interactions. *Storytelling.*

Ron's voice sounded clear, even though he was nine thousand miles away in a Filipino jail. "We need to get the State Department or the Embassy to send a letter to the Bureau of Immigration here in Manila telling them that I am no longer a fugitive of the United States. That is the only thing holding me here."

I took a sip of my coffee and washed down the remnants of the peanut butter sticking to the roof of my mouth. "Okay, I guess I start with the Embassy?"

Maria knew I was talking to Ron and sat down next to me. In the next few months, Ron and his incarceration in a foreign jail would consume not just my life, but hers, too.

"I think we need to start with everyone," Ron said. "I would call the Embassy and tell them the situation. I would call your contact at the State Department, the guy who helped you get my passport reinstated. Someone just needs to tell the Filipino government what is going on."

Ron's voice sounded desperate, ragged, strained. During the course of litigating his criminal case, Ron was confident. He is both a lawyer and a journalist. He has visited over one hundred sixty-seven countries and lived in a dozen of them. We strategized about his case, discussed questions to ask our expert witness, and decided what motions would be the most effective to file. I spent hour upon hour in that small office in the corner of the medical unit of the Pinellas County jail working with Ron. He was confident. We were a team.

"I don't know how much longer I can stay here," Ron's voice quivered.

At the time of his case in Tampa, Ron was in the medical unit of the Pinellas County jail, because he needed quadruple bypass surgery, a hip replacement, and the veins in his lower legs removed. He had high blood pressure, high cholesterol, and was at risk for nine different ways of immediately dropping dead. He shuffled into the Pinellas County jail on a walker.

Eighteen months later, when I resolved his case, he rolled out of the jail in a wheelchair. Ron's time in the medical unit was not a physical rehabilitative stay. Sure, the jail kept him alive, but his body slowly began to deteriorate.

At one point, I had to go to federal court to try and convince a judge that Ron was not receiving proper care—he needed to go to a specialist outside of the jail. Ron had developed sores on his feet and lower legs. Because of his hip, he was unable to bend down to care for the wounds. The jail nurse did apply ointment and changed his bandage every three days, but three days of festering in puss between cleanings caused his wounds to grow, deepen, blacken, and then travel up his legs. Ron went four months without washing his feet.

After a hearing in federal court—a much more contentious hearing than I had expected—all I wanted was to take him to a doctor. The Court granted my motion and allowed the appointment with a specialist. When the United States Marshal wheeled Ron through the back door of the doctor's office, it was the first and only time I would see Ron outside of custody.

I began with the United States Embassy to the Philippines, as Ron suggested. They had issued a letter to the Filipino government requesting Ron's arrest, so all they had to do was issue a letter to the Filipino government informing them Ron was no longer wanted by the United States—simple.

I called to make this simple request for a simple letter.

Working from my home in Tampa to secure Ron's release was difficult because of the time change. Manila is thirteen hours ahead. After a long day running the circuit as a criminal defense attorney, driving from court to court in county after county, and then running my kids to soccer practice, making dinner, and putting them down for bed, I had no desire to call the United States Embassy in Manila at 10 o'clock in the evening to talk about Ron.

If this were a novel, the attorney character would be living in some bad-ass condo, drinking coffee, and sitting next to a wall lined with documents outlining the strategy for getting Ron released from custody. The camera would show the clock ticking. The hours of the clock would turn as the attorney character diligently spent all his waking hours trying to secure his client's release.

However, this is not a novel, but a memoir, a true story, and all this really happened. I did not want to call the Embassy for Ron. I was tired. I wanted to read my book, snuggle with Maria, talk with her about her day, read a Bible verse together, love, and laugh.

I am not an attorney character in a movie. I am a man. I am selfish and self-centered to the core, spiritually sick, trying to work my recovery step by step, trying to build a relationship with my Higher Power, and trying to crush my ego, my self-will that had led my life down a path of alcohol and two failed marriages.

I am not the hero of this story. I don't have a bad ass condo. I don't own a damn thing. Everything is gone—wives, houses, beach condos, and my sanity. That last one, my sanity, I am trying to get back slowly, one day, one moment at a time. I am not a hero. I am a nobody, who is just beginning to understand that this is the key to my recovery.

"Hello," I said as the voice on the other line cheerfully chirped, "'Good morning, United States Embassy." I paused, where should I begin?

"I have a client who was arrested by the Filipino government at the request of the United States, based on an US arrest warrant. I had that arrest warrant withdrawn. The Filipino government is holding my client as a fugitive waiting for the United States to come pick him up and deport him to the United States. One problem, a big problem, is that this will never happen because the arrest warrant was withdrawn. So the United States is never going to pick up my client, who is just sitting in custody."

"What would you like me to do?" The voice on the other end of the line was young, high pitched. She spoke English very well, but I could tell her English was learned not in the home or on the streets, but at school. She spoke formally. Her grammar was perfect, as if she were reading her responses to my questions from a cue card.

"I would like you, or someone there, to inform the Filipino government that the United States will not be picking up my client, and that he is no longer a fugitive." I poured myself another cup of decaf.

"Sir, to whom would you like to speak?"

"I don't know—you tell me."

"How would I know that, sir?"

"Because you work for the Embassy and I don't."

"That is correct, sir." Silence ensued.

"So, since you work for the Embassy, and I don't, I want someone in your office to send a letter to the Filipino government telling them my client is no longer a fugitive of the United States."

"I can't do that, sir."

"Why not?

"I work the phones, sir."

"I understand that." I glanced up at the clock, almost 10:30 at night. My head hurt. "As I said, I don't really need you personally to inform the Filipino government that my client is no longer a fugitive, but I do need someone else to do that."

"To whom would you like to speak to, sir?"

*Was she kidding?* "Someone who can do what I requested."

"And what was that, sir?"

I paused. (*A technique I had learned in my recovery.*) I am trying to gather myself before exploding through the phone, the way I would have reacted before my recovery began.

"Sir, are you still on the line?"

"Yes, I am still on the line."

"Yes, sir, to whom would you like to speak?"

"Someone who can help me."

"And what do you need, sir?"

That was the first time I almost jumped out of my skin when speaking to someone at the United States Embassy in Manila, but it would not be the last.

"I need ... " Then I took a deep breath and ran my fingers through my hair.

Maria walked into the room. She was wearing a t-shirt and underwear. So flippin' cute. She could see something was wrong.

"What's going on?" she mouthed to me.

I shook my head back and forth, telling her it was too much to talk about now.

"I need," I continued with the young foreign lady on the other line, "someone who can assist me in getting my client out of Filipino custody."

"I can let you speak with Mark." She told me his last name. (I am not keeping his last name out of this book to protect him. Rather, I don't remember it, because he was worthless.)

"Okay. Let me speak to Mark."

"He's at the window." She did not continue, as if I should know to what "window" she was referring and understand the great importance of Mark being at that window.

"Can you get him for me?"

"No, sir."

"Why not?"

"Because he is speaking to someone at the window."

"Can you tell him I called?"

"Yes, sir."

"Will he call me back?"

"I don't know, sir."

"Can you make sure he calls me back?"

"I can only tell him, sir."

"Okay, will you tell him?"

"Yes, sir, but he's at the window now, sir."

"I got that. Let me give you my name and number." I told her my name and my number, and that I was calling from the United States.

"Thank you, sir. I will give him the message, sir." Throughout the entire conversation, her voice, the pitch and inflection, never changed, never wavered. She stuck to the cue cards.

"Thank you. Have a good night—I mean morning." I said.

My conversation with the contact I had at State Department in Washington, DC, the person who helped me secure Ron a new passport, went something like this.

"Hi, my name is Bill Sansone and you helped me get a passport issued for my client who was put into a Filipino jail about a month ago."

"Yes, I remember."

Thank God, he remembered. It had only been three weeks, but the minds of government employees work in strange ways, and I can freely say that, because I used to be a government employee. My mind would selectively shut down, depending upon who was on the other line and what that person's question was.

"Well, my client is still in custody. You see, I had the arrest warrant withdrawn. So you, the United States, are no longer going to pick him up and bring him back to the US, because he no longer is a fugitive. One problem is that the Filipino government still thinks that the United States is coming to pick him up to deport him back to the United States. However, that is not going to happen, so my client is just sitting in jail waiting for something that will never happen."

"I see the problem."

Thank God almighty, he sees the problem. An official at the State Department in Washington, DC. understands the issue, on the first call—Amazing Grace.

"What would you like me to do?"

I almost jumped out of my skin. Should I say, "Why don't you leave the office early, hang out with friends at a bar, get shitfaced, and forget that I even called?" *What the hell do you think I want you to do?* I did not say this, but wanted to. PAUSE. BREATHE.

"I would like someone at the State Department—it does not have to be you—to inform the Filipino government that my client is no longer a fugitive of the United States. Therefore, the United States is not going to pick him up at the jail." *There, that was it—clear and to the point.*

"We don't get involved in telling the Filipino government what to do."

"I'm not asking you to tell the Filipino government what to do. I am asking you to tell them the truth, a fact that the United States is never going to pick my client up. After that, the Filipino government can do whatever they want."

"So what is it that you want?" he asked.

*Was I not speaking English?* "I want someone in the State Department," and then I took a breath, and spoke even more slowly, "to write a letter to the Filipino government and inform them that my client is no longer a fugitive, and the United Sates is not coming to pick him up."

"We are not a law enforcement agency. We don't do that. You will have to get another agency involved to do that."

"Who do you suggest?"

"I don't know, maybe the FBI, or the United States Attorney's office. I don't really know."

"So the State Department is not willing to inform the Filipino government the truth about my client? Are you aware that the only reason he is being held in that hellhole is that the Filipino government is keeping him detained at your request and is waiting for you to come pick him up."

"Not me, sir."

"I know not you, personally—I mean the United States of America, but you do represent the United States of America."

As my voice rose again, Maria came back out of the bedroom. She mouthed, *"What's going on?"*

I mouthed back, *"Unbelievable."*

"Sir, the State Department doesn't send letters telling other countries what to do. You will need to contact another agency."

I said, "And you don't know who I should contact?"

"No sir, I don't."

"Do you understand that my client is seventy years old, and has to use a walker to get around? He is an American lawyer from Atlanta. The State Department requested that the Filipino government arrest him. He is in jail because of a warrant that was immediately withdrawn, but now he is classified as a fugitive of the United States. He has serious health problems and is dying in that jail. You're saying that the State Department won't simply send a short letter to the Filipino government informing them that my client is no longer a fugitive of the United States? Is that accurate?"

"Sir, we will not send a letter. As I told you, we are not a law enforcement agency. You will need to contact another agency. As for his health issues, we can help with that. If he is not getting the health care he needs, we can send an official to the jail to do an assessment, and make sure he gets the medical attention he needs."

"So you will make sure he is healthy in jail, but will not help him get out."

"Sir ... " Now, the voice on the other end sounded annoyed.

"Why don't you send the letter for which I am asking with the person who will go to make sure my client is healthy as he rots in prison?"

"Sir, we don't need to go over this again."

"No we don't. I understand that the State Department will not write a two-sentence letter."

"Sir, we are not ... "

" ... a law enforcement agency. I know. You have made that clear." *Was he also reading from cue cards?*

I hung up the phone. I looked at my watch—11:15 p.m. here, 12:15 p.m. the next day in Manila. Ron knew I was going to talk with the State Department that night. He was hopeful. I could hear it in his voice. Excited, like a kid a few days before Christmas.

I had gotten to know Ron quite well over the past two years. I saw his highs and lows, as his case wound itself through the criminal justice system. He was a lawyer and smart. He had lived all over the world. He was confident, but not cocky. However, he was in jail now, and some of that confidence that he had built up through his seventy years on this earth had begun to erode, washed away by wave after wave of setbacks in his case.

Sometimes as he spoke to me, I could feel the tears in his eyes and hear the pain in his voice. He was scared and vulnerable. There were many times I would sit with him in the medical unit of the Pinellas County jail much longer than I had planned, long after we had finished talking about his case, and just let him talk.

As he spoke, I would feel the pressure within him begin to lessen. When it had lowered to a tolerable level, only then would I rise and tell him that I had to go. He always thanked me for coming to see him, and I could tell that he meant for the visit, not just to the legal discussion about his case, but the visit, to keep him sane.

I went to bed that night after speaking with the man from the State Department, without talking to Ron. He would remain hopeful, with a childlike anticipation of the gift of freedom on its way until tomorrow. When I had to inform him of another setback, I would feel the tears begin to well up in his eyes.

The United States Attorney's Office didn't know what to do either. I never called the FBI. That was nonsensical. Ron's probation officer, the one who violated him for leaving the United States without permission, left me one voicemail, and then never returned another one of my calls.

So then I began to write letters to the State Department and to the United States Embassy in Manila, outlining my client's situation and begging for assistance. Months went by. My letters went unanswered.

I could feel the desperation in Ron's voice when he would ask, "How long am I going to stay here?" I didn't know. "I can't stay here. This place is a fucking shithole. I can't bend over. I haven't washed my feet in months. I don't have my medications."

I would sit at my kitchen table late at night, eating my green apples and peanut butter and drinking decaf coffee. I didn't like to remain silent when Ron would ask me, "How long am I going to stay here?" I wanted to give him some hope.

One night, he said, "I am either going to try and escape, or I'm going to kill myself. I can't take it here any longer."

I struggled to find something to say—some words that might keep him alive for a little while longer. Thereafter, some nights when he didn't call, I wondered if he had escaped or killed himself. The days turned into weeks and weeks into months. I prayed for him. I prayed for a solution. I prayed that I be given the wisdom to find the next step, and to take it boldly. Ron was running out of time, and that is the *only* thing I knew for sure.

And as the clock ticked, there Ron sat. A seventy-year-old man on a walker sitting in a Filipino jail waiting for the United States to come get him, something that was never going to happen. No one would do anything to help, not even send a simple two sentence letter.

Would Ron ever get out? Would he escape? Die? I didn't know then. I don't know now.

Now I am in Manila with Maria—a story-telling criminal defense attorney and a third grade school teacher. We travelled nine thousand miles to Manila to get Ron out. I had a plan to meet Chito, Ron's Filipino lawyer, in the lobby of the Bayleaf Intramuros Hotel at 2:00 p.m. on a Monday afternoon. That was the plan.

After months of phone calls to numerous government agencies, both American and Filipino, followed by a letter-writing campaign and numerous emails, all of which went unanswered, this was the plan. Meet a man named Chito at the Bayleaf Intramuros Hotel at 2:00 p.m. on Monday December 4 in Manila, Philippines. That was it. What would come next, we would figure out along the way.

*Day 1*

## Chapter Two

# Steppin' Out

WE STEP OUT of our air-conditioned hotel into the soup that is the Manila morning air. We have four hours until our meeting with Chito, so we decide to explore the city. The air is warm and wet, filled with exhaust and the smell of urine. Cars inch by. Maria and I hold hands and start walking. The sidewalk is in disrepair, as if the roots from a tree had begun to push through the concrete, crumbling it—but there are no trees, only concrete. The sidewalks are exhausted from years of use and neglect. The city is crowded. People are everywhere.

One block from the hotel, we see a long line of makeshift restaurants lining the sidewalk of a side street. They are more like hastily built shacks, all strung together. The food smells good and overpowers the exhaust.

Mostly men sit waiting to be served. They are dressed in construction gear and sit at card tables and folding chairs that are out in front of the kitchens. That's what they are—makeshift kitchens—just enough of a structure to provide protection for the grill and cooking gear.

At night, the restaurateurs lower a piece of plywood or cardboard over the front, giving protection from the rain. In the morning, they pull it back, set out a table and folding chairs, and begin to cook again. The men eat hungrily.

Children play with animals at their feet, mainly dogs and a few cats. These are not the construction workers' kids—just young kids, seven, eight, or nine years old. They are dirty.

*Stepp-in' Out. Maria waiting for a Jeepney.*

I look at my watch. 10:34 a.m. and these kids are already dirty. Most don't wear any shoes. Their toes are darkened by dirt and tar from the streets. I am wearing brand-new running shoes I bought for the trip. They are white, no dirt. My socks smell like Tide. I scrubbed my feet in the shower before we left the hotel.

"Why are these kids not in school?" This is the first of a hundred times Maria would ask this question as we made our way through the streets of Manila. Maria has a gift—a gift given to her—not one learned. Yes, she has learned how to effectively teach during her twenty years in the Hillsborough County public school system, but her true gift is not learned in a classroom or from an instructor.

She has a way with children, a way of understanding and relating to a mind not fully formed. Since my mind is still not fully formed either, her gift has also helped her in dealing with me, but it is in her interactions with children that I see nothing short of a true artist at work. Maria was put on this earth to protect, guide, mold, cherish, nurture, instruct, comfort, shelter, and love children. I have seen her artistry with my kids, when they are angry and cranky and I have lost all patience. However, Maria is able to redirect their thinking, easing their young minds, calming their breathing just by her voice and the way she looks into their eyes. The only thing for which Maria has no patience for is adults and teachers who have no patience for the kids in their charge.

"Why are these kids not in school?" Maria looks at her watch. "It's Monday morning. These kids should be in school." But they are not. They are playing with starving animals on the street at the feet of construction workers, who are eating food from these makeshift kitchens on the side on the road in a city of two million people, in a country being strangled by poverty.

I would not have thought about these kids not being in school. I would have looked at their dirty feet and walked on, as many others would. I would do this because I am not Maria. I do not have the gift, which at this moment must have felt like a curse.

"Oh, baby," I say as my put my arm around her. Tears are in her eyes. This is the first of many times Maria will cry for the forgotten children on the streets of Manila.

We make our way to the corner. The traffic is insane. There are cars, buses, mopeds, motorcycles, taxis, trucks, and Jeepneys everywhere. Jeepneys are the most common and cheapest form of public transportation in Manila. Originally, Jeepneys were made from leftover US military jeeps from the Second World War. In the front, they look like an American jeep, but they have been elongated to accommodate passengers.

Passengers enter the Jeepney from the back, just hopping in. They cram in and line the sides of the vehicle, which have long plastic-covered benches. People pay the fare, only five cents, by passing the money from passenger to passenger until it arrives at the driver, who does not look at who just jumped in, but is constantly looking at the street, changing lanes, which are really only lanes in theory, not in practice, inching through intersections, and pulling off to the side to allow more fares to jump in or out.

We turn at the corner and continue walking. A man on the sidewalk is fanning the flames of a fire made from scraps of wood. He has no fire pit. The fire is on the sidewalk. Food sits next to him. He has no shirt. His hair is long and a cigarette hangs from his mouth. He is cooking, right there on the sidewalk in the middle of the city at ten o'clock on a Monday morning. We look at him. No one else does. This must be normal. Where are we? What is this place? We walk on.

We see more children on the street. "Why are these kids not in school?" Maria walks in front of me. She walks quickly as if on a mission to get somewhere, but I know she doesn't know where she is going—neither one of us does—so we walk on as the city unfolds before us. There are not only children on the streets, but entire families sitting on the sidewalk. I don't know what they are doing, just waiting ... but for what? Maria and I keep walking.

We turn down a side street. People are everywhere, riding bikes, motorcycles, mopeds, walking, sitting, standing, and cooking. The smell of the food begins to overpower the smell of the exhaust. Everywhere people are cooking on the side of streets, and selling to those passing by. They have small carts, kind of like the hot dog vendors one sees on the streets of New York City, but these people are not cooking hot dogs. They are cooking various meats.

Raw meats sit in plastic containers next to the burners. Flies swirl around the meat. The food carts are all down the street. Traffic continues—cars, Jeepneys, and motorcycles, in and out, everywhere. Exhaust, the smell of raw meat, urine. Maria has tears in her eyes.

"What's the matter?"

"I can't take it."

"Take what?"

"All of it. It's overwhelming." The tears hang to the corner of her eyes, not wanting to come out. She pulls down her sunglasses that were resting on the top of her head. "I live for food, but this—I just can't take."

We walk for a few minutes. I stop and take out my phone. We stand in the middle of the road and I take a selfie. For some reason, I want to capture this moment. In the picture we are both smiling. I send the picture to my family and Maria posts it on Facebook. The caption reads, "We are definitely in a foreign land, let the adventure begin."

We are smiling, but not happy. Maria is spinning and I am not sure where she will land. She tells me she needs to go back to the hotel, that the city is too overwhelming. Too much, too fast. We did not prepare to come to Manila. I was busy trying to get Ron out of custody, and Maria only decided to come when we booked our tickets a week and a half before we left.

We did not sit on the couch at night sipping wine and drinking coffee with travel books in our laps, mapping our route through the city and country as we snuggled and imagined ourselves in this new place. We did not read about the history of the city, or ask people who might have travelled here.

We just bought plane tickets and came, for we did not come here on a vacation, but on a mission, a narrowly defined mission—to get Ron out of custody—that is all that mattered. That is why we are here. It is as if we went to bed in Tampa and woke up in some fairytale. But this is not a fairytale. This is reality, the reality of twelve million people living on top of each other in a city with no services to support the poor and struggling. People, families, men, women, children, dogs, cats, chickens, and rats must all fend for themselves, scratch a living from the dirty, cracking, and potholed streets.

As we continue to walk, Maria and I are not smiling, but seem to be the only ones. All of the people we pass in this crowded, congested, mosh pit of a city are smiling, happy. Happy that it's morning or Monday or not raining or that God has blessed them or that food is in their stomachs or that someone cares about them or that they are healthy or … I just don't know.

As we walk, the smiles of the people we pass are infectious, overpowering the exhaust, the flies, the dirt, and the stench. I am the only blond-headed person on the streets. I stand out, and all I get are smiles, smiles from everyone. Some nod as they smile. Some flash their teeth. Some just turn up the corners of their mouths. Some turn their heads slightly to the side as they smile as if slightly embarrassed, but all smile.

The men who are rebuilding a run-down building are yelling back and forth at each other, from floor to floor, directions or orders of what each should be doing. I look up. Each one whose eye I catch slides me a smile in between breaths and yells and orders. I feel welcome, strangely at home. I have been on the streets of Manila for ninety-seven minutes. I begin to smile, as if there was nothing else to do on this Monday morning in Manila but smile.

Maria walks ahead of me. We walk on and on. We walk past a school. Maria stops and looks in. The children are in uniforms. They are playing in a courtyard. "I wonder if they will let me in to observe a class." Maria says, not taking her eyes off of the children. A large banner hangs from the railing on the second story. It reads, "LEARN ENGLISH." Maria takes a picture. The schoolchildren have smiles too, just like the children on the street. I wonder if they are always smiling, or just at us, a beautiful American woman, with her blonde-headed friend. We walk on.

The streets wind through the city like tributaries to a river. Every street is crowded. The power lines overhead are like nothing I have ever seen. They resemble giant and intricate spiderwebs, with seemingly no purpose in design. Hundreds of thin black wires are attached to each pole, maybe thousands. It seems that when a wire stops working, the old one is not taken down, but a new one is just put up. After years of this, a literal spiderweb of black wires exists, hovering above the streets of Manila. Clothes hang from the balconies of buildings, slowly drying in the wet and exhaust-filled air. People. More people. Smiles. More smiles. We walk on.

Jollibee's Restaurant is the most popular Filipino fast-food restaurant, outpacing McDonald's and Kenny Roger's Roasters. We stop in a Jollibee's to use the bathroom, since they are clean and air-conditioned. No heat, no wetness, no exhaust, no urine. We reassess. Look at a map. Find out where we are. We are heading back to the hotel, but not in the hurry that we were in only a few minutes ago. Maria's discomfort is easing. I see it. I feel it. We walk on.

Crossing the street is difficult. There are no lanes, and cars, motorcycles, bikes, and people are weaving all over. The traffic signals are mere suggestions, not orders, and drivers seem to pay no heed to the suggestions as they inch through red lights.

I studied law in Oxford, England, and it took two weeks before I began to look in the correct direction before crossing the street in that city, but Manila was going to be even more challenging, because in Oxford, at least drivers follow traffic rules. Once those rules are learned, pedestrians can cross the street with the assurance that a bus will not run them over.

Manila is different. Maria and I look both ways five or six times and then do what we see other pedestrians doing—stepping out into the street, while holding out our arms with palms extended upward, like a traffic cop. However, we are traffic cops with no authority, other than the hope that drivers do not wish to blow up their day by running us over. We cross and walk on.

We walk past a park, where the park benches are broken and garbage is strewn about. Some of the garbage is recent, while large portions are covered in dirt and grime, having been left there for days or weeks. No grass is visible, only weeds and a few plants, but only plants that are hearty enough to fend for themselves, since no assistance, pruning, fertilizing, or watering is done. Plants are on their own, like the women who sit on the dead tree trunks with infants in their laps.

I don't get a good look at the women or their children, because I do not want to stare, do not want to invade their lives by having a blond-headed tourist gawking about. When I glance over, there are only smiles—all smiles. I smile back, but quickly. I feel embarrassed. Embarrassed by the money in my wallet, the hotel I am walking back to, the shiny running shoes on my feet, and my neatly coiffed and clean hair. I don't consciously think this, but I feel it quickly, all at once. I turn away. We walk on.

We see a child, about three years old, with a handmade broom, sweeping the sidewalk around a large cardboard mat, while a young man sleeps—hopefully he is the father. A bicycle with a sidecar is next to the man who is sleeping on the mat. He must give rides for a living, but is now resting, but who is watching this child?

What does the child do when the father is giving rides? I see no mother. Maybe she is working, making food somewhere for someone, and has no choice but to leave her child with the father who needs to sleep after a long night of giving rides to people like me who have money in their pockets and are too lazy to walk to their hotels. The child is sweeping the dirty and crumbling sidewalk. He must have seen his mother do this a thousand times, a thousand times in vain, for this handmade broom is no match for the dirt and filth of Manila, like dipping a bucket into the ocean hoping to get all the water out. But there he is. Sweep. Sweep. Sweep.

He smiles. Maria stops. She leans over and says something to him. I cannot hear. The boy's smile widens into a laugh. Maria reaches out and playfully pinches his stomach. His shirt is dirty, filthy. He wears no shoes. His toes are the color of the dirt he is sweeping. What is his life? What does he do each day? What chance does he have? Maria turns. The tears have returned. We walk on.

It is Christmastime, and the city is clothed in celebration. The Philippines is over eighty percent Catholic, though I am not sure who is counted in this percentage—the sleeping man on the mat next to his child, who is sweeping the dirt from one side of his father's bed to the next? Are they counted? Do they exist?

Christmas trees adorn the windows of businesses. There is a large one in the Jollibee's, a small one in a barbershop, a wreath on the door of a moneychanger, and a nativity scene outside the door of some type of government agency.

There is no separation of church and state in the Philippines. There are no fights over prayers in schools or Ten Commandments monuments outside of courthouses, or government funding of Planned Parenthood. The people in the Philippines do not need to wring their worried hands over that last one, for there is no Planned Parenthood and certainly no government funding for impoverished women seeking basic medical assistance for themselves. We walk on.

We turn onto a side street. Thousands of small colored tissues are strung together and hang in the air from one side of the street to the other. There is an orange section, then a pink, a green, and a blue, giving the feel of walking beneath a flower-covered field. The right side of the street is lined with café-style restaurants. Tables and chairs are set up on the sidewalk. People sit at cardboard, plastic, and homemade tables and sit on folding chairs, plastic chairs, wooden chairs, or bar stools. They lean over their food. The food smells good. Laughter and smiling.

Across the street, I hear a child. He is not laughing. He is not smiling. He is standing in the gutter, naked except for a pair of yellow flip-flops on his feet. He is screaming, bouncing back and forth from one leg to the other. He is wet. He is looking inside an open door. He is screaming at someone inside.

A man sits in a chair on the sidewalk next to the child. The man is smoking. He pays no attention to the child who is screaming and hopping from one foot to the other, maybe because he knows this child, maybe this is his child. Does this child scream naked in the gutter hopping from one foot to the other every day? Perhaps the child was getting a bath and ran outside, or is hungry or tired or wants to go to school. Maybe he wishes to leave this street, this place, this city, or maybe he screams because he does not know what he wants. He only knows what he does *not* want and that is this—standing naked and wet in a gutter, across the street from a sidewalk filled with people eating, underneath tissues of color on a Monday morning in the city of Manila—screaming, a cry of help, pain, or of desperation, or maybe it's just a child's tantrum. The man continues to smoke. The child continues to scream.

The windows above are boarded up with plywood, as if in hurricane preparation, but the weather is calm. This must be the child's home. There is a gap in between the two pieces of plywood. The gap is filled with cloths hanging from a thin metal pole. They are drying. I see a woman with a large bucket down an alleyway. She is scrubbing a wet pair of soapy pants with a brush and dunking the pants into a large bucket filled with water. The child continues screaming. The man is still smoking. The woman keeps dunking. The people are eating. The cloths are drying. The colored tissues are blowing. It is Monday morning in Manila. We walk on.

Maria slows her pace and we clasps hands. She returns her glasses to the top of her head. The tears in the corner of her eyes have dried. We near the hotel.

"I'm still overwhelmed, but …. " She does not finish the sentence. She does not look at me, but looks forward, then from side to side at the people, the traffic, the shops, the drying cloths, the wires overhead, the roaming animals, and the children—especially at the children.

She squeezes my hand. She does not speak. A smile creeps across her face. I know. I understand. I feel it, too.

## Chapter Three

# Bayleaf Intramuros Hotel

AT TWO O'CLOCK, I am scheduled to meet a Filipino lawyer named Chito in the lobby of the Bayleaf Intramuros Hotel, the old walled part of the city of Manila. Ron told me that he met Chito while at the jail, and after talking to him for a while, decided that this could be the only person he spoke with at the jail who might not be trying to screw him over.

Ron had heard numerous stories from other prisoners of lawyers who took money promising to help their "client," but were never to be heard from again, because who could the clients turn to when taken advantage of? They were locked in a shithole detention facility and obviously had no one looking out for their best interest or general welfare because they just gave their last peso to someone they happened to meet in the jail.

A month ago, when Ron told me he hired a Filipino lawyer to assist, I never thought I would have to make the trip to Manila to secure his release. I thought the lawyer would be able to navigate the stormy waters of the American and Filipino government agencies, and secure the letter from the US Embassy that would set Ron free.

Ron hired Chito to check with the Bureau of Investigation, the Filipino version of the United States' FBI, and find out if he had any charges pending against him in the Philippines. He could not be released from custody, even with that letter from the United States Embassy informing the government that he was no longer a fugitive, unless Ron had a clearance check from that bureau.

Chito had been unable to secure that clearance check, but Ron decided to pay Chito to "make introductions" for Maria and me at the various Filipino agencies with which we were going to have to deal upon our arrival.

Here is all we knew we needed to be able to do:

1. Acquire clearance letter from the United States Embassy informing the Filipino government that the arrest warrant for Ron had been withdrawn, so he was no longer a fugitive, but the United States was not going to pick him up for deportation back to the states.
2. Take clearance letter to the Filipino Bureau of Immigration (BI), the agency responsible for Ron's continued detention.
3. Obtain clearance from the BI for Ron and make sure BI also has a copy of that same document, so Ron could be released.

That was the plan. Ron hired Chito to help me, but getting everything together was not Chito's job—it was mine.

I stand in the lobby of our hotel in Manila. I am wearing a white button-down shirt and long khaki pants. My briefcase contains copies of all of the letters and emails that have gone virtually unanswered from the United States government, as well has the Filipino government.

For months, from my kitchen table in Tampa, I had been trying to secure Ron's release. Because of the thirteen-hour time difference, I had to work late at night, drinking decaf coffee and eating my Granny Smith apples with peanut butter. Phone calls to the United States Embassy got me nowhere. I could never get anyone on the phone with any authority to assist—only general workers, who, even if they listened to my story, just directed me to someone else.

After one night of complete frustration as Ron's lawyer, I was going into detail about his situation with a worker at the United States Embassy that sounded something like this:

| | |
|---|---|
| Lawyer: | So, what I need is for someone at the US Embassy to simply inform the Filipino government that my client is no longer a fugitive, so the US is not going to pick him up for deportation. |
| Worker: | I don't pick people up, sir. (The woman on the line is very young, and her English sounds learned, not natural. Every time I called the Embassy, it seems like the same young woman answered the phone.) |
| Lawyer: | When I say YOU, I mean someone working at the United States Embassy. |
| Worker: | We cannot tell the Filipino government what to do, sir. |
| Lawyer: | I am not asking you or the United States Embassy to tell the Filipino government what to do, but only to inform them that my client is no longer a fugitive of the United States, so the United States is not going to pick up my client for deportation. The Filipino government is then free to do whatever it wants, but, you see, the Filipino government is holding my client at the request of the United States and is waiting for the United States to come pick him up for deportation. This is never going to happen, because that arrest warrant has been withdrawn, and you, the United States government, will never pick him up for deportation. Make sense? |
| Worker: | Have you told them that, sir? |
| Lawyer: | Told who what? |
| Worker: | The Filipino government, sir. |
| Lawyer: | Have I told them that? They don't give a damn what some criminal defense attorney from another |

|          | country says about one of their inmates. You, the United States government, told the Filipino government to arrest my client, and you, the United States, need to tell them that the situation has changed. |
|----------|---|
| Worker:  | To whom would you like to speak, sir? |
| Lawyer:  | How would I know? I am nine thousand miles away. I am sitting at my kitchen table talking to you. It is just after midnight here. You tell me who I need to talk to. |
| Worker:  | Maybe Gerald Smith. He would know more than me. |
| Lawyer:  | Okay, please get me Gerald Smith. |
| Worker:  | He is busy, sir. |
| Lawyer:  | Can you have him call me? |
| Worker:  | It would be better if you call back. |
| Lawyer:  | Call back when? |
| Worker:  | When he is not at the window helping other people. |
| Lawyer:  | When is that? |
| Worker:  | I don't control his schedule, sir. |
| Lawyer:  | Do you understand that my client is a seventy-year-old lawyer from Atlanta, Georgia? He is on a walker. He is sick. He has been sitting in a Filipino craphole for over two months because the Embassy will not send a simple letter informing the Filipino government that he is no longer a fugitive, so you are not going to pick him up. |
| Worker:  | Not me, sir. I do not pick people up, sir. That is not my job, sir. |

Upon hearing that last statement from the young lady at the United States Embassy, I almost jumped out of my skin. Maria had just walked into the room. She stopped and mouthed, "What is going on?" She must have heard my voice rising. I clenched my fists, held my rage, and tried not to have a heart attack right there in my kitchen. When the anger subsided, I continued.

Lawyer: Well, tell Gerald Smith to call me.

Worker: It would better if you call back, sir.

Lawyer: (Holding at bay his rage as it began to resurface). Okay. I will call back.

And call back I did. Night after night. Decaf cup of coffee after decaf cup of coffee. Granny Smith apple after Granny Smith apple. "Please call back, sir." "No, he is not here, sir." "What do you want me to do, sir?" "That is not my job, sir." "Please calm down, sir." Always a different Embassy employee, though they must have all gone to the same English language academy, so they all had just a slight variation on the same seemingly scripted answers.

Months went by and there Ron sat, or more accurately, he sat there and rotted. On Thanksgiving Day, Ron emailed me a picture with the caption, "Thanksgiving Dinner." It was a picture of a large rat just outside his cell. "You have to get me out of here," he wrote underneath the picture. Ron had bribed a guard for the use of a computer and an internet connection. He was a resourceful man, but his most important resources, his life and his health, were running out.

Our hotel calls for a car to take us to the Bayleaf Intramuros Hotel. The car arrives and Maria and I get into the back seat and slowly pull out into a sea of cars. We turn onto Roxas Avenue, which runs parallel to the Bay of Manila. The street was named after Manuel Roxas, the fifth President of the Philippines, who assumed the presidency on July 4, 1946. At that time, the United States had sovereignty over the Philippine Islands, but relinquished that sovereignty in a grand ceremony on July 4, 1946, in which the American flag was lowered so that the flag of the Philippines could be raised.

Now both countries celebrate their independence on the Fourth of July. Maria bought a book about the Philippines a few days before we left, and brushed up on the history of the country as we travelled from one side of the of the world to the other. She told me what she thought were the most interesting facts as we sat next to each other on plane after plane, layover after layover, and city after city.

She now holds my hand. We are here. We only decided to come to Manila nine days earlier, and now we are on Roxas Avenue in Manila, by the South China Sea, on our way to Intramuros, the older part of the city, to the Bayleaf Intramuros Hotel, where we will meet Chito in the lobby.

The car pulls over just outside the walled gate leading to Intramuros. I pay the driver, and his car vanishes into the endless stream of cars, trucks, Jeepneys, and motorbikes. We have thirty minutes before we are to meet Chito, so we take the time to walk around Intramuros.

Maria is dressed in a black skirt with a beige top. Her hair is pulled back. She has sunglasses on. She is strikingly attractive, even more so than when I first laid eyes on her as I entered the halls of Plant High School in August of 1988. Maria and I quickly became high school friends, and ran with the same crowd. When that crowd went to Florida State University, she and her girlfriends lived in the apartment above me, and we continued our close friendship as we dated each other's friends, went to the same parties, and ate large breakfasts on Saturday mornings, hung over as we discussed the escapades of the night before.

After college, we went our separate ways. I am not even sure that I saw her before my first wife and I loaded our belongings into a Ryder truck and marched west to Portland, Oregon. Maria married, and I married. She raised three kids and I raised two. Twenty years later, we reconnected when she called in on a radio show that I co-hosted, a legal call-in show, and she had some fun with me, as she asked me some outlandish questions. When I figured out who the caller was, I couldn't believe it.

After the show, I sent her a Facebook message, telling her how much fun that call was, and I was so happy to hear from her. As it was December 23, we wished each other a Merry Christmas and all the best for the New Year. About a month later, I sent her another Facebook message. We soon met up for coffee and caught up on the twenty years that had passed since we last saw each other. She was going through a divorce, and so was I.

We began to spend time together listening to one another, crying to one another, offering advice when we could, laughing about the old times and crazy things we used to do, but there were times when we just leaned on each other for support during those difficult days, as we sat in coffee shops, restaurant, bars, and on park benches. We began to study the Bible, every Wednesday night. We started with Ephesians, next Acts, and then Romans. I was new in my recovery from alcohol abuse, and even though I had spent most of my life in religious schools, I was still searching for my Higher Power, a relationship with a God of my understanding. Maria has an amazing relationship with the Lord, a close and personal one, and I envied it and wanted the same.

As months passed, Maria became my best friend, the only really close friend I ever had. I could be vulnerable around her, and I needed that during those vulnerable days for that is all I could be then, vulnerable. I didn't have to think about what I said, I just said it, not caring how it sounded, only that it was the truth, and I needed someone to hear the truth. Maria listened.

What an amazing gift it is to have another human being really listen to what you have to say, think about it, and respond for your benefit only. I didn't know how to listen like that, to care about another human being the way she could—that type of selfless caring was one of the many things Maria unknowingly taught me, as I struggled to find the right path.

In the Bible, it says that when a man and woman marry, they become one flesh—the two become one. I heard this. I had been married two times, but I didn't think the passage was to be taken literally, but more as a parable about how a person should act, kind of like the parable of the Good Samaritan. It was a story to teach a truth, a way of living, but there really wasn't an actual Good Samaritan.

Maria and I nursed each other during these days and months. We were not dating—we were two people who came back together during very difficult times in our lives, and leaned into one another for support, guidance, strength, and yes, love, but not a sexual love. Rather, we had an agape love, a kind of all-encompassing love that as I sit here typing these words, I cannot seem to find the right ones to put down.

I do know that Maria and I became one, long before I kissed her goodnight as she stood in the doorway of her mother's home. It happened after we attended a concert on a cloudless night, as the moon cast its light softly across her face. When I returned to my car after that kiss, I sat breathless, held my hands together in prayer, in thanks, and in disbelief. I had found her. Oh my God, I had found her!

Maria reads from the book she purchased about their city and the country of the Philippines, "The Spanish settled the Philippines in the 1500s. They built a defensive wall around the city in the 1600s." She says, "It looks like the fort in St. Augustine."

Maria is right, the wall does. The Castillo de San Marco in St. Augustine, Florida, is the oldest masonry fort (1672) in the continental United States. The wall surrounding Intramuros and the Castillo does look like they could have been built by the same construction crew, even though these structures were built five hundred years later, halfway around the world from each other.

Maria snaps some photos. I pose for a picture next to a rusty cannon. Even though it is December, the sun is strong, the air is wet, and my undershirt feels as if it is pasted onto my back. We walk on.

Maria crouches down and takes a picture of plants growing out of the old rock that holds the wall together. Who were the men who built this wall? Were they Spaniards or locals? What were their lives like? Were they happy to have the work, or pissed to be in this hot and wet land building a wall for a king who was thousands of miles away and would never even see it? Were their families with them? If not, how did their families survive? Was work that scarce in Spain that these men would risk the dangers of the sea and the unknown?

I feel unsettled—not jetlagged, but jumpy, restless. What in God's name am I doing here, standing on this old Spanish wall in Intramuros about to meet a man named Chito, who is going to help Maria and me extract Ron out of a hellhole somewhere in this city of twelve million people?

"I was to meet Chito in the lobby of the Bayleaf Hotel in Intramuros, Manila at 2 p.m. on Monday, December 4." That was the plan Ron told me as we spoke on the cell phone that he had bribed a guard to let him use, as he sat on the edge of his bed in his rat-infested room.

That is his plan—really? It sounds like the first line of a bad detective novel, but this is not fiction and I am not a detective, so I don't know what the ending will be. This is reality. Ron is desperate, because he is dying. He is a trained lawyer and businessman, but distressed enough that he is relying on me to travel nine thousand miles to Manila with my girlfriend to meet Chito in the lobby of a hotel, and then somehow get him out of jail, where he has been rotting for the past four months.

He has no one else to help him, so here I am standing on this wall, sweating in my long-sleeved shirt and slacks, as I watch Maria snap some more pictures. I didn't tell any of my clients I was travelling to Manila. I didn't have the time. I just decided that I needed to come, and come now, so Maria booked the tickets as we lay next to each other in her bed, computer on her lap, and the dog between us. Nine days later, we are here. I look at my watch—1:35 p.m., five minutes until we meet Chito.

Maria and I head to the hotel to cool off before Chito arrives. The first thing I notice about the Bayleaf Intramuros Hotel is that it has air-conditioning. The sweat on my back, sides, legs, neck, and face mixes with the cool dry air and gives me a much-needed chill. The lobby is white, sleek, and fairly modern, much like any American hotel lobby. Maria and I sit in the chairs next to the piano, across the room from the registration desk. No one asks us if we belong, for we look like we do—well-dressed American tourists.

"So, we're here." Maria says as she crosses her legs and returns her sunglasses to the top of her head.

"Yep, we're here," I say.

Maria shakes her head slowly from side to side as her eyes widen and a smile grows across her face. I know what she is thinking.

"So," I continue, "all we have to do is meet Chito, go to the Bureau of Immigration, get someone to tell us exactly what they require to allow us to take Ron out of jail, run over the US Embassy to get that clearance letter, drop it back off at the BI, and then Ron flies out of here—right? That's the plan."

"Right, that's our plan. Should be done by 4:30," Maria says as she looks at her watch. "Then we can go out for a celebratory dinner and spend the rest of the week sightseeing. Perhaps Ron can come with us."

Was it only about a month ago that I posed this proposition, "I might just have to go to Manila. What do you think?"

Maria was standing in the kitchen preparing dinner. I sat at the kitchen table. After her divorce, she rented a two-bedroom condo in south Tampa. It was small, but cozy, and we spent all our time there when we did not have the kids. Maria wore a gray robe that went to her mid-thigh. She was cutting jalapenos, onions, peppers, and mushrooms to put into a crock-pot dish she was making for us.

"I don't understand why you can't do this over the phone. I mean, what are you going to do in Manila?" She was right. I didn't understand, either, but after months of banging my head against the brick wall that is the United States Embassy, I was running out of ideas.

I had also tried to call the Bureau of Immigration, to get someone on the line who knew something about Ron's case, and what the Filipino government required before his release, but those calls were worse than mine to the Embassy—but not because of the sheer unwillingness to help, as was my experience with call after call to the United States Embassy. This quandary was caused every time I called the BI and explained to the person on the other line what I needed. I guess my story sounded too crazy for the dazed employee who answered my call to even know where to send me.

*Bayleaf Hotel.*

A few calls to the BI did lead me to the same person's secretary. Homer Arellano was a BI lawyer in charge of deportation. I left a few messages with his assistant, but never received a call back, and didn't think I ever would. Whenever I left messages, the assistant could barely hear me over the cacophony of sound pulsating in the background. It was as if her desk were in the corner of an extremely boisterous bar at the height of happy hour.

"I don't know what I will do in Manila, but surely more than I can do here. Maybe I will go to Manila and just pitch a fit, and if I can do that in front of the right person, something good might just happen. Right now, *nothing* is happening."

In the months before the trip, I spoke with Ron at least three nights a week. Mostly, he talked about his living conditions, the filth, the heat, and the lack of medical care. We also strategized about who to call, where and to whom to send letters, and what to say in them. I never failed to carry out what we had agreed upon. I sent the letters and emails, and made the calls to the US State Department, the US Embassy, and the Bureau of Immigration in Manila.

I left messages for Ron's probation officer and spoke with the Assistant United States Attorney in charge of Ron's case. I did all of this after I had the federal judge in Tampa withdraw the arrest warrant, which was the sole basis for his arrest. Nothing. No movement. Not even a positive development to give Ron some hope—a reason to wake up in the morning, to hold back the tears that I could feel coming through the phone as I spoke to him night after night, week after week, and month after month as though nothing had happened. No one called and I received no response to any of my letters or emails. Nothing.

I have never seen a picture of Chito, so I don't know for whom I was looking, but I am sure he will find me, the only blond-headed man in the entire city of Manila. Just before 2 pm, a man walks into the lobby dressed much like I am in a pair of slacks and a buttoned-down shirt. He looks tired, as if the week has beat him down, but it's only Monday. He stops, puts his hands on his hips, and looks around. He is not here to check in.

"Chito?" I say as I approach him.

"Bill?" I extend my hand and we shake. "Welcome to Manila." We walk over, and I introduce him to Maria.

"Okay, so what do we need to do first? I brought copies of the court order withdrawing the arrest warrant. I also have a copy of the letter from the United States Embassy to the Philippine government directing them to arrest Ron. My understanding is that their government needs a letter from our Embassy stating Ron is no longer a fugitive, and he needs a BI clearance stating he does not have any pending charges in the Philippines. At that point, he should be released."

"Sounds so simple," Chito says with a smile.

"Really simple," I say and laugh. "Unbelievable that we had to come nine thousand miles to get this done."

"The first thing we should do is go to the Philippine Bureau of Immigration. They are the ones responsible for Ron's detention. Then we can ask exactly what they need for his release. Then we," Chito pauses as if thinking about some detail that he just cannot grasp, "go from there." He smiles.

Ron told me that Chito does not know much about this case, but enough to help, especially with introductions and navigating the local agencies. Even though every educated person in the Philippines speaks English, their native language is called Tagalog, so having someone with me to, in essence, validate my presence will be invaluable. I agree with Ron. Chito is essential.

We step out of the hotel lobby into the heat. "My car is just around the corner," Chito says. He stops for just a moment and looks at us. "You guys ready?"

Maria looks at me, and then back at Chito. "Sure, why not," she says.

# IT IS AN ANONYMOUS PROGRAM

I cannot tell the story of Ron and our time in Manila, without telling you the story of my journey into the rooms of Alcoholics Anonymous, for the stories are intertwined, inseparable. One of the bedrock tenants of AA is anonymity, but breaking that anonymity about one's membership in the fellowship is a personal choice.

While writing this book, I wrestled with whether to break my anonymity. If I decided not to, how would I write this book? Perhaps just include the story about Ron, Maria, and our journey through the maze of Manila? If I decided to break my anonymity, what would that look like? How would I weave into this story my very personal journey in the rooms of AA? If I decided to break my anonymity, what would people think? What would my family think? My colleagues? Judges? Prosecutors? Clients? Potential clients? Do I care? Should I care? These thoughts and others ran their way through the contours of my mind, and still do, even as I write these words today.

In the end, I made the decision to break my anonymity, for I cannot separate one story from the other. Ron, Maria, and Manila and what happened there cannot be told without sharing the other life and death journey I am on. AA has become a part of me, not as a separate story, but interwoven into everything I do, everything I think, and everything I hope to be.

AA saved my life, my physical life, but more importantly—my inner life, my spiritual life and taught me how to engage in conscious contact with my Higher Power. For me, that power is God and conscious contact with the God of my understanding is the whole point of being alive. I could not have gotten on that plane to Manila without the fellowship of AA. I would have been too wrapped up in my own life, my personal needs and wants to think clearly about Ron. Ron would still be rotting in that jail, if I had not walked into the rooms of Alcoholics Anonymous and surrendered to a power greater than myself.

What I have decided to share with you is what I have learned in Alcoholics Anonymous—about myself and others, about humanity, the human condition, and my relationship with the God of my understanding. I write these words as thanks, as forgiveness, as hope, and as a prayer.

"My name is Bill, and I am an alcoholic." I cannot remember when I *first* said these words out loud in an AA meeting, but I know that I did not believe them, not really. When I came into the rooms of Alcoholics Anonymous (any AA meeting is referred to as being in "the rooms"), I had a successful career operating my own criminal defense law firm, two kids, a house, money in the bank, and the respect of my professional colleagues, so how could I be an alcoholic? I tried to intellectualize this question, which is the first of many mistakes I made when first coming into the rooms, that is, I tried to use my sick and suffering mind to understand and then to heal my sick and suffering self.

"I am a grateful recovering alcoholic." "I am blessed to be an alcoholic." "I should kiss the ground of AA every time I walk through the door." These are just some of the phrases I heard people say when I first came into the rooms of AA, and I had absolutely no idea what they were talking about. Why would anyone be a grateful alcoholic? Why would being an alcoholic be a blessing? Why would anyone be so thankful to AA that they would want to kiss the floor? Now, after having some sobriety under my belt, I smile when I hear these phrases, and sometimes I actually say them myself, for now I understand.

Sebastian Junger wrote a book called *Tribe: On Homecoming and Belonging*. The book explores the human need to belong and identify with a group. He explains why young men who come back from deployment in Afghanistan volunteer to redeploy on that life and death mission—the brotherhood, the fellowship, the camaraderie, the tribe to which they belonged and felt while fighting on the front lines cannot be found back home. So these young men drift, searching for that which they cannot find, until they find it again after redeploying to the battlefields of Afghanistan. Junger explains how some American soldiers who were captured by the Native Americans in our own homeland during our war with them chose to stay with their captors after having been "rescued." The brotherhood, fellowship, camaraderie, and the tribes of which these captured men became a part were something they knew they would never find in the first-world society for which they had been fighting.

As my days of sobriety began to mount and my mind started to clear and open, my ears began to listen and my mouth began to close. I came to realize that the fellowship of Alcoholics Anonymous is my tribe. I have belonged to many groups throughout my life—sporting teams, a college fraternity, a church community, and many professional organizations, but I never found a fellowship, never felt at ease. I was always posturing, sizing myself up, and comparing myself with the person on the left and the person on the right. I spoke as I thought one was supposed to speak, never mentioning how I really felt or was really thinking. I was always alone—even sitting at a table of ten in the middle of a room filled with people, I was alone.

In Alcoholics Anonymous there are no leaders, no directors, no hierarchy of any kind, no one has more authority or more of a say than the next person. A person who has been in the program for thirty years is just the same as a person who wanders into the rooms for the first time. AA does not accept any outside contributions or take a stand on any outside issues. AA has one purpose and one purpose only—to help the sick and suffering alcoholic who still suffers. AA's success is based on a simple principle—one alcoholic talking to another alcoholic.

AA was started in 1935 by Bill W., an alcoholic stockbroker and Dr. Bob, an alcoholic physician. Four years after starting AA, Bill W. put down on paper how the first one hundred members managed to stay sober, and thus, the *Big Book of Alcoholics Anonymous* was born. *The Big Book,* which contains the *Twelve Steps,* has been translated into over sixty languages, and AA meetings are in 180 countries around the world.

There is no president of AA. No one governs. There is no press secretary, and no directors. There are no dues or fees. There is only one requirement for membership—a desire to stop drinking. No one can be refused membership, no one can get kicked out, no one is forced to stay, and all are welcomed back. AA essentially runs itself, in the small meeting rooms around the world. I have been to AA meetings in Tucson, Kenab, Manila, Hong Kong, and even on a cruise ship off the coast of Mexico. In the most important ways, all AA meetings are the same—one drunk sharing his experience, strength, and hope with another drunk.

All around the world, an AA meeting generally works as follows: The meeting begins with reading the first few paragraphs of Chapter 5 entitled "How It Works." These paragraphs contain the *Twelve Steps*, which are the foundation of the spiritual program. Then, if the meeting is a literature-based meeting, people take turns reading from either a section on the *Big Book* or from a book of the collected writings of Bill W. entitled *As Bill Sees It*, or some other book that the fellowship approves as AA literature.

After the reading, the meeting is opened up for discussion about the reading or anything else someone might want to share with the group. If it is a speaker meeting, a speaker will share his or her story and within that story share his or her experience, strength, and hope with the group. Then, the meeting is open for discussion about the speaker, or about anything else a person might want to share with the group. AA meetings do not center around war stories of a person's drinking days, "drunk logs," but on the solution, and experience, strength, and hope. Meetings last one hour, and usually end with the group holding hands in a circle reciting the Lord's Prayer or the Serenity Prayer.

I have decided to share with you the experience, strength, and hope I have heard from others during my time in the rooms, once I learned how to sit with my mouth shut and my ears open. I have three college degrees, a Bachelor of Arts, a Masters, and a Juris Doctorate, but the wisdom that follows imparted to me from a bunch of drunks sitting around a table in a run-down building is far more valuable, far more meaningful, and far more useful than anything I have ever heard or learned in a classroom. If I repeat myself in the chapters that follow, it is because I need things to be repeated, over and over, until I let go and let God. I want you to walk with me and share in this journey. So open your mind and heart and let my brothers and sisters in.

# GET HONEST WITH YOURSELF

Roger says, "You ain't gonna to learn a damn thing until you start being honest with yourself." Roger sits in the corner. He always sits in the corner.

"I had to start getting honest with myself and realize that the real problem was me. My thinking was the problem." Roger wore a faded red baseball cap and a t-shirt with a front pocket where he kept his cigarettes. He was an old timer with a lot of sober years under his belt.

"I was the problem—not everyone else. When I first came in here, I didn't like anybody. I didn't even like people I hadn't even met yet. Everyone was out to get me. That's why my life was so screwed up. Everything that was wrong in my life was because of someone else—not me. If people would just leave me the hell alone, I would be just fine." Roger leaned back in the folding chair, his mustache stained with years of exhaling cigarette smoke. He glasses sat slightly crooked on his face and seemed to prop up the bill of his baseball cap.

"When I came into these rooms, I weighed 92 pounds and was a mess. My life was a mess. I had to start getting honest with myself. I had to realize that *I* was the problem, not nobody else, and until I could do that, I wasn't going to get any better. You see, I was suffering from a hopeless state of mind and my thinking was all screwed up. Until I realized it was my thinking that was problem and that all my problems were because of me—nobody else, I wasn't going to get any better. Start being honest with yourself—that there's the key. I mean, get *really* honest with yourself—then just maybe you can start getting better."

I sat in a folding chair on the other side of the room. Roger sat in the corner by the water cooler. "I've been sitting in this chair for two decades now," he would say, but I didn't have a regular seat. I was too new.

In the room, there were four folding tables pushed together to make one large table in the center of the room. Sometimes I would sit on the left side of the table in the middle, sometimes on the right. Folding chairs lined the walls. I don't like to sit in those chairs because there is no place to put my book, or put my head when the day had weighed me down, or I wanted to cry or pray. Two chairs were next to the water cooler. Roger sat in the one on the right—always the one on the right.

"No one comes in here on a winning streak." Roger would say that sometimes. Michael, who sat in the chair next to Roger, would nod his head in agreement and with a deep understanding forged by years of being outside these rooms, and after years of being sheltered and guided by the people within them. Michael wore a baseball cap, too. He was a few years older than Roger and walked with a limp. He wore a t-shirt with a front pocket where he could put his cigarettes. Sometime he would speak after Roger. I always liked that.

"Like Roger said, I had to start getting honest with myself. I was a sick puppy, when I first came in here. I didn't like nobody and everyone was picking on me. Everyone else was the problem, not me." He would lean back in the folding chair and cross his legs. "But it was my thinking that was the problem. When I realized that and kept coming around here and listening to people, instead of always talking, I started to become happy." Michael rode a small scooter to the rooms of AA. He lost his driver's license years ago and given up on getting it back.

"W.A.I.T. (Why Am I Talking)? I like that one, because before I came in here, I was always talking. I always had something to say. I sat my ass on a barstool at the place just around the corner and talked for years, but never said one word that was worth a shit." Roger nodded his head in agreement.

"So I came in here and started listening. For the first time in my life, I started listening to what other people had to say. And I started listening to the people in these rooms, because I wanted what they had. Sure I could go back to the bar, and they would be happy to give me a full refund on my misery, but I didn't want to live like that anymore. And I could not begin to get better, until I started being honest with myself.

"My problem was me, and for the longest time, I could not understand why wherever I went, I always had problems. That's because I was always there, and until I started to change myself and change my thinking, I was never going to get any better. My problem wasn't alcohol. My problem was being sober. My sickness was in my mind."

Michael spoke with a raspy voice. He didn't look at his hands or at the floor when he spoke like others did, but he looked around the room, catching the eyes of those sitting around the tables. I don't know what he did for a living, but now he was a teacher.

"And to you newcomers, just keep coming around. Give this place a shot, and things will get better. Start getting honest, really honest with yourself, because until you can do that, you don't stand chance." He sat forward and unfolded his legs. "That's all I have."

"Thanks, Michael," the room said.

Honesty: what is that, really? How am I supposed to know what is honest and what is a lie? I had been a liar for so long, on so many levels, how can I determine the truth?

"A sick mind can't heal a sick mind." I'm not sure if Roger or Michael said that, or maybe someone else did. It doesn't matter. I like it. But where does that leave me? One Friday night at 5:45 p.m., Roger answered that question.

"You don't have to try and control things anymore—that's what I learned. Me trying to control everything led me to losing my house, my wife, my job, and damn near my life." He pointed across the room to the wall where a banner hung containing the *12 Steps of Alcoholics Anonymous*.

"It's all right there." Many in the room nodded their heads in agreement. "My life had become unmanageable, and that is because of me, what I had done. My life sucked because of me, ain't nobody else. And until I could admit that to myself, and give up trying to do

51

what I wanted to do, and listen to others for a change, I was never going to change. I didn't have a chance. So I had to give up control, and put someone else in charge. My way just wasn't working. My way led me to these rooms with a foot and a half in the grave."

At the time, I was new to the rooms, and it seemed that Roger and Michael were talking to me—trying to help me as they continued to help themselves. They actually understood me, so I could relate to them.

Before I came into the rooms, I would have thought Michael, Roger, and I were from different planets, but inside these rooms, we became brothers. There were others, too—others who were new to the rooms. Kurt worked construction. His shirt was always filthy and so were his jeans. His blonde hair was caked in fine dust from cutting cinder block. He lived in the sober house down the street. I would give him rides to meetings sometimes. We didn't talk much. He would just sit in the passenger seat and look out of the window.

"How are things going at the house?" I would ask.

"Not bad. Same old shit. Some new guys."

I would drive on. To break the silence, I would ask, "How's Johnny doing?"

"He went back out." Kurt bowed his head and looked at his hands. He picked at the nail on his thumb. "A real shame. He's got kids and all, but just can't keep it together. Always blaming everyone else for everything." I nod. I have nothing to say. I am too new. I am still blaming others. I don't even know what honesty is. I am a self-centered son of a bitch and a liar. I am sick, mentally and spiritually. I came to the rooms because everyone I loved had thrown me out of their rooms. I came to the rooms like everyone else—broken, desperate, lost, with nowhere else to go.

Our Club, my AA home group, is located on the south side of town next to a dog groomer. The lady who owns the grooming business rents the room to the club. The club pays rent, and everyone chips in to help out. I think that is the seventh tradition—self-sustaining.

I have lived in south Tampa most of my life. I have driven by these rooms ten thousand times and never once looked at this small one-story building with an old sign out front that reads, "Our Club." The first time I walked into the rooms, I was there to meet David.

I had known David for over ten years. He used to live across the street from me, before he moved out, and before I was thrown out. I am not sure where he lives now. He knows where I live. He helped me move my things into my place, the place I got when I had no other place to go. David knew me better than I knew myself. He knew I was a sick and selfish liar on a path that would lead to misery and death, for he had travelled down that path. He asked me to meet him in the rooms, because that was the only place for me to be. All other places had failed. When I met him that day, he wasn't happy.

"So you fucked up, again." His tone shocked me—stern, tense, bubbling with anger. "You just couldn't help yourself, could you?" He was pulling copies of the *Big Book* out of the closet and placing them on the tables before the meeting. His eyes didn't meet mine when he spoke, and I knew it was not because he was ashamed, or embarrassed, or uneasy with what he was saying to me. I knew that if he looked me in the eye, he might just beat my ass. David was angry.

"How many times have you reached out to me over the years? How many?" He placed a *Big Book* before every chair at the table. He wore sunglasses on the top of his head. His skin was tan from years of working on roofs and building decks under the blistering Florida sun. He wore a gold cross around his neck, always had as long as I had known him. He is the eleventh child in a family of twelve, which made him a tough son of a bitch, always having to fight, earn, and scrap for what he had. His mother once told me that each baby only got two minutes on each boob, and if they didn't start eating when it was their turn, that was their fault. David took nothing for granted, and had no patience for those who did.

"How many times?" he asks. I didn't answer—a child with nothing to say.

"You come to me and say, 'Hey, maybe I could come to a meeting with you sometime. What's the *Big Book* all about?' And I always say sure, come on. Now I'm not going to force anyone to do anything. They need to come in here on their own, because if they don't, they're just taking up a seat that some other sick and suffering individual could use, someone who really wants to change. What do you want? Why did you even meet me here?"

I did not answer—I'm an ashamed, cowering child. David pulls out a binder from the cabinet. He walked to the head of the table and places it at the seat on the right. He pulls out three separate laminated sheets of paper and places them in the middle of the table. We are still alone in the room.

"You need to start being honest with yourself or stop calling me." He looked at me in the eyes for the first time that evening. "Do you want to get better? Do you even know how sick you are?"

I had never considered myself sick—that was my biggest problem. How could I begin to heal, if I didn't even know I was sick? How could I look for a solution, if I didn't know the problem? People started to filter into the room.

"Just listen tonight, okay?" As David asked this his face softened, and I could feel the compassion in his voice, the voice of a father frustrated with his son, but willing to go to any length to help him.

David introduced me to a few people as they came in. "This is Bill, a good friend of mine." Everyone welcomed me. A line formed at the coffee pot, and people began to take their seats. The wall unit kicked in and cool air began to circulate. The ceiling tiles were stained and two of the florescent light bulbs were out, giving the room a small more intimate feel in the soft light. The Twelve Steps and the Twelve Traditions were printed on large banners and hung on one side of the room. Other words to live by hung in various size frames around the room—the Serenity Prayer, Live and Let Live, Pause, One Day at a Time.

Forty-five years on this earth, two marriages, four cities, nine jobs, and two thousand sleepless nights led me to the chair next to David that night. A guy in military fatigues picked up a bell and rang it. The room fell silent.

"Let's have a meeting," he said as he placed the bell back on the table. The time to get honest with myself had just arrived ...

Chapter Four

# Bureau of Immigration

CHITO OPENS THE DOOR TO HIS CAR and tells Maria and me to wait to get in. He climbs into the driver's seat on his knees to remove items from the passenger seat and place them on the floor in the back. The interior looks much like mine, for our law practices are similar. We are both solo practitioners running around from courthouse to courthouse, jail to jail, and city to city, appearing before various judges, visiting clients, always back in the car, answering calls and emails as we drive to the next stop on our over-scheduled day.

Our cars became our second office, or more correctly, our main office. The passenger seat is a working desk, files piled next to a sandwich and a bag of nuts, a newspaper, a magazine for lawyers, a judicial directory, and bottles of water. Just by looking at the items that Chito removes from the passenger seat, I know we have much in common. Our daily workdays, even nine thousand miles apart in different worlds, are quite similar. This familiarity brings me a sense of ease and comfort as Chito unlocks the car and tells us to get in.

"I must apologize," Chito says as he starts his car and pulls out into the ceaseless river of cars, trucks, Jeepneys, and motorcycles.

"No need to apologize—my car looks just the same," I say.

"No, about my country." He looks over at me. "The corruption here is terrible. Everything and everyone is for sale. Ron should have been out a long time ago. Navigating the Filipino government agencies is difficult, maddening, and slow."

"No need to apologize. My country is the one who won't write a three-sentence letter to the Filipino government stating that the arrest warrant was withdrawn, Ron is no longer a fugitive, and the United States is not coming to pick him up for deportation. Talk about difficult, maddening, slow, and completely ineffective." Chito smiles. The professional bond that already connects us tightens.

"So the Bureau of Immigration needs a letter from the Embassy, which Bill and I will hopefully get, and we need to get a BI clearance from the Filipino government stating Ron has no charges against him in the Philippines. Is that it?" Maria asks. She did not take a week off from school for a vacation. Manila is not a tourist destination.

Maria came to work, to assist me with the logistics of travel and anything that might come up, since we had no idea what would come up. She knows all about Ron's case. She read the order withdrawing the arrest warrant. She read my letters to the Embassy, the State Department, and the Filipino government. We discussed endless ways of handling Ron's situation over decaf coffee late at night. She heard the strain, fear and despair in Ron's voice as he spoke to me on speaker phone from his cell night after night. She booked our flights, our hotel room, and arranged transportation from the airport to the hotel, and from our hotel to the Bayleaf hotel to meet Chito.

Now Maria sits in the back of Chito's car in Manila, Philippines, on her way to the Bureau of Immigration to help secure the release of a seventy-year old lawyer from Atlanta. She is dressed as any professional woman would dress, ready for business—not sightseeing. Maria said she was coming to Manila for me, but I also knew she was coming for Ron, even though she had never met him, and didn't know if she ever would. Her faith in and her love for people is strong and comes from the close relationship she has with her Higher Power, Jesus Christ. I envy her that relationship, for it is real and powerful and a guiding force assisting her as she travels down her path.

"Yes, Maria," Chito replies.

"How do we get that BI clearance, and why hasn't it already been done? Ron has been in custody for months." See, Maria is here for

Ron. When I told my dad that Maria was coming with me to Manila, he replied, "Nice to have a travelling Della Street." (Later, Google reminded me that Della Street was Perry Mason's secretary).

"The National Bureau of Investigation is not the most efficient agency," Chito replies looking at Maria in his rearview mirror. "Some people wait months, even years, for an BI clearance."

*Years?* I say to myself as we continue the drive towards the Bureau of Immigration. We need Ron's clearance by Friday. How the hell is this going to happen?

"After we go to the Bureau of Immigration, and find out exactly what they need to release Ron, can you assist us with getting his clearance at the National Bureau of Investigation, or at least make introductions and show us where to go and who to speak with?" Maria asks. "We will handle getting the letter from the US Embassy."

Maria's mind is working. You didn't have to go to law school to formulate a plan to get Ron out of custody—all you need is to make a checklist and just make damn sure all those items are checked off. (Della Street is making a checklist.) We have until Friday to get all the items checked off.

The Bureau of Immigration is on the north side of Intramuros and sits on the edge of the Pasig River. The building is a massive four-story structure and looks like it was built in the 1960s. Chito parks the car just out front. I grab my briefcase, take a deep breath, and step out of the car.

We walk through the main entrance into a dizzying array of people, sounds, smells, and heat, always heat. The air is stale, wet, warm, and filled with the odor of the exhaust from outside, and the sweat of many people, people everywhere.

Chito talks to one of the guards manning the front entrance. He converses in Tagalog and as he speaks, he occasionally points over to me, then to Maria. The guard nods his head in agreement or in understanding. I look around. Many children are sitting on the floor next to women who are holding younger ones. Men of all ages are standing in large groups. The scene looks like the floor of the New York Stock Exchange during a heavy trading day. People yelling to be heard, talking with their hands, crammed in next to one another trying desperately to get someone to listen.

Everyone is here for a reason, and so are we, but we don't have time to stand in one of these groups, to yell over the person next to us. Ron is dying. We need to talk with someone, and talk with that person *now*. However, I feel as if I am late to catch a plane and just got rerouted off the interstate due to a terrible car accident up ahead. How are we going to quickly navigate this chaos? Chito motions for Maria and me to come with him.

We pack so tightly into the elevator, it is as if we are trying to win a carnival prize for the team who gets the most people jammed into an elevator at one time. I pray the elevator does not break as I hear it creak and slowly climb from one floor to the next. I would be the first one to die of thirst, or anxiety, or lack of clean air.

My prayers are answered, and we get off at the fourth floor, which is eerily similar to the first floor—people everywhere, sounds, smells, and heat, always heat. The fourth floor is lined with offices on both sides and the end of the hallways are open to the outdoors, so the wet and warm breeze blows in. It seems as if every building in Manila is open to the elements, as if the cost to air condition the structures outweighs people's need for comfort from the wet heat.

So Maria and I sit and sweat and watch Chito as he walks up and down the halls, seemingly lost. "What is he doing?" Maria asks.

I'm not sure what he is doing, but he'd better be doing it fast. I look at my watch, 3:37 p.m. Our first day is almost gone, and all we have done for Ron is make it to the fourth floor of the Bureau of Immigration like half of the other inhabitants of Manila. Chito waves us over. He is talking to a man who is holding a clipboard. Chito tells me that he has explained what we are here for, but the man he is talking to does not seem to understand.

"My client," I begin hoping this man understands English, "was arrested by your government because the United States issued an arrest warrant and asked you to take him into custody. I had the arrest warrant withdrawn by a judge in the United States." The man nods seemingly comprehending my explanation.

I pull out a copy of the order issued by the United States District Judge withdrawing the warrant and continue. "I am providing a letter from the Embassy informing your government that the arrest warrant has been withdrawn, and the United States is not going to pick up my client for deportation back to the United States.

Our understanding," and I look to Chito and then Maria, "is that your government requires the BI to check to ensure that my client does not have any pending charges against him in the Philippines, before he is released. So we are here to get a list of exactly what documents the Filipino government need so my client can be immediately released. He is seventy years old and in terrible health." The man continues nodding as I continue speaking. If he tells me he does not understand English, I am going to cry. I wait for a response.

"You need to talk to Homer," and with that we are ushered down the hall to another office. The name is on the front door, HOMER AREALLANO, leads into a two-room office. The first room leads into the second and both are filled with people. Again, it seems they are trying to set a carnival record for jamming as many people as possible into a small office space.

I peer in through the window. Stacks of disheveled papers are piled on top of old computers, filing cabinets, desks, tables, and on the floor. The man who is holding court in the second room is surrounded by people, who are all talking to him at once using their hands to try and get his undivided attention. He smiles and shakes his head, as if these men just asked him for some ridiculous request, like a ride to the moon .

Chito opens the door and squeezes in. He knows Homer—not well, but he does know him. I see Chito slice though a myriad of individuals before reaching Homer. As he speaks, Homer looks over to Maria and me, and then he begins to usher the other people out of his office. Every man in the group continues to talk as they are literally pushed out into the hallway by a young woman named Jodie. I know this is her name because Homer has said it at least thirty times since we stopped outside his office door. Jodie is Homer's assistant, and she tells us to come in. Thank God for Chito.

Homer motions for Maria and me to take a seat. His office is air-conditioned. I feel the sweat covering my entire body begin to chill. "So you came all the way from the United States to see me." Homer is still smiling. The time is 4:05 p.m. Day One closes in fifty-five minutes.

"We sure did," I reply.

"So what can I do for you?" Homer sits down at the seat behind his desk. My head is spinning. Where do I begin? I am beyond jet lagged. My body is flipped inside out. I have travelled nine thousand miles to sit across the table from someone who can actually help Ron, and here I am. I can't think. My mind is frozen. Homer shuffles a few papers on his desk, leans back in his chair, and looks at me. "How can I help?"

"The United States asked your country to arrest my client based on an arrest warrant that was issued by a federal judge in Tampa. I had that arrest warrant withdrawn."

"The warrant was issued by mistake, so the judge withdrew it," Maria adds. Maria is trying to alleviate any probing questions Homer might have into why the arrest warrant was issued in the first place. She wants Homer to stick to the important facts. (Della is smart. Perry never would have made it without her.)

"Yes, Maria's right. The warrant was issued by mistake, and the court withdrew it." I reach into my bag and pull out the order from the federal judge withdrawing the warrant. I place it on Homer's desk and turn to the last page. "See here," I point to the last few sentences. Homer reads the documents with interest and attention.

I continue, "my client is now sitting in custody and your country is waiting for the United States to come pick him up to deport him back to the United States as a fugitive, but that is never going to happen, because the warrant was withdrawn. The United States is not going to pick him up, which is the only reason he is still in custody."

I don't even know if what I am saying is making sense. I have told this same story so many times to so many people in the form of letters, emails, faxes, phone calls, and even to random people in my dreams, with either no response at all, or the, "I can't help you, sir. That's not my department, sir. I am not responsible, sir. Please calm down, sir. Don't yell at me, sir. My supervisor is not here, sir. Call back again tomorrow, sir. Yes, I understand the English language, sir."

I stop speaking. Homer is silent. Chito is silent. Maria is silent. Did he hear me? Does he understand? Is he the right person to whom I should be talking? Does he care? Why should he care? Who am I? I just showed up at his office on a late Monday afternoon throwing papers in his face, and asking him to release my client from a jail where he has been sitting for the past five months. I am a nobody. Does Homer know that?

"I see. Yes, it was withdrawn. Okay," he sits back in his chair. "Just get me something from your Embassy that tells me he is no longer a fugitive, and that should do it."

"That's it?" I ask.

"Well, has he had his BI clearance yet?"

"No," Chito responds, "we are going to BI to check on that tomorrow."

"Perfect. Get me those two things, and I don't see a problem."

There must be some kind of catch that I am not picking up on. Homer sounds too relaxed.

"Get you those two things? That's all?" I pause and add, "Can you call BI and get Ron's BI clearance done?" (I swing for the fences.)

"No, it would better if you go in person. Things somehow get done more quickly in Manila that way." Homer smiles.

"Okay, Maria and I will go to the US Embassy tomorrow morning, and then we will all go to BI in the afternoon, say two o'clock?" I say looking at Chito. Chito nods to affirm the time. "Then we will check back in with you tomorrow, and let you know our progress." And with that Homer stands up and places his hand on my shoulder.

"Yes, come back tomorrow and let me know your progress."

"If we get you those things, do you think my client can be released by the end of the week? And if he is released, can he just walk out, and go back to his home in Angeles City (just North of Manila)?"

"No, that is not possible. He will have to leave the country. Because of his arrest, he has been placed on a blacklist. For him to stay, you will have to get him removed from the blacklist, and that will take some time."

"But can he leave the jail and go to another country by the end of the week?" Maria asks.

"Sure, no problem, just bring me those two documents."

"We leave Saturday morning. Can we get all this done before then?" Maria continues, not quite believing what is going on.

"Well, you will need to get me those papers by Thursday at the latest, if you want him out before your return to the United States."

I look at Maria. Maria looks at Chito. Chito looks at Homer. Homer yells, "Jodie!" Jodie walks in.

"Jodie, see our wonderful friends out. They will be visiting us again tomorrow." And with that I put my papers back in my briefcase and follow Maria who is following Chito as he navigates past the room full of people waiting to see Homer. I turn to Homer and say, "Thank you so very much for your time, sir. My client and I are so appreciative."

Homer's smile broadens across his face. "No problem. No problem at all. See you tomorrow. Good luck."

The hall is still filled with people, too much sound, and lots of heat—wet heat. We set another record for the most people packed into an elevator, as we creep our way down, floor by floor, back to the main lobby, which is still a mosh pit of people, sweating, yelling, and smoking in the wet heat. Women are still holding babies. Children are still running around the women. Men are still huddled in groups, talking in loud voices, and waving their hands. All these people must be here for a purpose, but they are not talking to officials—only to themselves. I start to think about why the woman standing with a half-naked child in her arms might be here, but I can't. I'm too tired, too flipped upside down, too wet, and too hot—the heat, the heat, the heat. We make our way outside and onto the street.

"How do you think that went?" I ask because I am literally unable to process information.

"Well, very well." Maria looks at Chito for his assessment.

"Yes, that went well."

"Better than well. I can't believe it. Thank you so much Chito. We now have a plan for tomorrow. One day at a time." We continue walking towards Chito's car.

The traffic is even heavier than when we went in, which does not seem possible. How could any more cars fit on these roads,—but they do—always more cars, trucks, Jeepneys, and an endless stream of mopeds and motorcycles carving their way through the impassible Manila streets.

We say goodbye to Chito. I tell him that Maria and I will catch a car back to the hotel. We shake hands, and even though I have known Chito for only three hours and six minutes, I feel like we already have a history together, shared some time in the trenches. Chito is a good man, the first person I met in Manila, a Filipino lawyer, father of two, married, with a sister who lives at the edge of town. I am blessed, so blessed that God and Ron put him in my path. I look forward to seeing him tomorrow.

"Hey, there's a Starbucks right there," Maria says as Chito edges his car into the traffic. I didn't see it, but it is not a standalone building, like one sees in the United States with a parking lot and a drive thru. This Starbucks is seemingly part of the old wall of Intramuros and perhaps the space used to be a storage unit where munitions and gun power were kept.

Maria crosses the street, opens the door and we walk in. It is air-conditioned. My sweat begins to chill. The inside is exactly as one would expect to find a Starbucks in the United States. I grab a seat and Maria stands in line to order. She does not ask me what I want. She knows.

I look around and see that most of the customers are young, late teens or early twenties. They are on their phones, tablets, and computers with textbooks and notepads covering the table. They are not drinking coffee, but fancy and complicated concoctions that I assume must have some amount of coffee in them, but cannot be sure.

These kids do not look poor. They did not grow up on the streets. Their mothers did not hold them on her hip, half naked in the lobby of the Bureau of Immigration yelling to seemingly no one in particular, but in a general fit of desperation. These kids slept in beds, brushed their teeth at night, and went to school. They have iPhones, tablets, and computers. They can read, for they went to school during the day and did not have to assist in finding water to wash clothes. They did not grow up among dogs, cats, chickens, and rats fending for themselves, scratching a living from the dirty, cracking, and potholed streets. They are not forgotten. They have been given a chance, and are using it wisely. They are smiling. That is the one thing they share with the street children of Manila. The smiles. Always the smiles.

"Lover, where did you go?" Maria sits down at the table with our coffees.

I had not physically left the table, but my mind had, and Maria knows this. She can see it in my face, in my eyes as they lose focus and cast more of a blank stare. I am trying to recover from a hopeless state of mind, as Roger said as he sat in the corner, next to the water cooler. A hopeless state of mind. A mind that will not relax, will not calm down, will not focus on what is real, will lead me to a place of restlessness, irritability, and discontentment, all of this without even getting up from my chair.

I am the king of catastrophizing. I can take any situation, any comment, no matter how slight, and weave a story in my head that involves people out to harm me, to interfere with my life, cause me grief, pain, and trouble. I will believe the lie I create in my mind, and then act upon that lie as if it were true.

For example: Maria does not text me goodnight when she is at her home with her kids and I am at home with mine on a Monday night. My mind immediately starts churning, the symptom of a sick and suffering person. I think to myself, Maria is upset with me. Churn. Churn. Churn. She is punishing me for something she thinks I have done, but I have not done a thing to her, so why is she mad? She has no right to be mad at me, to make me suffer. She doesn't want me to sleep.

That's it. She wants me to lie awake all night and think about what I did, but I didn't do anything. How dare she mess with me like this? Doesn't she know I have a big hearing in the morning? Maybe she just doesn't care. That's it, she doesn't care.

Well, I'll show her who doesn't care. I'm not going to text her either. When she wakes up in the morning she will see that I didn't text her, and she will wonder what I am thinking. She will text me, asking me what is wrong. I will not respond, so she will go to work and keep wondering. I will not respond. I will let her suffer as she is making me suffer.

Maybe she doesn't love me—she only says she does because she was lonely and searching for a way out. I bet that is it. I wish she had the guts to just tell me she doesn't love me. So she would rather get married, buy a house, and then drift away into her own life, where we either stick it out in a miserable marriage, or both get divorced again? Is that what she wants?

That's sick. I can't believe she would do that. Well, I'm not texting back. I'll show her. I'll live my own life within this relationship and go my separate way. Do my own thing and live my own life. My own free life! Yes, freedom, that is what I will have.

If people would just stop interfering in my life, I could be free. I have never had one freakin' day of freedom, because someone is always trying to control or manipulate me—well, that's over. I'm done with that. From now on, it's FREEDOM!

Maria texts me early the next morning. She tells me that she fell asleep reading her book. She tells how much she loves me, and dreams about our life together. She reminds me to work for the Lord and to have a good day.

See what I did? Catastrophizing. Selfish and self-centered. A hopeless state of mind, as Roger said. In the past, I would reach for anything to calm my mind, the real source of my misery. I would reach for booze, pills, homes, cars, jobs, women, and nothing would fill that hole or calm my mind. I tried desperately to fill it, but nothing worked. I kept pouring things in and those things disappeared in the black hole within me. Since I have started working the program and actually listening to other people and getting out of my own way, my mind has begun to settle.

People are not out to get me, as I thought for so many years. I have given up trying to control other people, control outcomes and situations. I have given up control of myself and my life to my Higher Power. This takes a daily effort to smash and re-smash the ego, the self that has caused me so much pain and hardship. I am still a child in my recovery, taking baby steps, but I am moving forward. My mind still drifts away, but not as often and not as far into the lava pit of despair, anger, and rage.

"Lover?" Maria takes a sip of her coffee. She smiles. "Where did you go?" I sit back and smile. My eyes refocus. I take a sip of my decaf.

"What the hell are we doing here?" I smile. Maria shakes her head and laughs. "What are we doing in Manila, Philippines? What did we just do today? What are we going to do tomorrow?" I lean forward and grab her hands. "Do you think I am crazy? I just shut my law practice down and travelled halfway around the world to help one of my clients get out of a Filipino shithole." I smile. I squeeze her hands. "Actually, you are the one who is crazy."

"Why is that?"

"Because you took a week off from school to come with me halfway around the world, to get a man you have never met out of a Filipino shithole. Now that is crazy." Maria smiles and looks around.

"I sure did, and here we are. Sitting at a Starbucks, outside the Bureau of Immigration in Manila after a meeting with Chito and Homer. Tomorrow we go to the Embassy to get that letter and then the National Bureau of Investigation to get Ron's clearance. What else would I be doing?" She laughs and holds her coffee mug with both hands as if trying to warm up from the cool air blasting from the vents in the ceiling.

"What are Maria Giglio and Billy Sansone doing?" I say. We both smile. I go by Bill now and her last name is Cavallaro (has been for twenty years), but Maria Giglio and Billy Sansone are the two Plant High School buddies, palling around at football games and weekend house parties. Our lives separated after college, and we lived a life apart, without even a thought of each other.

Now we are here. Sometimes, when I look at Maria, I see that girl who I used to sit next to in the hall before the bell rang signaling first period. When I see that girl, I am amazed at where we are—not just in Manila, but in life, holding hands together on our spiritual journey, teaching each other along the way, crying on each other's shoulder, and holding on for stability during the storms that always come.

"Maria Giglio and Billy Sansone," Maria says. "What are those two kids doing here? Are they playing grown up? Does everyone know we are just two kids? Are our parents going to come through that door, and say, 'What are you guys doing in Manila. Get to your room. You are grounded.' "

We sip our coffee slowly, mostly in silence, enjoying the moment, resting comfortably in the bond that holds us together, holds us upright, as we walk through this part of our journey. We finish our coffee and head outside into wet heat. The traffic is continuous. We catch a cab. Maria tells the driver where to go.

I sink into the back seat and watch the cars, trucks, Jeepneys, motorcycles and people, so many people, go by. We leave Intramuros and cut through Rizal Park, back onto Roxas Avenue and past the US Embassy, where we will begin our day tomorrow. *Maria Giglio and Billy Sansone—who do they think they are?*

## Chapter Five

# Miles to Go Before I Sleep

I AM IN THE SHOWER and Maria is blow-drying her hair. I let the water hit the back of my neck as I replay the events of the day. At first, I cannot remember how it began, our first day in Manila, but then the smell of exhaust and urine, the heat, traffic, people, and children, yes—the thought of that small child holding a broom and sweeping the dirt from the sidewalk to the street as his father lay sleeping on a flattened cardboard box comes flooding back in.

Was that today? Seems like so long ago. Where is that child now? What is he doing? I am in a clean shower wasting clean water because it feels good on the back of my neck, and I am tired and had a long day. Soon I will walk into a restaurant, where I will order anything I want without looking at the price. Then I will come back to this air-conditioned hotel, maybe even shower again, and then slide in between soft white sheets as I wrap my legs around Maria's and quickly drift off to sleep, my head cradled by two plush pillows.

I will sleep, thinking only of myself, my problems, my hardships, and my minor hills in life that for too many years I have struggled so strenuously to push upward into steep cliffs, so I can obsess even more about *my* problems, hardships, and little tiny hills. And that little boy—what will he do tonight? What will he eat? Where will he lay his head? What will he do tomorrow? Keep sweeping the never-ending dirt from the sidewalk into the street? His shirt was so dirty and his feet were the color of the dirt he was sweeping. I turn off the water. I have wasted enough.

"What are you going to wear?" Maria asks.

"Clothes," I answer.

"No, really."

"I don't know. You?"

"Jeans and a black top. Do you think it will be too hot?" Maria asks holding the black top up to her shoulders.

"It will be too hot if we both leave the hotel naked." I place my wet towel on the hook on the back of the bathroom door. Our room is like any other hotel room I have stayed in before, complete with robes in the closet and a Gideon's Bible in the drawer next to the bed. Maria and I picked a nice standard hotel, because we came to Manila on a specific mission, and did not want our accommodations to prove difficult or challenging. That, and the hotel has a rooftop lap pool, so I will have a place to swim, which Maria knows is vitally important to my well-being and mental health.

We finish dressing. We are very close to the Aristocrat Restaurant, so we decide to walk there, which with the endless traffic, might actually save us a great deal of time. The man at the front door opens it for us, and we step out into the excessive heat, wetness, exhaust, and traffic. The sidewalk is cracked and crumbling, so I watch my step and grab Maria's hand as we make our way down the street.

A man is pulling a blue tarp over his small stand where he sells cheap trinkets, bottled water, newspapers, and cigarettes. Four folding chairs are on the side of his stand and a woman in a stained yellow dress sits in one chair, knitting. The shadows are deep, so I cannot tell how old she is, but a small child of maybe five years sits next to her. The little girl has short brown hair and is holding a plastic cup, squeezing it to make a strange, crinkling noise. The man looks at us. He is wearing a Chicago Bulls t-shirt, darks shorts, and no shoes and has a cigarette hanging from the right side of his mouth. He smiles and nods. I smile and nod back.

"Good evening," Maria says as we pass.

"Hello," says the woman, taking a break from her knitting to smile. The child turns her head, quickly turns it back, smiles, and then hides her face. This is a family. This stand is their family business. Behind the folding chairs are a few pieces of cardboard laid on the sidewalk. I squeeze Maria's hand. This is their home. This is where they live. An emaciated dog comes around the backside of the stand sniffing the ground for anything that might be edible.

"Hi," I mouth to the woman. She smiles broadly, her head tilted to the side with her hands folded in her lap on top of the yarn.

"Hello," she says smiling even more broadly. She looks happy, as does the child and the man—happy being on the side of the street on that cracked and crumbling sidewalk next to the traffic and the exhaust, in this heat. Where do they shower? Where do they get water? Clean their clothes? Eat their food? Go to the bathroom? Privacy? Ever? Where? When?

That child. What does she do all day? Does she have friends? Hopes? Dreams of the future, a future beyond tomorrow, beyond helping her dad sell his trinkets, water, and cigarettes? Does she ever pretend to be a princess, as my daughter does? Has she ever seen a princess? Where would she have? At the movies? On television? In a book? She has no access to those mediums, or any other mediums, other than what is right before her now, on the side of the road, next to her father's stand, sitting on a folding chair with her cardboard bed behind her.

I pull out a fifty-peso note. Two American dollars. I hand it to the child. She hesitates, looks at her mother, who nods approvingly, and then reaches for the bill. Our hands slightly touch as she takes the bill from my hand. Her eyes are cast downward, but I can see she is still smiling. So is her mother. So is her father, who has stopped covering his stand with the tarp to watch our transaction.

"Thank you," the child says.

"You are certainly welcome," I reply. The child holds the bill up for her mother to see. The mother laughs and places her hand on the back of the child's head. The cigarette is still dangling from the side of the father's smiling mouth. This is a family. They appear happy on the side of the road, next to the traffic, in the heat, the exhaust, among the street vendors and the people—so many people.

I squeeze Maria's hand. She is smiling too. So am I. We are all smiling, sharing this time, this moment of reprieve from the world around us. Maria and I walk on and the moment passes. There are more street vendors closing up for the night, more emaciated animals, noses to the ground, hoping that the next piece of dirt or pebble is a piece of food fallen from one of the food carts that line the street.

A police officer is on the other side of the street. He is in uniform, wearing a badge and a gun. He is relieving himself against the side of building. His urine forms a stream and runs across the sidewalk and into the gutter, mixing with other forms of water, dirt, and garbage. Maria sees the officer, but does not speak, only squeezes my hand in shared disbelief and disgust.

We walk past the Malate Church. Malate is the district of Manila in which Maria and I are staying, the district to the south of Intramuros. The Malate Church is constructed in the Baroque style and rises elegantly above the neighborhood. Its stones, blackened by years of exposure to exhaust and dirt, give the house of God lines of character, showing that the structure is part of this neighborhood.

A mission is located in the building next to the church. The mission is having a fundraiser and the gift is a new car. The car sits in the side courtyard. It is shiny and new, two qualities we have not come across in our first day in Manila. A security guard sits in a folding chair next to the car. He is smoking a cigarette and looks bored. A placard describing the history of the church is mounted on the wall just to the right of the front door. I should go read it, get some understanding of the role this structure has played in the district of Malate during the wars, famines, fires, and uprisings. However, Maria and I have not eaten since our hotel meal after our morning walk. My body's need for fuel outweighs my need for understanding and context. We walk on.

# 5 DAYS IN MANILA

The Aristocrat Restaurant is located on Roxas Avenue, overlooking Manila Bay. We walk in and are greeted by a friendly young man, who grabs two menus and takes us to our seat. Our waiter comes. Maria orders a beer. I order a water. The restaurant is almost at capacity, which is nice for a Monday night. People of all ages are eating, drinking, and laughing. Smiles, smiles, smiles. Ever since we landed in Manila, less than twenty-four hours ago, all Maria and I have encountered are smiles.

We landed in Manila just after midnight. The airport was packed with people, so we were at the back of the endless sea of individuals waiting to go through customs. I was giddy with lack of sleep, and I kept telling Maria that when I got to the front of the line, and they asked me what I had to declare, I would answer, "I have nothing to declare except my genius," which is what Oscar Wilde said when he passed through customs on his first trip to the United States.

Of course I didn't. By the time we reached the customs official, I was no longer giddy, but tired—tired from the twenty-six hours of travel that it took us to get from Tampa to Manila. The airport was packed with people. Where were they all coming from, and at this hour? We exited the airport into the wet heat. People everywhere. Maria had arranged for a car from the hotel to come pick us up.

We jostled our way across the street to the duty-free store, where the car was supposed to be waiting. A man was there ready to take our bags and our bodies to the hotel. (Della Street had come through again.) Just before we got into the car, I realized that I had dropped my phone, which contained all my business contact information, and Chito's information, and who we were to meet the next day in the lobby of the Bayleaf Hotel.

I panicked, as I made way back across the street, past people and more people. I had no plan, I was just walking back. Right as I entered in main terminal, I saw a policeman holding a small iPhone. I had kept my phone for years, and as technology had improved along with it, so had the size of the phones, but I kept my old reliable small one.

I went straight towards the officer. No one uses a phone that small anymore. That is *my* phone.

"Hey, I think that is my phone," I said as he was looking through it.

"Can you prove that it is yours?" As he handed it to me, I pulled up a picture that Maria took of me about an hour ago standing in the back of the immigration line and showed it to the officer.

"Ha. It is yours," he said with a large smile. Another officer came by and he was smiling, too. The one officer told the officer the story of how he had found my phone on the ground and picked it up. I shook their hands and I smiled. The one officer smiled. So did the other one. I went back to the car. Maria saw that I had my phone and she smiled. So did the driver. Smiles, smiles, smiles—Manila.

Our waiter returns. He is smiling. Maria places our order. She always does. She knows that I don't like anything with a heavy sauce, cooked in butter, or made with a lots of salt, carbohydrates, or starches. This usually narrows the choices on a menu, but as she orders, she looks at me and smiles.

"So," she says as she reaches across the table and grabs both my hands, as if about to start a prayer.

"So," I reply.

"We are in Manila. We met Chito at in the lobby of the Bayleaf Hotel. We then met Homer at the Bureau of Immigration. Tomorrow we go the United States Embassy to get a letter stating Ron is no longer a fugitive, then to the National Bureau of Investigation to get Ron's clearance done, and then hopefully, back to Homer to give him those documents." Her smile turns into a laugh. "What the hell are we doing here?"

"We have a plan, don't we?"

"We sure do." Maria takes a sip of her beer. Her face shows that it tastes good. "What a day. Seems like a week ago we were walking through that neighborhood. All those people, and the children. What about those children? Why aren't they in school? They are so poor. I couldn't take it. It was all too much. The people, the filth, and the smell—I was overwhelmed."

"I know you were. I could see it and feel it. Seems like you have bounced back a bit."

"Yes, I think it helped that we actually had something to do to take my mind off of things." Maria pauses and looks around the room. " ... and the people—everyone seems happy. Everyone is smiling. Even those families living on the street. The people are so sweet. In the midst of the heat, the exhaust, and the stench and filth, the people are smiling—happy for what they have."

Maria looks around. "This is quite a place. I have never seen anything like it. Never experienced anything like it. I was a bit worried this morning, worried that I wasn't going to make it here."

"That was just a few hours ago."

"I know. There is something about this city. I don't know how to explain it." She doesn't have to. I know. In this immensely foreign land, with foreign people, foreign ways, foreign landscape, foreign manner of living, foreign food, and foreign smells, there is something familiar, comforting about Manila. It feels like a place I am returning to after many years away.

Our food is fantastic, filled with spices, vegetables, chicken, rice noodles, and a few things I am not sure what they are or how to describe them. We eat in silence, pausing only long enough to tell each other how good the food tastes. So much food, not just on our plates, but everywhere.

Manila is filled with people cooking food at all hours of the day in restaurants, cafes, and on the streets. The city streets are lined with people cooking on small stoves, burners, over wood, coals, or anything else that will burn. So much food, yet so much hunger. The food and the hunger lay next to each other, like oil and water, touching at the edges but not mixing. I can't eat anymore. My plate is still half-filled. This food will be tossed in the garbage, placed out back for a family on the street to later sift through, pulling out the edible parts and serving it up to their family to get them from one day to the next.

"I can't eat another bite," Maria says as she puts her fork down. "Let's put this in a to go box, and give it to a family on the street on our way back to the hotel." This is why I love Maria, and need her teaching ways in my life. I was just thinking about how a family would be sifting through the garbage to find the remnants of my dinner in the dumpster at the back of the restaurant in the early hours of the morning. Maria is thinking about serving that same food to a family while it is still hot, fresh, and not mixed in with other garbage.

"Can we get plastic forks with our to-go boxes?" Maria asks our waiter and the waiter cheerfully says yes. Maria also wants the family to eat with a bit of dignity. There is a big difference between making a decision and taking an action. I have always made decisions in my life, decisions big and small, but I am only now learning how to take action.

In the rooms, Mike tells it this way: "There are three frogs sitting on a log, and two decide to jump off. How many frogs are sitting on the log? Three. A decision needs to be followed with an action." Maria instinctively moves from a decision to an action. I am learning this skill, this manner of living, and it is hard, unnatural for me, for it requires one to stop being selfish and self-centered and those are two personal characteristics I have spent the past forty-six years mastering.

We have spent less than twenty-four hours in Manila, and I am already becoming accustomed to being hit in the face with the wet heavy air when I step outside. Then we are met with the exhaust, the sounds and smells, and the people—people everywhere. I hold the bag of food in one hand and Maria's hand in the other. I look up. There are no clouds, but there are no stars either.

I smile. I know that this selfish and self-centered alcoholic is blessed—blessed to be holding Maria's hand as we walk the sidewalks in Manila. Also, blessed to have a brother and sister, and two parents to model my life after. My mother is ill with Parkinson's and dementia, but even in her illness, she carries a message of strength, hope, and courage.

I wish she could see me now and realize that I have come to know God. We have the same Higher Power, but I wasn't able to share that with her. She drifted off before I woke up. I have spent so much of my life with one foot in tomorrow and the other foot in the past, continually pissing on today.

Right now, I am in Manila. I am holding Maria's hand. I am here to secure Ron's release from jail. I am sober. I gave myself up this morning to my Higher Power, as I try to do every morning. Sweat is collecting at the back of my neck. My hamstrings hurt from the hard run I did in the gym before dinner. A warm breeze blows my hair. I am not trying to be somebody. I am not trying to get anywhere. I am me, and for just this second, this fleeting moment, that is all I need. I am not pissing on today. I am here. Right now. Here. Peace. Finally. Let go.

"Let's give the food to a family with a small child." There is so much going on in Maria's sentence: the love and compassion she has for others; the action she always takes, reminding me to move forward with my decisions; and the knowledge that we will not only see homeless people on our way back to the hotel, but we will see a homeless family with a small child.

I watch my step, for the lighting is poor and so is the sidewalk. The security guard still watches over the car in the courtyard of the Malate Church. The church stands guard over the neighborhood as it has for centuries, as the political winds blow from left to right, ever changing, yet still the same.

Across from the church is a small park, littered with trash and packed with people, people who are finding a place to lay their heads for the night. Everyone in the park could use the food that I am holding. They all need it and deserve it. So do the animals, the cats and dogs who are circling the people, still hoping for that scrap of something to fall from somewhere, maybe from the church itself, if God would only provide.

The air is heavy. Maria and I continue on, stepping over puddles that have formed in the potholes on the sidewalk, although it has not rained, so the water has come from an unknown source. We pass people sitting on the sidewalk. We exchange smiles. Some of them hold out their hands, hoping for some scraps to fall from somewhere, maybe from the blonde-headed man with the pretty woman on his arm.

The lady in the dirty yellow dress is still sitting on the chair. The man now sits next to her, the tarp secure over his business. The child lays on a piece of cardboard between them. The child is asleep, the plastic cup she was playing with is next to her small hand. I give the bag to Maria. She hands it to the woman. The woman takes it gratefully. She smiles. Her husband nods his head in a show of appreciation and thanks. He smiles. Maria smiles. I smile. Just as we did on our way to the restaurant, we are all smiling again. Sharing another moment of grace and thanks. We walk on. I turn and see the woman wake the child, for the child must have fallen asleep hungry. I spend my day worrying about converting my decisions into actions. They worry about survival.

Our hotel supplies each room with two complimentary water bottles per day, for it is not recommended that one drink the water from the tap—just another reminder we are in a third world country. I take one of the bottles, open it, and take a long drink as Maria readies herself for bed. I check my briefcase to make sure all Ron's documents are in order. Tomorrow we head to the Embassy. I check my phone. I have no emails, texts, or missed calls. I look at my watch and see that it is 9:30 p.m. Monday night here, which means it is 8:30 a.m. Monday morning in Tampa. My world of clients, lawyers, bondsmen, detectives, judges, courtroom deputies, scared moms, and nervous dads whose kids I represent, are just waking up, drinking coffee, and walking out the door into the world that awaits them. I put my phone on silent.

I resist the urge to take another shower. Though I am sticky from the short walk to the restaurant and have a faint smell of exhaust swirling about my head, a shower somehow feels too decadent, too wasteful. I brush my teeth and rinse using the water from the tap.

"Did you use the tap water to brush your teeth?" I yell to Maria from the bathroom.

"No," she replies from the other room. I have only read about people contracting dysentery in third world nations, and my mind begins to churn through the possible calamities that await me as the unfiltered water runs through my system. Normally, my sick and suffering mind would spend the rest of the night and into the sleeping hours playing out the catastrophes that await me: painful stomach, then a trip to the hospital, IV bags hooked to my arms, Maria crying, my father on his way to Manila to see his son one last time, and a life flight back to Tampa. The possible outcomes are endless and my mind would usually run through all of them, not ceasing until sleep brought me reprieve, but not tonight.

My mind is still, replaying only the smiles I saw on almost every face I encountered on my first day in Manila. Smiles from the construction workers, the ladies cooking food on the sides of the street, the children on the streets, the children in the schools, the men who ride bikes with passenger sidecars, the security guard at the Bureau of Immigration, Homer, his secretary, Chito, the kids in Starbucks, our taxi driver, the ladies at the front desk of our hotel, our server at dinner, the entire restaurant, and the family to whom we gave the food on our way back. Smiles amidst the heat, exhaust, dirt, garbage, stench, poverty, hunger, but not amidst hopelessness and despair. The smiles are genuine, not forced, but naturally growing across each face. The smiles are an outward sign of an inner strength, one I do not have, but one I ask my God to grant me if I could only surrender myself to His will, not mine.

Maria is already in bed. She has her book in her lap, and reading glasses on, but her eyes are closed. I slide in next to her. I pick up my book, Hue 1968 – The Turning Point in the American War in Vietnam. I place it back on the nightstand. Not tonight. I will check in with the young men fighting against the North Vietnamese's Tet Offensive tomorrow. I lay my head against the pillow. Maria wakens just enough to take off her glasses and turn out the light on her nightstand. She snuggles in close, laying her arm across my chest. I feel the pressure building within. I try and hold it down, or in, or stop it coming from where it is bubbling up, but cannot.

"What's wrong, baby?" Maria senses the pressure.

"I don't know. I feel like crying." Tears have gathered at the corners of my eyes.

"Then go ahead and cry, sweetheart." Maria doesn't ask me why. She doesn't need to. She slowly rubs her hand across my chest as my tears make their way down the sides of my face and onto the pillow. Day One in Manila has come to an end.

# DON'T SWEAT THE SMALL SHIT AND IT'S ALL SMALL SHIT

I am trying to recover from a hopeless state of mind. This hopeless state of mind keeps me separate, blocked from my Higher Power. Really, that's what it's all about, just like Peter would say. Peter is an old timer with over thirty years of sobriety, so I listen to him. I am forty-six years old, a criminal defense attorney, so it is my job is to counsel people who are in crisis, both in the criminal justice system and in their lives. People come to my office in tears, in shock, in denial, in debt, in over their heads, and in trouble. If not, they would not be coming to my office.

I usually see new clients on the weekends. The ones who are not in jail, cannot or should not, take the time off from work, and the ones who are in jail, well I wait until it is a good time for me to see them, because it's just too hard to get to the jail during the week.

So I spend my weekends counseling drug addicts, alcoholics, wife beaters, child abusers, child pornographers, fraudsters, armed burglars, and yes, innocent citizens accused of crimes they did not commit. They come in all shapes and sizes. The State of Florida does not discriminate against those whom it chooses to charge with crimes.

I represent blacks, whites, Hispanics, Asians, Africans, Native Americans, Russians, rich, poor, tall, short, fat, thin, and Christians to agnostics. Their stories are different, yet somehow the same. What they did and how they did it will differ, and even why they did what they did will change from person to person. However, when I peel back all of the layers, the crap that covers a person after years of walking on this earth, I begin to see the sameness within: fear, loneliness, addiction, restlessness, a searching, a hopeless state of mind.

How am I to counsel these people, if I am one of them? I am not talking about the law. Sometimes very little of what I do is about the law. I counsel people in crisis. The law is the law. The facts are the facts. I will figure that out. Most of my clients don't care what motions I file, or what I discuss with the prosecutor, but they do care about how they feel, the despair, and the fear of both the known and the unknown. They do care about that, and they want me to make it go away.

Many can't turn to their spouses, moms or dads, aunts, uncles, cousins, or even friends. Those relationships have been tested over the years, and the reason for them sitting in the chair across from me at the conference table is because of the most recent event after thousands of other ones. The most recent fuck up after years of fucking up. I am the one to whom they are looking to make it all go away, to ease the pain. Most listen to me, really listen, as if I am explaining to them the secret pathway that will lead to a new and difficulty-free life. They listen, maybe for the first time.

When I first came into the rooms of Alcoholics Anonymous, I hadn't listened to anybody in years, not wives, not friends, not family, not even myself. I didn't know myself, but I relied on myself, my thinking, my way, and that way lead me to two failed marriages, broken friendships, and tension within my family.

"No one comes in here on a winning streak." I am not sure who said that. Maybe Frank. He sits on the right side of the table, on the opposite side from the person chairing the meeting. His hair is short and looks dirty. He works construction. He drives an old van with faded flames on the side. He did not paint the flames on the side of the van—the previous owner did. The van was the delivery vehicle for a barbeque restaurant. The place went out of business, and so did the reason for the van. Frank bought it for $800. He paid in cash. The most money he had ever had in his hand in his life.

Frank was proud of himself, and he should be. He beat back the demons, came into the rooms, and listened, and after a while, things began to change. He began to experience that spiritual awakening that is the last promise of the 12 steps, the promise that if we just shut up for once, listen a little bit, follow a few steps, maybe our lives won't suck anymore. Maybe we might not feel so bad. Maybe we might start thinking clearly. Maybe we can mend some of those relationships. Maybe we can stop being so selfish and self-centered.

"Don't sweat the small shit, and it's all small shit." Frank said this to me after a meeting one night. He didn't have to take the time to come up to me after the meeting, but he did. Step Twelve—having had a spiritual awakening as a result of the steps, we bring our strength, hope, and experience to other alcoholics. I had shared with the group that night. I don't remember what I said, but I remember what Frank said. At that time, I did sweat the small shit, because the small shit affected my life—or so I thought. I was the director trying to control everyone on the stage, worried about what everyone else was doing, and how their decisions would impact my life, my plans, my existence, and my quest to take care of myself, my happiness, my peace—me, me, me! I'm so tired of me. So I have chosen to fire that director and try and turn my life over to the care of God. Then my life will not be run by an idiot anymore.

"A sick mind can't heal a sick mind." David told me that, and that's what Frank was also telling me then—just in a different way. We can't control other people. We need to stick to our side of the street. Make sure our side is clean.

I call it catastrophizing, and I was the king of it. It goes like this: My wife comes in the back door with groceries in her hand. She places them on the kitchen floor. I am on the couch watching some sporting event. I am soaking in gin. She comes back in with another load. I don't move. I'm busy soaking. Another load. She opens the refrigerator, places a few items in it, and slams the door shut. She has ruined my soaking. She is angry. She wants me to do something. Why can't I just soak in peace? She does not want me to soak. She doesn't leave me in peace. Well, that's fine. I will live my life within this marriage and she can live hers. I will turn her off.

Just because she decided to go to the grocery store, am I supposed to just stop what I am doing and help her? I could have helped later, when it was good for me. Now, I am not going to help. I am through helping. We will live separate lives, and that will work just fine. I have my books to read at night. We don't need to talk. Weekends, I will work out early in the morning, and then I don't care what happens. Vacations, I will work out early in the mornings and then I don't care what happens. I will drink my gin and live my life, how I want. Holidays, I can work out early in the morning and then I don't care what happens. I will drink my gin and soak. Read my books. Soak, work out, read, soak, soak, soak, soak. Damn it!

She just screwed up my soaking by slamming the refrigerator door! Banging all those groceries around. How dare she? Maybe I should leave her? Soak by myself. Workout without the guilt. No. Don't want to do that. I'll just live my own life within this marriage. That's what I'll do. That will work. If she would just finish putting up these goddamn groceries and go upstairs, so I can soak. She is so selfish. She'll probably go upstairs and start banging around because I forgot to make the bed. Who cares about making the bed anyway? It just gets messed up again. I bet she will. I bet she will bang around up there to keep me from peacefully soaking. Why won't she just leave me alone? What did I do to her? I was just sitting here—soaking. What's wrong with that?

I didn't know she was coming back from the grocery store. Am I just supposed to stop soaking because she decided to go to the grocery store? Why couldn't she go later, or tell me so I wouldn't be soaking? But she didn't, no. She had to go on her time, when she wanted to, and I'm supposed to just stop what I'm doing and do what she wants when she wants it. Is that it? Is that how she thinks this marriage works. Well, screw that. I'm just going to live my own life in this marriage. Soak when I want. If she would just go upstairs. I can't even enjoy my soaking anymore. She ruined it. She is so selfish. What did I do? Nothing. I wasn't doing anything. I was just sitting here. Soaking. If she would just leave me alone. If she ...

I don't soak anymore. I sit in the rooms and listen. I let my mind follow the wisdom of the people who talk in these rooms. I have three advanced degrees, but I have gained more wisdom listening to these bunch of drunks than all of my professors combined. Honesty. Selfless honesty. That's what I found in the rooms. That's what Frank was sharing with me after the meeting that night.

"Bill, you can't control other people and their actions—only yours and how you react." His eyeglasses are chipped and sit crooked on his face. "If you try and control other people, and what they're doing, you will drive yourself crazy. Focus on your Higher Power, and ask Him for guidance. You are not in control, so let it go. Enjoy the freedom of not being in control. You work for a new employer, your Higher Power. Enjoy that freedom." Frank's shirt is dirty. His shirt is always dirty. His face is lined with age, sun, and years of abuse. He puts his hands on my shoulders. His eyes are blue. He looks directly into mine. Men don't do this, do they? Frank does. "Let it go, brother, or it will eat you alive. All of the shit you have been carrying around in your mind, let it go." He squeezes my shoulders. "I have been in and out of these rooms since I was nineteen years old. I have spent over half my life trying to control others, trying to control shit I just can't control.

It wasn't until I realized that I can only control how I act and react to situations that my life began to get better. It wasn't until I sat my ass in these rooms and started getting honest with myself, and realized that I was the problem, and no one else, that my life started to turn around. It wasn't until I gave my life and will over to my Higher Power, and started working for him, not for me, that my life started to get better.

Get honest with yourself. Let all that shit you are carrying around in your mind go. You don't have to fix the world and all of the people around you. Just focus on yourself and what you can do, and the miracle will begin to happen. Once you start focusing on yourself, and taking time to work the steps, and staying in touch with your

Higher Power, a miracle will happen. You will start to become selfless. You will start to care for others. You will walk this earth with a smile on your face. You take direction only from your Higher Power. All the crap that used to keep you up a night, all the crap that kept you drinking, will vanish. None of it will matter anymore. Your mind will clear. Your heart will open. Love will grow inside your heart."

The only person still in the room is Ken, an old timer. He is cleaning out the coffee pot and preparing it for the next meeting. Frank takes his hands off my shoulders. He smiles. His teeth are tiny, worn down, and stained from cigarette smoke. We walk out of the club together into the warm evening. The sun has just set. People are sitting on the back porch smoking cigarettes and laughing, sharing stories, and engaging in the fellowship, when my sponsor walks up to me. "Everything okay?"

I tell him yes. He can tell if I am bullshitting—and he knows I am not. He smiles. He puts his arms around me. "You're doing just great."

I walk slowly past the porch. I hear Roger telling a story about a Firebird he once owned. Stacie is sitting next to him. She has been in and out of the rooms for years, and is living in a woman's shelter. Mike lights her cigarette. He is in the Air Force. Pam is talking to Rick. Pam just got a new job. She lost her last job, a sales job, because she got another DUI and lost her license, so she couldn't drive to meet customers anymore.

I hear her say she doesn't like her new job, but it's okay for now. Peggy is sitting next to Michael. She is laughing. Michael is talking. I can't hear what he is saying. Frank has made his way over to his van. Mike, a young kid who is living in the sober house down the street, hops into the van's passenger seat. Frank is giving Mike a ride home so he doesn't have to walk. Frank hops into the driver's seat, rolls down the window, and lights a cigarette. He starts the engine and begins to pull out. As he rolls past the porch, he glances in my direction. He flashes me another smile and then looks the other way.

Sarah, an older lady with short white hair, comes up next to me. "How you doing this evening?" Frank pulls out onto the road and is gone.

"Pretty damn good, Sarah. Pretty damn good."

Sarah smiles.

## Chapter One

# United States Embassy

MARIA'S ALARM GOES OFF. The room is dark. For a few seconds, I am not sure where I am. I get up and shut her alarm off. Maria doesn't move. I check my phone. It is 7:00 a.m. Tuesday morning in Manila, 6:00 p.m. Monday night in Tampa. While I slept, my criminal defense life was in full swing as evidenced by the emails, text messages, and voice mails I received concerning the following: court dates, offers from state prosecutors, scared parents wondering what is happening with their son's case, notification that my transcript request in a deposition of a medical examiner in a case where my client caused twenty-eight rib fractures to his seven-week old child is ready for pick up, a lunch request from a fellow criminal defense attorney who wants to talk to me about a legal issue in one of his cases, six calls from the Hillsborough County jail asking if I will accept charges from an inmate who is trying to reach me, and a scared truck driver who just got arrested for driving under the influence and is panicked about losing his commercial driver's license and his whole livelihood. All of this happened while I slept soundly next to Maria on the other side of the world, our legs intertwined, my mind whirling about, attempting to make some sense of the impossible task we have travelled nine thousand miles to accomplish.

    I start with the emails. I respond to most requests indicating that I am out of town and will get back to them next week. The more pressing matters, I hit head on, either answering the questions, or directing them to contact my buddy, Dominic Fariello, a lawyer who said he would cover for me if any of my clients needed assistance while I was gone.

*Bill waiting for a meeting at the U.S. Embassy.*

    I make a list of all of the promises I make to my clients on a legal pad as I sit at the desk in the hotel room, and will address these promises when I return to Tampa. I put new deadlines and court dates in my phone and my paper calendar. The chief complaint people have against their lawyers is not the manner in which they handle a case, but a lack of communication, so I respond as promptly as I can, even if this requires getting up early to reply to messages so my clients will have some response before going to sleep. Almost all of my clients come to me in crisis, for they have been charged with a crime.

    The uncertainty of their lives rests not just with the outcome of the case, but with their jobs, finances, family, and their sanity. I am a counselor at law, but also a counselor of people. My clients are looking over the edge and all they see is the abyss. My job is to bring some comfort, some level of certainty during this chaotic time. Many of my clients are battling with substance abuse and having to deal with this demon, as their case and their future grind its way through the criminal justice system. They look to me to quiet their troubled minds, calm their frantic family members, relax their employers, and reassure the investigators at the Department of Children and Families that my clients are not bad parents, just going through a bad time.

These skills are not taught in law school, for these tasks have nothing to do with the law. However, performing them on behalf of my clients, many of whom are sick and suffering, is the reason why I am sitting at this desk in a hotel in Manila early in the morning.

I know what it is like to have one's mind race out of control as your head hits the pillow, leaving you to toss, turn, and worry your way into another day you are unable to manage. So a simple text that reads, "I called the prosecutor last week. I think we are going to be able to work a deal. Relax. Everything is going to be fine. I've got you covered," can get that hamster off of the wheel, and allow my client to drift off to sleep and be better able to deal with the myriad of issues that will still be there at first light.

When I finish, I see that Maria is still sleeping, and, thanks be to God, in a few hours my Tampa clients will be, too, so the emails, texts, and phone calls will stop. I sit quietly at the desk and work my program. "God grant me the serenity to accept the things I cannot change, the courage to change the things I can, and the wisdom to know the difference." We say this prayer at the beginning of every AA meeting. It's a short prayer and easy to say, but as Bob said (Bob is eighty-four years old and sometimes sits next to me), "I still have to work on the serenity, the accepting, the courage, and the wisdom parts. Other than that, I got it all figured out."

"Hey, lover. Whatcha doing?" Maria asks, as she stretches herself into the day.

"Doing my thing." I organize my papers on the desk, check one last time that I made contact with everyone who contacted me, lay my pen on top of my TO DO list, and get back in bed with Maria.

"Oh, my God, I love you so freakin' much I can't stand it," I say as I pull her tight.

"That's so sweet, baby."

"No, it's not sweet. It's just true." I sit up. "What the hell are you doing here?" I smile. "What the hell are you doing in a hotel in Manila, Philippines?"

"Going to the United States Embassy to get a letter that is going to free Ron from jail. That's what I'm doing."

"Oh my God, you are so freakin' awesome." I pull her tight again, and she is awesome, and we are awesome, and I am awesome when I am by her side. I don't like the word awesome, but that's what comes out, for I lack the ability to describe my feelings towards Maria. I love her so much, I sometimes want to be her.

"I want to be you, baby. I literally want to crawl inside you and become one with you."

"Samsies," she replies.

I have no filter when I am with Maria, for she knows me so well I might as well say what I am thinking because she already knows. I have never known such freedom in a relationship, such peace. I have had two wives and many girlfriends, but my relationship with each of these diverse women ended exactly the same way. Some of these women, who are nothing alike, even said the same things to me at the end. All the while, I just thought I had gotten involved with five of the craziest women in a row. How unlucky was I?

A few years ago, I was listening to Terry Gross interview Greg Allman of the Allman Brother's Band. At the time, Greg was in the middle of his sixth divorce. Terry said, "Greg, I have to ask you, what goes through your mind in the middle of your sixth divorce?"

Greg paused and then replied, "Terry, I'm beginning to think it's me." For many years, in many relationships, I thought as Greg Allman did.

"So, shall we get ready?" Maria asks as she pulls herself from the sheets. She leans over and kisses my lips. She smiles.

She is not here for Ron. She has never met him. She is not here to visit Manila. Manila is not a glamorous tourist destination. She is not here to get spa treatments and sit by the pool. Maria is here to meet with Chito at the Bayleaf Hotel, go to the Bureau of Immigration, then the United States Embassy, then the National Bureau of Investigation, in the heat, the dirt, among the people, the animals, and the poverty. Maria is here to do whatever it takes. Maria is here for me. PERIOD.

Breakfast is included in the price of the room, so we head to the hotel restaurant before stepping out into the unknown. Maria and I sit at a table next to a window that overlooks the street outside. Cars, trucks, Jeepneys, motorcycles, mopeds, and bicycles are lined up and slowly roll by carrying people who have somewhere to go and something to do, people carrying their fears, concerns, dreams, regrets, anger, and happiness. Halfway around the world, my clients, my parents, and my friends are getting into bed as the day comes to an end. Their heads hit the pillow and they think about where they have to go, what they have to do, carrying their fears, concerns, dreams, regrets, anger, and happiness. All around the world, in the most important ways, we are all the same.

"Lover, where did you go?" Maria asks with a smile. She knows that my mind has drifted off somewhere, rolling through various scenarios of countless concerns about numerous people doing many things.

"I'm right here, baby. Right here." She smiles for she knows that I was not right here, but in some far off place and that she has just pulled me back. We get up and go to the buffet. The offering is not of the usual food one finds in a western hotel restaurant. The dishes include rice, pork, fish, salad, fruit, and noodles, along with eggs, bacon, and sausage. I don't usually eat much, so I select the fish, fruit, and salad. Maria puts a little of everything on her plate, which is exactly how she lives her life—loading up with a little of everything.

We eat hungrily and in silence. The coffee is good, and I motion to the waiter to bring me another cup.

"How do you feel this morning? Jet lagged?" I ask Maria as the waiter refills my cup.

"No. I feel great. I slept like a banshee."

"And how does a banshee sleep?"

"Oh, stop."

"I mean, I'm not even sure what a banshee is. I have never seen one, or at least I don't think I have, and I know I have never seen one sleep. Even if I did, I'm not sure I would know how soundly or unsoundly that banshee was sleeping."

"You are impossible," Maria smiles.

I wonder, "Who is the first person who said, 'I slept like a banshee?' And did the person hearing that say, 'Wow, what a great analogy. I think I will use that next time.' I guess it is better than, 'I slept like a rock.' Who was the first person who said that? Because if someone said that to me, I'd have to tell them that is the dumbest thing I ever heard. Makes no sense at all. Sleeping like a rock."

"It's because a rock doesn't move. Get it?" Maria takes a sip of her coffee. "It makes perfect sense. If someone sleeps like a rock, that person is so sound asleep that the person appears to be an inanimate object, like a rock."

"Yeah, that makes some sense, but how did it catch on? It's not so clever that you would think that it would become a cliché said round the world for generations to come. 'I slept like a rock.' Pretty silly. I like 'I slept like a banshee is better, if in fact banshees are known for sleeping. Are they?"

"I don't even think a banshee is a real animal, but some mythical creature."

"Then it makes even less sense. 'I just slept like a mythical creature.' What does that mean?"

"It's a saying."

"Why?"

"Because people have sayings. People just say stuff."

"Why?"

"You know why. It's just the way people are. You are the same way, too, so don't go thinking that you are above using clichés. You use them just like the rest of us."

"Yes, but the ones I use at least make sense."

"Make sense to you, maybe, but not to others."

Maria takes another sip. "How do you feel?"

"Great. I slept like an inanimate object or a mythical creature."

"Would you stop?" Maria laughs and puts her coffee on the table. She is strikingly beautiful, even more so than when I met her thirty years ago. She was always cute and pretty, but time has crafted an elegance to her. She is wearing her hair up, so the outline of her cheeks and jaw line are more clearly visible. Sometimes when I look at her, I see that child who I meet in the halls of Plant High School in 1988. We were such good friends back then, but now we are inseparable lovers.

God required me to forge a path, walk through many valleys and fall off many mountaintops, endure numerous sleepless nights, imprison myself with my own thinking and selfish actions, endure the wrath that came as a consequence of my actions, so that when I reunited with Maria after a lifetime of stepping in the wrong direction, I would be ready, ready to be a partner, ready to be the "ONE" discussed in the Bible when two people become one flesh, ready to love another human being, and in that love to lose the self—Agape love.

"Where did you go, lover?"

"Just thinking about how beautiful you are."

"Yeah, right."

"Yeah right. It's true."

Maria gives me a half smile. We finish our breakfast and linger over coffee. Though unspoken, we are both delaying our step into the unknown.

Maria knows that I have spent months trying to get the United States Embassy to inform the Filipino government that Ron is no longer a fugitive. The results of my efforts are that we are sitting in a hotel in Manila about to take a car to that Embassy to try and obtain that letter, which will hopefully set Ron free.

After letters, emails, and phone calls, the first direct response to my pleas to the Embassy came only after I sent an email demanding a sit down meeting with the US Ambassador to the Philippines on December 5th, because I was coming to Manila to discuss the issue of my client's intolerable situation and his unexplainable, unjustifiable, and prolonged imprisonment.

The response was very governmental and bureaucratic. Actually, it was a cover your ass response, in that it deflected all responsibility for Ron's situation onto the Filipino government and its system of government—total crap.

Ron is seventy years old. He is an American lawyer from Georgia. He was arrested on a United States mistaken warrant, which was withdrawn in two days. He has been sitting in a shithole for four months since the warrant was withdrawn, as he labors to get around that shithole on a walker. The United States Embassy gives me excuses and spends their time deflecting responsibility, rather than working with me to get this American senior citizen out of jail.

"Let's go to the Embassy, baby." I stand up and Maria follows suit. We are off. The distance to the Embassy from our hotel is less than two miles, but the ride seems much longer. Our car inches into the stream of busses, trucks, cars, motorcycles, and Jeepneys—Tuesday morning in Manila. We have four days to get Ron out.

The United States Embassy sits on an impressive piece of property on Roxas Boulevard overlooking Manila Bay on the backside, and

Rizal Park on the other. The Embassy consists of many separate buildings, all white with turquois-colored roofs. The buildings are also impressive. The people I have dealt with behind these impressive walls are not.

The guards out front of the Embassy are wearing United States uniforms, but look Filipino. "I am here to get some information about my client who is in Filipino custody."

"Please go to that gate. You will need to speak with someone in American Citizen Services."

"Thank you." And with that, Maria and I proceed into the United States Embassy. We show our passports, and then go through security. A man tells us that American Citizen Services is on the second floor. We will need to take a number and wait to be called. We take the escalator to the second floor, which is a large room with chairs in the middle and twenty separate service windows taking numbers as they are called. I take a number and sit next to Maria. The room is already filled with people, most of whom are holding on to small children.

"What's their story?" Maria glances at a man wearing a backpack and holding the hand of a small child who is crying. The man looks American. He has a military-styled flattop haircut, but his hair is gray. He has tattoos on both forearms, but I am too far away to make out the design. He looks fit, but not the kind of fit that comes from taking body pump classes at the YMCA on Monday, Wednesday, and Friday, but the type of fit that comes from strenuously working one's body on a daily basis over the course of many years. His face is weathered but chiseled, his skin light. The young child is wearing a dress. Her skin is dark. Her hair is dark. She is maybe three years old and is crying. The man is looking at a document in one hand, and with his other, he holds the child. What is their story? Maybe ...

Perhaps he is an American serviceman who was stationed in Manila years ago. He met a Filipino woman and married her. The two moved to the United States, maybe North Carolina. They had a child. He recently retired from the military and is receiving his full pension, a pension that will go a lot further in the Philippines than in the United States. He is estranged from his family, his brother and sister, and mom, who is still alive. His family lives in San Diego. He has not seen them in years. They do not approve of his marriage. His wife has a huge family and they are very close. They all have accepted this American military man into their arms and hearts.

This couple with their young child decides to move to Manila. His pension is more than enough to live on, and he can probably pick up contract work either at the American base, or maybe at the Embassy he now stands in. They have been living in Manila for almost a year now, but need to return to the United States. He is here trying to get the proper documents for his wife and young child. Paperwork. Always paperwork. His mother is sick, and his brother reached out for him to come home. He agreed. Now, he is here. His backpack has lots of patches sewn on it. I cannot get a close look, but when Maria and I were hiking the national parks in southern Utah, we saw many people with backpacks that had similar patches.

The patches denote all the places that the person had hiked: Canyonlands, the Hoodoos, Arches, the North Rim of the Grand Canyon. This man hikes alone. The canyons, cliffs, toe paths, ice fields, and rivers are his church, his places of solace and meditation. He is not religious, but he has a Higher Power. He served many combat tours, saw a great deal of action, and killed a few people. He does not go to counseling, even though he still has sleepless nights, but he does hit the trails, with his backpack filled with maps, food, water, a change of socks, sunscreen, bug spray, a first aid kit, and a compass. He wears a knife strapped to his lower left leg. One time, when he was hiking in Denali, he came across a …

A woman comes up behind him. She is holding a small boy. She is Filipino. The little girl releases her grip and goes to her. The man shows the woman the documents he is holding. So they have two children, this ex-military man and this Filipino woman. She is young. Happy to be back in her country. She …

"So, what do you think?" Maria asks.

"About what?"

"Their story," she says as she glances over at the family of four.

"Oh, I have it all figured out."

"I know you do. You have been staring at him for the last ten minutes."

"Is it that obvious?"

"Yes, it is." Maria smiles. I put my head on her shoulder and wait for our number to be called.

It is time to talk about the charge—Ron's charge. I was not going to include his charge in this book, because it shouldn't matter. Maria and I sit in the United States Embassy in Manila, not because of his charge, but because of the arrest warrant that was mistakenly issued, Ron was arrested, the warrant was withdrawn, and the United States has not informed the Filipino government that Ron is no longer a fugitive, so there he sits, and here we sit, in the Embassy with ticket in hand, waiting for our turn to be called.

Ron was charged with the possession of child pornography. Sounds terrible, and the child pornography industry is—terrible, insidious, despicable, and those dealing in it should go to prison. PERIOD. The facts behind Ron's charge are not the ones that might jump to the forefront of your mind. In 1995, Ron was living in Havana, Cuba, as a journalist. One night, some prostitutes came over to his apartment. Ron ended up having sex with one of the prostitutes, and the act was filmed. The woman was young. Just how young would be the subject of a fierce legal battle twenty plus years later in a federal courthouse in Tampa, Florida.

That film, for reasons unknown, ended up in a storage room in Ron's T-Mobile store that he owned in Spring Hill, Florida, in 2008. At that time, Ron had an employee stealing from him. He filed a police report against her, and somehow (the circumstances still unknown) that employee got her hands on that film and turned it over to the Hernando County Sherriff's office, stating that it contained child pornography.

The State Attorney's office reviewed the tape and decided not to prosecute Ron, for the woman in the film was post-pubescent and her age was not readily ascertainable—was she fifteen or nineteen? If she was fifteen, then a crime had occurred, not for having sex with a minor, because that act occurred over twenty years ago in another country, but for possessing child pornography in 2008. If she was nineteen, then no crime occurred. The girl's identity was unknown, so the government was going to prove her age by the video itself, which the State Attorney's office concluded that it could not do beyond a reasonable doubt.

Then, somehow, the tape ended up in the hands of federal agents from the Department of Homeland Security. This began a six-year surveillance investigation into Ron's movements and activities. Ron traveled all over the world, and federal agents were certain that they had a sex tourist on their hands, a person who travels to countries for the purpose of having sex with young girls. They followed Ron from Cuba to Bangkok, Ron never being the wiser. His bags were searched upon reentry into the United States. Over the years, after countless trips abroad, after taxpayer money being spent in search of some sexual deviant, the United States government found ... nothing.

So, the United States government decided to leave Ron alone, right? No. In 2015, seven years after taking possession of the old tape, the United States of America indicted Ron for the possession of that old tape. At the time, Ron was living in the Philippines and got word that he had been indicted. Rather than hide, and clearly thinking the case was ridiculous, Ron flew from Manila to Tampa to self-surrender. Then things got really crazy.

I was not involved in the case at the time, and at first appearance, Ron's lawyer argued that he should be released on bond. He was sixty-seven years old at the time, in need of a hip replacement and bypass surgery, and the case against Ron was ludicrous and vindictive, but the unthinkable happened. The court found that he was a flight risk based on the government's recitation of all of the countries he had visited and lived in over the years, so the court ordered that Ron be held in the Pinellas County jail without a bond.

I met Ron three months later in the medical wing of the Pinellas County jail. A friend called and said Ron was looking for new representation and had given Ron my name. I went to the jail for my "interview."

I approached the guard desk in the middle of a large open room that was filled with what looked like cubicles, but were the individual "rooms" for the sick inmates. I told the guard whom I was there to see, and he responded, "The old sick guy?"

Having never met Ron, I just nodded my head. The guard walked over among the cubicle rooms, and then I saw an elderly bald man struggle to stand up. He grabbed onto a walker and slowly made his way to a room next to the showers. The room had a desk and two chairs.

Ron got to the door, stuck out his hand, and said, "I'm Ron. Thank you for coming." I helped Ron into a chair and once settled, he looked at me and said, "I'm not even sure where to begin."

So he began at the beginning, telling me where he was born, a bit about his childhood, then his college days, and off to law school. He told me about a few large cases he had tried, and some of his victories and crushing defeats.

Ron described how later he decided to stop practicing law and began life as a journalist. He went to live in Cuba on a journalist Visa, where he interviewed Fidel Castro, wrote stories about food and culture and a book about wine, married a Cuban woman, had a child, travelled the world, got divorced, got together with another Cuban woman, smuggled her into the United States through the Bahamas and then Bimini, started a business in Ft. Lauderdale, and moved to Spring Hill to open a T-Mobil store. That is when the events leading up to his arrest took place.

He told me about the employee who was stealing money from him, whom he fired. He called the police, which is when she turned that old tape of Ron and the prostitute over to the Hernando County Sherriff's office. Ron was unaware how the tape ended up in the hands of federal agents. He knew the State Attorney's office had declined to prosecute, so Ron resumed his life, with federal agents secretly in tow.

He was informed seven years later that he had been indicted for possession of child pornography. Possession of that twenty-year-old tape of him and the unknown Cuban woman was in the hands of the United States Attorney's Office for the Middle District of Florida.

Ron hired a lawyer and flew from Manila to Tampa. Ron actually made some doctor's appointments for his return to the States, never thinking that he would he held without bond, and live for the next eleven months in the Pinellas County jail, as his spirits and health rapidly declined.

I enjoyed listening to Ron, and I could tell from the way he crafted the story of his life that he was a good trial attorney and an excellent journalist, both storytellers by trade. Ron and I got along immediately, despite our age differences, and two days later I was hired .

Now, I could write a separate book on the litigation that ensued over the course of the following eleven months. We had hearings to readdress Ron's bond status—denied; to allow Ron to be escorted by the United States Marshals to a heart specialist, because his lower legs were turning a dark purple and sores were opening on his ankles and feet. It was granted to remove the United States Attorney's office for the Tampa division for violating Ron's right to protected attorney-client communication. Granted (are you beginning to see how I could write a book?) to disallow the United States' expert who stated that the woman in the video in question was fourteen, a conclusion our expert in child development called "ludicrous" and never heard by the Court for a plea agreement that was reached, a plea agreement that involved multiple lawyers and all levels of the hierarchy within the United States Attorney's Office.

Now, for most of my representation, Ron was insistent that we go to trial, but the downside of losing at trial was catastrophic. "If we lose, you will spend six years or more in a federal prison." Ron was insistent that he had done nothing wrong, and I truly believe that he had not.

On a Friday afternoon, I went to view the original tape along with the expert we had hired. At first, I did not recognize Ron in the video, he was so much younger, dark hair, dark beard, bounding around the room, far from the bald man with a white straggly beard shuffling across the jail pod on his walker.

Then I saw the woman. She was young, but how young was the critical question. We could see when she shed her clothes that she was fully developed. It was then that our expert said it would be impossible to pinpoint exactly the age of this woman, since she was past puberty. He agreed that she could be 14, but also, 15, 16, 17, 18, or 19. Remember, Ron was not charged with the sexual act, but having a video that depicted a sexual act with a minor.

After months of negotiating, Ron agreed to plead guilty, because the plea deal would secure his release from jail, and allow him to return to the Philippines, where he had a girlfriend and a child. Ron was not at all that concerned about being a convicted felon, since he was retired, so we crafted a deal with the United States Attorney's office for a plea to time served, and five years of supervised release with the caveat that he could return to the Philippines whenever he wanted.

It was this last piece of the agreement that never made its way to the probation office in south Florida, so his probation officer violated Ron for leaving the country for Manila without permission, which led to his arrest at his home in the Philippines. Now, my successful motion to have the warrant for his arrest was withdrawn. Months passed of unanswered pleas to get the United States government to assist me in getting Ron out of that Filipino detention center, until, ultimately, Maria and I boarded a plane and travelled nine thousand miles—all to get Ron out of custody before he died.

So the underlying charge, possession of child pornography, does not matter, or shouldn't, because Ron was not being held in a Filipino jail for possession of child pornography. He was there because an arrest warrant was executed, and then withdrawn. However, the charge, possession of pornography, did matter to US officials in charge of his release, as you will see.

We are still waiting for our number to be called, so my head is still on Maria's shoulder, as the room fills with people. Ron is stuck in jail, while the air outside still warm and wet, while the streets are filled with trucks, cars, Jeepneys, motorcycles, and children who are not in school, but struggling to make it through the day just to sleep, wake up, and make it through the next day.

"NUMBER FIFTY-FOUR," the voice yells our number from window two. Maria and I get to our feet and walk to the window.

"How may I help you?" I take a deep breath and remember what Ron first said to me over two years ago, "I'm not even sure where to begin." I look at Maria and begin again.

The person behind window number two gets quickly overwhelmed with the information and paperwork I present: an order from a federal court, an email from the supervisor of his division explaining why the Embassy has not assisted in securing Ron's release, my letters to the State Department, to the United States Attorney's Office, and to United States Probation, who sent the initial letter of violation to the Federal Judge in Tampa.

"Sir, you need to speak with a supervisor. I cannot help you with this."

"Can I actually speak with Ms. Erica M?" (Yes I will protect her identity, though I would like to call her out). "She is the one who sent me this email stating why the United States government is not to blame for my client's continued incarceration, and that it is the fault of the Filipino government that he is rotting in a jail."

The man behind the window gives me a quick look, picks up the phone, and holds up one finger indicating that I should wait. After a few minutes, he places the phone down, and gathers up the documents that I provided to him outlining the chaotic and quixotic journey that lead us to his window nine thousand miles from my home. He tells me to wait just one more minute, and in about one minute exactly, he returns.

"Yes, you can speak with Erica M. She is going to be waiting for you. Please go back down to the first floor, walk to the end of the hall, where you will see a number of rooms. Please go to Room Number Seven. She will be there in a few minutes." He looks flustered.

"Can I have my documents back?"

"Yes, sir, of course, sir." He slides the documents under the glass and motions to the escalator. "Downstairs and to Room Number Seven at the end of the hall."

"Thank you, sir, you have been very helpful." And he has. He did not tell me that he could not help me and leave it at that, as had the employees with whom I had spoken at the State Department, the United States Attorney's Office, the United States Probation, and the Embassy during the months prior to my coming to Manila. The employee I spoke with at the State Department was the most frustrating and maddening of all. My conversation with this State Department employee over the phone went something like this:

"So, what I need now (this came after I detailed the events that lead to Ron's arrest) is for you to send a letter to the Filipino government stating that my client is no longer a fugitive, and the United States will not be coming to pick him up."

"Not me, sir. That's not my job." The voice on the other side sounded young, very young—not a good sign, for I needed someone to take control of this situation.

"When I say 'YOU', I mean the United States government, the State Department—not you personally."

"We are not a law enforcement agency," he said and then paused as if that should mean something to me.

"Okay. What does that mean? I am not asking the State Department to arrest anyone."

"You will need a law enforcement agency to do that."

"Why?"

"The State Department does not tell other countries what to do."

"I am not telling the State Department to tell the Filipino government what to do. I am telling the State Department to inform the Filipino government that my client is no longer a fugitive, and the United States will not be coming to pick him up and deport him back to the United States. So, I am asking the State Department to just inform the Philippines of a factual situation. The Filipino government can then do whatever it wants. They can hold or release my client or do whatever. Understand?"

"That is not the State Department's role."

I placed my head in hands. "Whose role is it?"

"A law enforcement agency. Maybe the FBI? Have you tried them?"

"Doesn't the FBI only work within the United States?"

"They might be able to assist you better."

"Well, I am sure of that. I don't see how the FBI has any control over this situation at all. Let me ask you, do you, and when I say you I mean the State Department, agree that the arrest warrant that lead to my client's arrest and incarceration has been withdrawn, that my client is no longer a fugitive, and that the United States government is not going to pick up my client to deport him back to the United States?"

"From all the documents I have seen, yes, I agree with that."

"Then why can't you, the State Department, just send a letter to the Filipino government informing them of this?"

"This is not the State Department's job. We are not law enforcement. We do not tell other countries what they can and cannot do."

"I am not asking you to tell the Filipino government ... " I stopped in paralyzing frustration. "So let me get this straight, my client is seventy years old, just had bypass surgery and a hip replacement, is on a walker, and he has been unnecessarily detained in a Filipino prison because no one in the US government will inform the Filipino government that he is no longer a fugitive, so there he sits, dying."

"We can help if he needs medical attention."

"What?"

"If your client is in need of medical attention, we can send someone from the Embassy to make sure he is getting the medical care he needs. Do you want us to do that?"

I could barely breathe at this point. "Ummm, the State Department will go to the prison in Manila to make sure my client is getting medical care, but will not tell that same prison that the US government is not coming to pick him up, and if that is the only reason for his prolonged detention, he should be released."

"We will not tell the Filipino government what to do, sir. How many times do I have to tell you that?"

"But the government will make sure that my client has proper medical care to stay alive so his unnecessary detention in that Filipino shithole is prolonged, along with the violation of civil rights. Is that what YOU are saying?"

"I don't like your tone, sir."

"My tone? My client is dying in a Filipino prison for no reason."

"And I already told you, we can send someone from the Embassy to make sure he is receiving the proper medical care while in custody." At that point, I almost succumbed to an apoplectic shock.

Maria and I find Room Number Seven at the end of the hall on the first floor. We open the door and step inside. There are two chairs next to each other facing a bulletproof glass window. Maria and I sit down.

"Bulletproof glass? Are you kidding me? Didn't we have to show our passports to get in here, and then go through a metal detector? Now, we can only speak to Erica on the other side of bulletproof glass?"

"Baby, you need to take it easy." Maria puts her hand on my leg. "All we need is that letter, and we have a meeting with the person who might just be able to write it."

"Bulletproof glass? Really?" I say half under my breath, not yet ready to let go of my anger and frustration. "I'm sure the employees here do need to sit behind bulletproof glass, because they don't do shit and drive ordinary law-abiding citizens into deranged lunatics ready to take a human life."

"Bill Bill," Maria sometimes calls me that because she knows my mother used to do it. "You need to calm down. If Erica walks through that door and you start with your attitude, we aren't going to get anywhere. That will not help Ron. You need to focus on the goal. We are in the United States Embassy in Manila, Philippines." She places her arm around my shoulders.

"If this goes poorly, we have nowhere else to turn. Our goal of getting Ron out of jail could end right now. You need to keep that in mind, keep Ron in mind. He is the reason we are here, and if it takes sitting in a room sweet-talking some bureaucrat from behind a bulletproof window to get Ron out, then that's what we are going to do. I know you are frustrated, but this is not about you. This is not about lazy and incompetent government workers. This is about Ron, and we are here to do whatever it takes to get him out. He is relying on us. Okay? Can you focus for me?" Maria slightly squeezes my neck.

"Bulletproof glass, as if," I say sliding Maria a smile so she knows that she has broken through the thick layer of anger that was encasing me. We sit in silence. My breathing regulates. A door on the other side of the bulletproof glass opens, a light switches on, and a middle-aged American woman enters and sits in the seat across from us.

"Good morning. I am Erica. I am the director of American Citizen Services here at the Embassy. I understand that you are here about your client."

"Yes, we are." I look at Maria, take a deep breath and begin. "I am not sure how much you know, or remember about my client's long ordeal, but you did send me an email about two weeks ago." I reach into my bag and pull out the folder containing all my documents. I grab a copy of the email in which Erica basically deflected all responsibility, and I place it flat against the bulletproof glass for her to inspect, the same way I do when visiting my clients at certain jails around the state of Florida.

"Yes, I am familiar with that email. I remember your client's situation. The problem is ... " the adrenaline begins to flow even before she finishes her sentence, "that the Embassy does not control the Filipino government. We cannot direct the Filipino government to do anything, especially to release your client. So I am not sure that the US government can help."

I lean forward before repeating what I have said, written, emailed, and faxed what seems like ten thousand times. "We are not asking you to tell the Filipino government what to do. All we are asking is that you send a letter to the Filipino government informing them that my client is no longer a fugitive, because the arrest warrant was withdrawn, and that the United States is not coming to pick my client up to deport him back to the United States. Then, the Filipino government can do whatever they want, and I realize this is out of your control."

"Please don't say *me*. I am not the one who is responsible for this."

"When I say *YOU*, I am referring to the United States of America, of which you are a representative."

She looks down at some papers she brought with her. "I see that your client was charged with possession of child pornography. Many times the Filipino government will hold such undesirables in custody because of a charge like this, and there is nothing that the United States can do about it."

"Fair enough, but the United States still needs to inform the Filipino government that the United States is not coming to pick him up to be deported back to the United States, because there is no longer a warrant out for him. We can all agree that if this never happens, then my client has no chance of ever being released."

"We went to the Bureau of Immigration yesterday," Maria begins, "and we were told that we need a letter from the United States stating that our client is no longer a fugitive, because that is the reason he is still being held." Maria looks at me and then back to Erica M. "So, it sounds like our client is not being held for any charge he might have had in the United States, but because the Filipino government still thinks he is a fugitive, and that you, I mean the United States, is coming to pick him up to deport him."

"Well, the Filipino government might have told you that, but they still can hold him as an undesirable, " Erica adds.

"We know that, and completely understand that, but if the Filipino government does not get the letter from the Embassy, they will never know." This third-grade teacher from Tampa, Florida, is doing a much better job at discussing the state of Ron's incarceration with an official from the United States Embassy than her legally trained boyfriend.

"The Bureau of Immigration said that they need a letter from the United States and an BI clearance, and we have an appointment at BI this afternoon at 2 o'clock. So, we just really need that letter." Erica M. sits in silence sifting through the paperwork that lay on the table before her. Maria outlined the situation in a such a simple and straightforward manner that Erica seems to be searching for a reason to say that the United States does not have any responsibility in the matter. She flips the papers, straightens the papers, and pretends to read the papers.

"My department is not the department that would even write such a letter. You would have to get something from law enforcement, and they are not in today. They are in the field in some type of training."

"Will they be back tomorrow?" Maria asks before I have a chance to say something condescending to this woman, and therefore, damage our chances on this life-and-death errand.

"I think so, but they are very busy, and very hard to reach."

I slip my hand into my bag and pull out a copy of the Summary Deportation Order issued by the Filipino government to Ron. In the order, it say that Mike R., an attaché for the "United States Department of State, Diplomatic Security Service Overseas Criminal Investigations, Manila, informed the BI that Ron is a fugitive from the USA for violation of probation in relation to his original charge as a sex offender." I place the letter against the glass. "Will Mike R. be in tomorrow? He is the one who informed BI that Ron is a fugitive. Now, BI wants him to inform them that Ron is no longer a fugitive before they will release him."

"Well, Mike R. is the chief of the Criminal Investigations unit, so it will be hard to contact him. He has a lot on his plate right now." Erica M. sits back in her chair as if she is tiring from this conversation.

"All we need is a short letter," I say.

"Let me think outside of the box for you," Erica responds. "I know how the Filipino government works, and maybe there is something you can do that will speed up this process." For the first time in months, someone in the United States government has my undivided attention. A possible solution. Speeding up the process. These are good things, great things—not "I'm sorry, it's not my job, not my department, not my problem, not a good time, not going to happen, not … not … not.

Erica sits up, places her elbows on the table and clasps her hands as if about to start a prayer. "Why don't you write the letter? Sometimes all the Filipino government wants is something with a stamp on it, and we will do that."

"You will co-sign a letter I write?"

"No, we will notarize a letter that you write." All the blood leaves my head, and I almost fall out of my chair. Is this woman crazy, insane, mentally deficient, or is she just playing a cruel joke on me? Maria can sense the rage emanating from every single pore in my body.

"You want me, Ron's criminal defense attorney from Tampa, Florida, to write a letter to the Filipino government telling them that even though the United States State Department informed them that Ron is a fugitive from justice that the Filipino government should release him because I, his paid criminal defense attorney, says so. Is that what you are suggesting?"

I can't breathe. "That is … nonsensical." I am surprised that such a kind word came out of my mouth, and so is Maria for she steps on my foot as if trying to thwart the next word from coming out, a word that will not be so kind.

"That makes absolutely no sense at all. We have travelled nine thousand miles to get you, the United States of America, to write a simple letter to the Filipino government. We came to the United States Embassy for help, and your suggestion is that I should write a letter. Is that the official position of the United States as to my client who is a seventy-year-old American lawyer from Georgia, on a walker and rotting in a Filipino detention facility due to a mistaken warrant that was withdrawn over four months ago? Is it the United States' official position in this dire situation? That his criminal defense attorney should just write the Filipino government a letter, and then my client will magically be released with a plane ticket to the country of choosing in one hand and a letter of apology from the Filipino government in the other." Maria presses harder on my foot.

"We just don't think," Maria begins, more to stop me from speaking than to add something to the conversation, "that the Filipino government will accept a letter from us, because we were told yesterday that we need something from the United States government, not from us."

"Sometimes they just want something with a stamp on it," Erica adds, insulting the intelligence of the entire Filipino government as she does.

"That was not our impression from yesterday," Maria continues. "The gentleman in charge reviewed all of the same documents that you just viewed, and he was very specific. His government needs a letter from our government stating that Ron is no longer a fugitive, and he needs an BI clearance, which we are getting today. Those are the *only* two things that the Filipino government needs and will accept before releasing our client."

Silence. Maria and I watch Erica shuffle through all the papers again as she sits on the other side of the bulletproof glass. Maria and I received handshakes and warm welcomes from the Filipino government, but we get a lady sitting on the other side of bulletproof glass telling us, "It ain't our fuckin' problem," from our own government.

"I will see what I can do. I will try to contact Mike R. today. I can't make any promises."

"That would be very helpful," I say in a genuinely thankful way, trying to repair some of the damage I might have caused, so as to not blow up the bridge that Maria just built.

"Yes, that would be very helpful," Maria adds, relieved that I did not throw another grenade. Erica M. picks up the papers she has been nervously fussing with during our entire conversation. We cannot shake hands because we are separated by bulletproof glass. I say, "Thank you very much. I apologize. I am just a bit stressed over this situation, and a bit tired from the long flight." Erica M. does not deserve an apology, but I am here for Ron, not me. Maria and I are in Manila on a life-and-death errand. This is the best I can do. Maria also thanks Erica M., who vanishes out a side door and into the abyss that is the United States Embassy fortress.

"I think that went well," I say to Maria as she places her hand on my shoulder and laughs.

"Yea, you almost got us arrested. Can't wait until we meet the Filipino officials at BI this afternoon. You might just get us shot." We laugh and head back outside into the heat, the traffic, the smells, the garbage, and the people that make up the city of Manila. I am beginning to like this place.

# WHO ARE YOU, CREEPO? WHO ARE YOU?

There is a scene in the movie *Rocky* that I think about from time to time. Rocky is walking down the streets of Philadelphia and comes across some kids hanging out in front of a liquor store. They are yelling insults at him, and then Rocky notices a young girl he knows, Marie. He tells Marie that he wants to walk her home, and on their way to the young girl's house Rocky imparts to her his philosophy. The following is not a direct quote (you will need to rent the movie for the exact words) but this is how I remember the scene:

Rocky: Marie, what are you doing hanging out with those coconuts?

Maria: They're my friends?

Rocky: (After taking a cigarette from her mouth) Don't smoke these. It will make your mouth smell like garbage.

Marie: I like garbage.

Rocky: No one likes garbage! Marie, if you keep hanging out with those yoyos, you're going to become a yoyo. See, if you hang out with nice people, you'll have nice friends. If you hang out with smart people, you'll have smart friends. If you hang out with yoyo people, you'll have yoyo friends.

Now I have to use a bad word—whore. If you hang out with those guys, no one will remember you, but they will remember the rut. Someone will say, "Remember Marie?"

"No, I don't remember her."

"She's that whore who used to hang out on the corner."

"Now, I remember her."

See they won't remember you—they will remember the rut. You see …

| | | |
|---|---|---|
| Marie: | | I know. |
| Rocky: | | What? |
| Marie: | | If I keep acting like a whore, I will become one. |
| Rocky: | | Something like that. |
| Marie: | | Hey, Rocky (She says as she stands on the stoop outside of her home). Screw you, creepo! (She flips him off, turns, and goes inside). |
| Rocky: | | (Turns away and slowly bounces his racket ball on the ground. He says to himself). Yeah, who are you to give advice, creepo? Who are you? |

This clip stuck with me long before I started working the AA program and before I understood how selfish and self-centered my life, my actions, and my thinking are (I almost typed *were*, but must write *are*—the program calls for rigorous honesty). I'm not sure why the scene resonated with me in the past, because I did not live a humble life. I did not wake up and make a daily concerted effort to smash and re-smash my Ego. I did not live a life that demands rigorous honesty.

I like the scene because it shows Rocky's humility—not mine. Rocky questions who is he to give advice to anyone, even a twelve-year-old girl hanging out on the street with a bunch of coconuts. In that moment, I used to think that Rocky realized that he was a nobody, a two-bit leg breaker working for a loan shark and dreaming about becoming somebody when he laces up the gloves at Mickey's Boxing gym. Who is someone like that to give advice? Now, I think differently about this scene, since I came to the rooms and started working the program.

"I'm not in control anymore. I gave that job back to the one who always had it in the first place—God." Paul sits in his usual seat at the far end of the table. "Life was hard, when I was trying to control everyone. I always had advice to give (or what I used to call advice). It was more like stage directions to all the actors around me, and if they just did their part like I wanted, everything would be fine. But they never did, and my life sucked."

Paul sits back and adjusts his baseball cap. It is too faded to read the logo from my seat on the other side of the room. I sit in between Diane and Dan. Dan is a retired marine and wears Harley Davidson gear to every meeting. He is a large man with a handle bar mustache that matches the handlebars on the bike he parks in the parking lot at the efficiency motel next door. He wears a silver skull ring on his middle finger. He looks like he would break your neck for asking him which way to the nearest gas station, but when I first spoke to him his eyes lit up and a smile grew across his face. Dan is a wonderfully gracious human being with twenty-three years sobriety. He loves the Lord and the fellowship of Alcoholic Anonymous. He spends his time riding on his Harley and sponsoring others who are sick and suffering. He has ceased fighting anyone and anything. Dan said he owes everything in his life to God and these rooms.

"This bad ass mother fucker now spend his days with the Bible in one hand and the Big Book in the other." Dan quit smashing others and now smashes himself, his Ego, and he walks this earth with a strength and a power he never had when he frequented the biker bars. He no longer drinks. He prays every morning to do God's will, not his. He helps any and all who ask, but he does not offer advice. That's not his place, not his way. He does not have a way—rather, he gets up every morning and asks the God of his understanding for help, direction, and guidance. Dan is a peaceful and loving man and has found true freedom. I want what he has.

Diane is a mother of three. She was sentenced to these rooms by a judge, but now is here to try and save her marriage, her family, and her life. Last year, she got pulled over for speeding. She was drunk and had her seven-year-old in the car. Her husband let her spend two days in jail before he bailed her out.

Diane always looks put together on the outside—the diamond ring, the purse, the hairstyle, the earrings, the makeup, the shoes, and the dress, all perfect. She has masked her chaotic life well. She is here for the same reason as Dan, though they literally come from different universes—they are both searching for freedom, freedom from the self and the unbearable weight that comes with it. Dan and Diane are friends. I have seen them talk, laugh, and embrace. The bad ass biker and the soccer mom on the same life and death errand, taking time to help and guide each other along the way.

When I first came into these rooms, I wasn't sure what I needed. I wasn't drinking, and wasn't that enough? The more I sat and listened, actually listened for the first time in my life, I began to understand what I wanted, what I needed. I wanted what others in the room had. I wanted what Bill W. had and why he wrote the Big Book to guide others. I wanted—freedom.

Though I was divorced for the second time by the time I stepped into these rooms, and only had my kids fifty percent of the time, I was not a free man. I was a slave to myself, to my wishes, to my desires, to my excesses, and to my mind. Even waking up on a Saturday morning by myself with nothing to do that day, I was not a free man. I was locked inside myself. My mind held me prisoner and tortured me slowly throughout the day. I would go for a long run, swim, or a bike ride, sometimes in succession, but I was not free, for I was always there.

In the rooms, there is a picture of Bill W. on the wall. He is sitting at his desk in his office—he named the picture, "At Wit's End." Bill is smiling, reclining in his chair. At the bottom of the picture it reads, "And I knew I was a free man ... " Freedom from the self. What is that really? What does that look like? What does it feel like?

Sometimes I think about Jesus, my Higher Power. I think about the people he hung out with when he walked the earth, the poor, the prostitutes, the sick and suffering, the ragamuffins. If he came back today, I am certain Jesus would sit next to Roger by the water cooler amongst us modern-day ragamuffins. Jesus did not have an ego. He completely denied the self and gave his life to his Father in heaven, doing God's will, not his.

Unlike me, Jesus actually had the power to control others, to be the director of his play and order others to move around the stage as he wished, but Jesus didn't do that. He asked, never ordered. He listened before he talked. He gave of himself completely, he turned the other cheek, and in doing so he was free. He was not beholden to this world or anything in it. He reminds me that my life is like a mist, a mere vapor, shooting forth one second, gone the next. No matter who you are or who your Higher Power is, absolute freedom in the rooms is the goal. This is the freedom we all want and what we all strive for. This is why we work the program and will continue to do so for the rest of our lives.

Rocky had it right. He did not get angry when Marie flipped him off and called him a name. He smashed his Ego, rather than giving in to it, and in that moment, Rocky was a free man.

"Who are you, creepo? Who are you?"

## Chapter Two

# Rizal Park

MARIA AND I did not have much time to research Manila or the Philippines before our trip. We decided to come nine days before takeoff, and in that time we both had to get our lives in order.

Maria had to create a week's worth of lesson plans for her substitute teacher, make sure her ex-husband was willing to take her son on her days, and find a dog sitter to take care of Domino, Maria's fourteen-year-old deaf and blind Shi Tzu Maltese mix.

My ex-wife agreed to take my kids on my days. I made multiple calls to multiple criminal defense attorney friends to get all my scheduled court dates covered, asking them to simply tell the court that I had to take an emergency trip out of the country on behalf of a client, and to just get a new court date.

Attorney Dominic Fariello, better known as The Dom, would handle any legal emergencies that came up for my clients while I was out of the country. I rent space from Dom, and sometimes appear as a guest on his weekly radio show, The Ask the Dom Show.

This legal call-in show brought Maria and me back into each other's lives when she called in one night and had some fun at my expense. Maria had seen on Facebook that I was co-hosting the radio show, so she and her friends decided to call in. She was with seven of her high school friends at a get together, "girls' night," two days before Christmas.

When Maria called in, she was on speakerphone, and I quickly knew that something was up when I heard all the laughter in the background. Maria asked me some made up question about getting her husband deported. Cackles of laughter exploded in the background as she explained her dire situation.

Even though I had not heard Maria's voice in many years, I quickly realized that the caller was Maria Giglio. The laughter in the background belonged to the other seven of the "Great Eight," a clique of eight girls that ran together in high school.

I finally asked, "Wait, is this Maria Giglio?" Laughter pulsated across the airwaves. Dom asked me if I could name all eight girls, and even though put on the spot on live radio, I was able to somehow remove years of dust from my mind, and name every single one.

When Maria told Dom, "You should ask Billy how many of the Great Eight he has dated," the heat from my red face could be felt burning through the radio waves. After that night, I contacted Maria via instant messenger to tell her how much fun I had had.

A month later, for reasons unknown to me, I contacted her again, God inspired I now know, to ask if she and the Great Eight wanted to get together and reconnect. I was in the middle of my second divorce and had just moved into a rented condo.

Maria and I then began the sweetest courtship ever to take place on this ball we call Earth, talking over coffee, walking down Tampa's River Walk, going to movies, playing board games, starting a Bible study, leaning on each other's shoulders when the weight of our divorces almost pushed us to the ground, all the while never even holding hands, me only lightly pecking her cheek each time we would say goodbye when the late night hour forced us to separate.

It was during this sweet and innocent time that I came to understand that I had the God-breathed capacity to completely love another human being. I thanked God for Facebook and the radio, the new and the old mediums of communication that brought two old friends together on God's time, not ours.

Even though Maria and I did not have much time to prepare for our trip to Manila, Maria conducted some research on the city and country. Maria ordered a map of Manila, a quick and easy guide to the city, and *Noli Me Tangere*, or *Touch Me Not*, a novel written by Jose Rizal, the Philippines most important national hero. The novel was published in 1887 and described the social inequities brought about by the Spanish Catholic church and the government.

Jose Rizal was a doctor, a writer, a poet, and a political

*Rizal Park*

reformer during the time of Spain's colonial rule. *Touch Me Not*, although fiction, created a social movement within the country and ultimately lead to Rizal's execution at the age of thirty-five by a firing squad. The site of Rizal's execution is located in a park in the center of Manila. The execution spot now pays tribute to the man who set in motion the Philippines' separation from Spanish rule and towards independence.

Maria started *Touch Me Not* the day before we left for Manila and made her way through it as we travelled from Tampa to New York, New York to Taiwan, and Taiwan to Manila. On December 30, 1896, Jose Rizal wanted to face his executioners, but was denied his request. He was shot in the back. His last words were, "It is finished," the same words that Jesus uttered from high on the cross the day he breathed his last breath.

The site of Rizal's execution, brought about by cowardly individuals afraid of losing a grip on some small sliver of earthly power, now stands as a national shrine to courage, independence, and freedom. Jose Rizal never bore arms, only a pen, but as the Good Book and the Big Book have shown me and millions of other sick and suffering people, the pen, when God-breathed, contains power beyond our limited understanding, a power greater than the guns and bombs we build to guard and hoard our earthly treasures.

Jose Rizal believed in something, and didn't just make a decision to do something—he took action and did something. The line between making a decision to do something and actually taking the action of doing that something can be as wide as the Gulf of Mexico. I have spent most of my life stuck on the Gulf's shore staring out across the water, making lots of decisions with my feet safely planted in the sand, only to return to the beach house to sip a cocktail as I let those decisions fade and those dreams stay just that, dreams.

Jose Rizal's remains were moved from an unmarked grave and placed at the current site, within a stone monument resembling a miniature version of the National Monument in Washington, DC. At the base of the monument, there is a statue of Rizal standing tall, looking over the city and the country that he wrote into independence. To his left, there is a statue of children kneeling while reading a book, to his right a mother holding her infant son.

Right before his execution, a Spanish surgeon took Rizal's pulse—remarkably, his pulse was normal. His work was finished, with the decisions he had made and turned into actions. He left this earth to the care of others, with the hope that they wouldl not stand on the shores of the Gulf of Mexico with their feet in the sand, and a drink in one hand, but rather to take action and step faithfully, willfully, and joyfully into the deep water.

Maria and I wander through the grounds of Rizal Park. Even though it is December, the air is warm and wet. Sweat begins to gather on my forehead, the small of my back, and on my feet, which are stuffed into leather shoes. Maria decided we should do some "power sightseeing" in between our meeting at the Embassy and the National Bureau of Investigation.

We learn that on July 4, 1946, the United States, who was operating as a protectorate of the Philippines, turned over sovereign control to the people of the Philippines at the site of Rizal's Monument. We snap some photos, but my mind is not on the history of Manila, its people, or even the amazing short life of Dr. Jose Rizal.

My mind churns and churns, hitting replay again and again on Erica M. and the interaction we just had at the Embassy. Who the hell does she think she is? She actually told me to write a letter to the Filipino government telling them to release my client, a man whom the United States government told them to take into custody?

Me? A stamp? Really? That's all the Filipino government wants? Some notary stamp, and they will release Ron? Is she serious, stupid, conceited, or just that condescending? I'll bet my life savings that dimwit has never been to the Bureau of Immigration, never spoken with a Filipino representative, never once got her ass out of that chair and out from behind the bulletproof glass where she pretends that she is important and in need of protection. I travelled nine thousand miles for her to tell me to write a letter? Does she think that I am just as dimwitted as she is?

"Bill Bill, where did you go?" Maria brings me back to Rizal Park, stops me from hitting the replay button. My mother used to call me Bill Bill. She is sick and no longer speaks, but Maria has called me this ever since I spoke to her about my mom, and her affectionate name for me, Bill Bill.

"Erica M.—I just can't get her out of my mind," I say, looking up at the large Filipino flag, which sits at the site of the American transfer of power to the Filipino government.

"I know. She was rude to us and condescending to the Filipino government, but you know what?" She waits for me to look at her. "We might still need her. Remember the mission. It's to get Ron out of jail, and we will need that letter. She said she is going to try to find the right law enforcement person—Mike R., right? He is the one Homer referred to in his deportation order. She said she will try and get in touch with him. He's the law enforcement guy we need, right?"

"Yes, you're right, and I need to stop letting Erica rent space in my head. It's just that we travelled nine thousand miles. We are at the United States Embassy. I am an American lawyer. Ron is an American lawyer. He is sitting in a Filipino shithole because of the Embassy, and Erica gives me crap as she sits behind bulletproof glass. Who in the hell … " Maria places her hands on the sides of my face.

"Let it go, baby. Yes, she's lazy and had an ego the size of Texas, but what can we do about it other than press forward?" She feels the tension begin to slowly drip out of my body and removes her hands from my face. "Now get out your camera and take a selfie of us in this amazing park."

"Yes, Ms. Street. Will do."

In the rooms, we learn that to live a more spiritual and free life, we must work the steps and the principles that are associated with them in all our affairs. The teachings do not stay in the rooms, and by teachings, I mean the steps as outlined in the Big Book of Alcoholics Anonymous, which is the roadmap to recovery for the sick and suffering individual.

It's what the people in the rooms say about their experiences in life, how they are working their program, and how they have grasped a manner of living that demands rigorous honesty. How they take time to make a daily inventory of the harms they have caused, and struggle not just to remain sober from alcohol, but to live with a sober mind, a mind that is not driven by ego, rage, and lack of understanding, but a mind driven by compassion, love, and humility.

The rooms have no instructors, but all who sit in the rooms are teachers, and for the first time in my life, I have taken the time to listen and to allow the words of other human beings to seep into my mind.

Rigorous honesty. Can I live a life of rigorous honesty in all of my affairs? Rigorous honesty? I have been rigorous in many areas in my life. Rigorous with drinking, with women, with exercise, with work, but rigorous with honesty? An honesty that begins with the self and then with others. Am I capable of living that way? What does it look like? How does it feel?

There are those in the rooms who can and do live like this, and I want what they have, so I listen to them. I listen to the retired construction worker, the mechanic, the electrician, the CPA. I want what they have, but am I willing to go to any length to get it? What do I thirst for now that I no longer drink?

Erica M—maybe she is sick and suffering, too. Maybe she needs the steps. Maybe she is blocked from the sunlight of her Higher Power. Maybe she needs for me to pray for her rather than curse at her. Maybe she needs compassion—not judgment.

What I do know is that I am not supposed to allow Erica M. to rent free space in my head. I only have so much room up there, and Erica M. has no place in that limited space, but yet, I allow her in, and along with her comes anger, rage, and judgment.

"What I am trying to recover from is a hopeless state of mind." Roger said that sitting in the chair next to the water cooler. Before I walked into the rooms, I thought AA was a program to get you to stop drinking and then you were "cured." "Quitting drinking was the easy part." Roger again.

"Once I stopped drinking, I then had to deal with myself, my mind. That was the hard part." So I stand in Rizal Park in Manila, Philippines, on a life-and-death errand, and I am letting Erica M. into my head, as I have let in so many others before. I have wasted so many years, so much time, and a tremendous amount of energy, hitting that replay button. Each time I hit the button, the scenarios get worse.

By the time my mind is finished with Erica M., she will have told me to "Go to Hell!" and then I will have busted through the bulletproof glass and armed guards will have pulled me off before I could strangle her to death. I no longer drink, but am I working the program? Am I living a life of rigorous honesty? Am I being selfless? Putting my trust, my will, and my life in the hands of my Higher Power? If not, then what am I doing? Where am I going, other than down the same road? Where does that road lead? Unfortunately, I already know. I am so tired of that road. I have been travelling on it for years, passing by the same sad places again, and again, and again.

Maria and I wander through the park, holding hands. I used to watch couples holding hands, and would think to myself, I am just not a person who holds hands. There are people like that, right? People who just don't care for holding hands. People who would rather walk next to the person they are with without holding hands. That's fine, right? Normal, right?

As we wander through the gardens, past the vendors selling various wares, foods, and souvenirs, Maria and I continue to hold hands. I am a hand holder, I think to myself. I am one of those people, one of those countless couples I have seen over the years. Maria and I hold hands, always. Billy Sansone is a hand holder. Too funny. And he is holding Maria Giglio's hand, as he walks through Rizal Park in Manila, Philippines, after leaving the United States Embassy on our way to meet Chito at the Filipino National Bureau of Investigation to get Ron cleared to leave the country. After all this time, I am a hand holder—I just never had the right person to reach out to and grab hold of.

"Let's grab a Jeepney, and head to Intramuros. We have some time before we need to meet Chito. We could walk, but it's too hot," Maria says as she looks at her watch.

"It's 11:45. That will give us plenty of time to get there and walk around the area before meeting Chito at 2."

Maria and I head to Maria Orosa Street, which cuts through the middle of Rizal Park and leads to Intramuros, the old walled part of Manila. We stand on the sidewalk and watch the dizzying array of trucks, cars, Jeepneys, and motorcycles make their way through the lane-less streets. Maria holds out her hand as if hailing a cab. Is that how you get a Jeepney? Is it like a cab? Just stick out your arm and jump in the back? How much is the ride? How do we know where the Jeepney we jump into is going?

I am certain that Maria doesn't know the answers to any of these questions, yet I am just as certain that she doesn't care. In the same bold manner in which she lives her life, Maria is holding out her hand, going to flag down a Jeepney, jump in, and figure it out. And that's exactly what we do.

The Jeepney is not crowded when we climb in through the back, so Maria makes her way to the front behind the driver and pulls out her purse. "How much?" she asks.

"Twenty pesos." The Jeepney is moving. The driver did not wait for us to pay first. The driver holds his hand back over his head and Maria places the money in his outstretched hand. He does not count it, rather places it in a cigar box that rests on the dashboard.

The inside of the Jeepney is lined with long cushioned benches that go the length of the vehicle, so the people sitting on the left side will face the people sitting on the right side. The driver cuts and weaves his way through traffic, coming so close to other cars that I brace for impact, yet we somehow glide on.

As if guided by an internal sonar device, the driver knows which people standing on the sidewalks want to be picked up, so he cuts through the traffic, stops just long enough to pick up the passenger, then starts out again. The new passengers pass the money from one passenger to the next until the one closest to the driver taps him on the shoulder and the driver puts out his hand, the money is handed over, and it goes into the cigar box, without being counted.

I quickly realize Jeepneys operate on the honor system. With each stop, people jump in through the back and the Jeepney starts moving before the last person is seated. The people then pull out their wallets, or find change in their pockets or purses, and hand the money to the person sitting next to them, who hands that money to the next person, until the money reaches the driver and it goes into the cigar box—an honor system taxi service in a city of twelve million people.

Can you imagine such an honor system in New York, or Miami, or Chicago, or even Mayberry? I look at the people who have joined us on our ride, and they look at me. I stand out. My hair is blonde, on the longish side, and combed back up over my head, a sight not seen in Manila.

All these people are going somewhere. They carry with them the same types of worries, concerns, pains, uncertainties, fears, loves, and longings as everyone else on the planet, yet all stop and smile, not the quick type of smile one gives or gets when catching someone's eye in an elevator or standing in line; rather, a smile that says "Hello, I hope you are well. God be with you and keep you today."

"How do we know where to get out?" I ask Maria. There were no signs on the Jeepney stating where it was going. We never told the driver where we were going. The Jeepney was headed in the direction of Intramuros, so we jumped in.

I pull out my phone and check my GPS. I see the blue dot that signifies my exact location in the world, and I zoom in, trying to locate Intramuros in relation to our location.

Maria has another idea. She leans forward, places her hand on the driver's shoulder and says, "We are going to Intramuros. Isn't that just up here? Where should we get off?"

Interesting idea. Ask the driver where to get off. (Della Street has saved me again.)

"Just around the corner. I let you know," the driver says without turning his head. And he does … the driver does let us know.

A few minutes later, he pulls off to the side of the road, leans his head back, and says, "Get out here." Maria and I make our way to the back of the Jeepney, step out onto the street, and watch as it quickly vanishes into the traffic.

## Chapter Three

# Billy and the Barber

MARIA HAS AN ELEGANCE, a grace, a delicate ease about her. Sometimes that is all I think of when I look at her. My mind empties of anything and everything else. She can hold my gaze like a sunset over the Gulf of Mexico or a cloudless starry night in Moab, Utah, where I get lost in vastness and beauty. She is wearing a black and white striped blouse with a black skirt and tan shoes. Her hair is pulled back into a bun, and sunglasses adorn her head. She wears small gold-hooped earrings and a thin gold necklace. Simple, elegant.

There are a number of Spanish-style cafes that line the outer edges of Intramuros. I watch Maria as she navigates past the tables where young students are having lunch across the street from their school. Thirty years ago, I would see this same woman, then just a girl, navigate past tables where young students were eating lunch at Plant High School. Thirty years have passed. We collectively have had five children, three marriages, two recovery programs, and one God-breathed love affair.

I know that I can only truly rely on my Higher Power, God. All humans are just that—humans, bound to make mistakes, show anger, jealousy, and exhibit that deadliest trait of all—selfishness and self-centeredness. I am supposed to give myself completely to God, to do His will, not mine, but He gave me Maria, and I have come to rely on her.

By letting myself depend so much on another human being, I have opened myself up to being hurt, but I am tired of walls. Over the years, I have built walls stronger and thicker than the one the Spanish built around the city of Manila. I would not let anyone in. This is where I lived, alone and isolated. I try daily to improve my conscious contact with God, but for me, that is not enough, though I know it should be. Maria is the one person whom I have let through this high wall. Though I am slowly dismantling the entire structure, years of building have made the wall high and thick, and it will take time to tear down. Maria came in through a door I did not know existed—a hidden door, through which she quickly opened and passed with ease. There is no wall between us, no space at all, just a closeness where not even light can escape.

"Grab a table—I'm going to get us a drink."

I do and she does. Maria brings me a large glass of freshly squeezed lemonade and we cool ourselves as we listen to students talk about the things that are most important to them at that time. Maria looks over at them as she rests her head in her hand.

I know what she is thinking—why is it that these kids are in school, and so many others are not? If I wasn't sitting next to her, in love with her, trying to become one with her, I would not think about this. I would have sat here next to the old wall in Intramuros, enjoying my cool drink, thinking how pleasant the breeze is, and how the shade brings relief from the sun, and what I was going to do next, and what that means for me.

If I did think about the kids around me at all, I would think how nice it was that they were able to spend time together before going back to class. But I am not by myself, I am with Maria, so I wonder, as she does, about the massive disparity in wealth on the streets of Manila—how some kids are openly bathing in gutter water, while others are in neatly pressed school uniforms with the latest in technology in their hands.

Other cities have wealth disparity, but never have I seen it on display like it is in Manila. In New York, you will not find a half-naked three-year-old child picking through garbage on the sidewalk of a major intersection. If you did, you would call the police, who would come and then call Child Protective Services. The child would be taken into custody and charges could be filed against the parents, who might have their parental rights taken away for neglecting their child. In Manila, that child is left alone to pick through the garbage, eat whatever she finds, as she exhibits the most basic animalistic instinct of all—the instinct to survive.

"Billy," Maria says without looking over at me.

"I know."

We finish our drinks and begin to slowly wander the neighborhood streets. There is color to Manila, every color, everywhere. The umbrellas that are placed above the food stands are red, yellow, and green. The plastic chairs at the tables next to the stands for the customers are green, white, and black, The motorcycles that line the streets are black, red and blue. The street food that the men and women are cooking cover all the colors of the rainbow with red, orange and yellow peppers, green produce, blue-colored fish, indigo spices, and violet fruits. Manila is alive.

Even with the extreme poverty, there is a gaiety amongst the people—all the people. It is as if the people of Manila have learned what the Apostle Paul learned: to be content in any and every situation, whether hungry or well fed, tired or rested, or in want or with no needs. The girls in clean pressed school uniforms walk gleefully hand in hand. The girls wearing filthy clothes with no shoes walk arm in arm smiling and laughing. They seem to live in the present, a place where I am just learning how to dwell.

The buildings that line the streets have shops on the ground floor and living space on the second floor. Outside the second floor windows, clothes hang from steel rods, slowly blowing dry in the damp air. There is no design, pattern, or cohesive plan to the buildings. It is as if they were built as needed—as if someone said, "Okay, we must put up another structure right now," and the structure went up and was used for the purpose it was intended. Nothing is wasted in Manila—

not space, food, water, or even garbage. Unfortunately, there is not enough of the first three, and too much of the last.

The buildings are separated by narrow alleys, and along these alleys are apartments and rooms for rent. In many ways, these homes are like any other homes. They have potted plants outside their doors, bicycles lean up against light poles, brooms and dust pans evidence that chores are underway, and small tables with chairs are there for coffee in the morning or a relaxing drink in the evening.

However, in some ways these homes are not like others. They are jammed into small alleyways, where laundry dries hanging from every pole and available hook. Filthy water fills the potholes in the crumbling concrete. I stare too long and catch the eye of a young woman washing clothes in a rusted aluminum bucket. She pauses to smile at me. I smile back. This woman is working—really working. She cooks, cleans, washes clothes, and lives day to day, taking each one as it comes. Maybe that is why she lives so firmly in the present, or at least seems to me to be doing so. She does not have the luxury to dwell on yesterday, or the precious time to fret about tomorrow.

Maria and I continue to wander. Food is everywhere, being cooked over wood, coals, hot plates, or whatever will generate enough heat to get the job done. I'm not sure for whom all of this food is intended—I mean, who is buying and eating it? Everyone seems so poor and thin, but food is omnipresent, as if the neighborhood is preparing a feast for a national celebration, but it's just a Tuesday.

As we continue to walk, I see a sign that says, "Barber Shop." It hangs on a piece of wood that is crudely attached to the building. One blue plastic chair sits outside. An OPEN sign hangs in the window beneath an air conditioning wall unit, which must not be working because the day is hot, all doors and windows are open, and the wall unit is silent.

"Hey, do you think I should get my hair cut?" I ask, as Maria stops and turns toward me.

"Sure, we have a bit of time." I step into the small room. There are two barber chairs and no one waiting. The man inside springs to life.

"Can I get a cut?"

"Sure, sure," he replies as he wipes the barber chair with a towel. I sit and tell him to just give me a trim, not to take too much off, and he nods in seeming agreement and understanding, but I am not too sure of either. Hair grows back, right? The man begins to cut, and I state the obvious, "I am just visiting Manila." I am the only blonde-headed person I have seen in this city of twelve million people, and maybe the first blonde ever to sit in this chair.

Maria stands outside, as the room is small and hot. I take off my glasses and the world becomes a Monet painting. I ease back into the chair, tired and content. I close my eyes and breathe, trying to empty my mind. A peace comes over me, as if I have been here before and am comforted by the familiarity of my surroundings. The barber continues to cut, and I keep drifting.

The man works quickly and methodically. I am in no hurry, so I wish he wasn't. Maybe he thinks that because I am an American, dressed in a nice shirt and slacks, and carrying a leather case, that I am here on important business and must be in a hurry. He has no other customers, no one waiting in line. He is the only barber in the shop. I really don't want him to hurry. I want to sit and drift in and out of myself, out of my head and the incessant running of my mind.

I hear the sounds of the scissors clipping. My eyes are closed. Clip, clip, clip, clip. I feel a heaviness, a weight behind my eyes brought on by months of fatigue and forty-eight hours of travel. I let the weight take hold. My mind is clear. Only the weight. I give into it. It pulls me down and I let it take its course. The weight, the clipping, the clearing of the mind. I sit. I drift downward. Slowly, and heavily, and peacefully.

There are not too many places or times or circumstances when my mind will relax and let go of its stranglehold on me, but I find them all here in this barbershop, a perfect confluence, as I sit in a chair in this shop on a street in Intramuros, in the heart of Manila on a cloudlessly warm day in early December. I drift, down, slowly ....

"Haircut finished," the man says as he takes the apron off me. I feel as though I was forced to ascend from depths too quickly, being pulled back into myself, into my mind, a place I was content to leave, even if for a short while. I put my glasses on and return to Intramuros Manila.

*Bill outside the Barber Shop.*

"It looks great." And it does. "How much?"

"Fifty pesos." I shake my head in disbelief. One US dollar? Four quarters? His time is worth more than that. His talent is worth more than that. I pull out a one hundred pesos bill and hand it to him. He reaches into his pocket searching for change, and I tell him I don't need any change. He smiles broadly and puts his hand on my shoulder. I paid and gave a one hundred percent tip, and it cost me two dollars.

"May I take a picture with you?" he asks reaching for his phone.

"With me? Sure." The man pulls out his phone and motions towards Maria.

"Maria," I call, "can you come in here and take a picture of us?"

Maria steps inside, and the barber hands his phone to her. The two of us stand next to the barber chair and I place my arm around his shoulder. He is a small man, and so am I, but I am a good bit taller than he is.

He flashes a thumbs up at the camera, and Maria snaps a shot.

I thank him again, and consider giving him more money, but I don't. We say goodbye. I shake his hand and, with the other, I wrap around him in a hug. He leans into the hug as if wanting me to squeeze him closer. We look at the photo on his phone and laugh.

I have been in his shop for less than fifteen minutes. We barely spoke, and I feel a connection, a bond with this barber. We lock eyes, and I say thank you once again. I tell him that when I come back to Manila, I am coming for another cut, and I mean that (if I can ever find this place again). I step outside into the warm air with my fresh cut. I wonder where that picture will go, the picture he took of the two of us, and to whom he will show it, and why he even wanted it.

"He wanted his picture with you, because you are the first blonde person who has ever walked through the door of his barber shop," Maria says when I ask her these questions.

"You think so?"

"Of course. Look around. When is the next time a man with wavy blonde hair will walk into his shop?" Maria pauses. "The next time *you* are in Manila," she says answering her own question, *Della* will know how to find the barber.

As we wander through the streets of Intramuros, my mind stays with the barber. I never even asked him his name, nor did he ask me mine. Maria stops to take some pictures of kids playing some sort of game on the sidewalk. It is Tuesday afternoon and they are not in school. This would not have occurred to me on my own, but I know it troubles Maria.

I wonder if the barber was a street kid. If he grew up playing games on Tuesday afternoons while other kids learned to read and write. If he was left to entertain himself while his father gave rides on the side car of his motorcycle, and his mother cooked food on the sidewalk over coals. Where did he learn to cut hair, and from whom? Why did I only give him a dollar tip? I like to think that the picture of us will not stay locked in his phone, but will make its way into a frame and be placed on the shelf next to the broken television in his shop, so he can tell his customers about the time when the blonde American came in for a cut. I hope he finds peace in the memory of our brief time together, as I find a peace as I walk back into my mind, searching for these words to write.

Maria finds us another Jeepney. We jump in the back and are gone.

## Day 2

## Chapter Four

# National Bureau of Investigation

MARIA JUMPS OUT of the back of the Jeepney and I follow. "We are a bit early, so let's see if we can find some street food," Maria says, as she takes my hand and leads me down the sidewalk. About twenty-four hours ago, Maria had tears in her eyes as she walked the streets. She covered her mouth with her hand to keep the smell of exhaust, urine, and garbage from her nose. She looked panicked and overwhelmed.

Now, she guides me confidently down a street she has never seen, in a place she has never been, among a mass of people she has never met. She acts as if she has returned to a familiar place after years of being away, as if she were walking through a town she lived in and loved many years ago and is eager to show me all it has to offer and tell me the stories of what she did as we pass those places along the way.

I understand her change. I feel it, too. In a few short hours, Manila has reached out and put her arms around me, taken my hand, and comforted me. I feel as if I have returned to a place of my childhood, a place tucked safely away in my memory for comfort when the world presses in. Why? How? Manila is a third-world New York City. Twelve million people live here, foreign in every way from every place I have ever known or visited, yet I feel the same comfort and ease that I know Maria feels as she holds my hand and steps confidently over the holes in the sidewalk and maneuvers through the never ending avalanche of people moving towards us.

"There's the BI," Maria says as she points to the large complex of buildings across the street. Maria's voice brings me back to the errand we are on, back to Ron, Chito, Homer, Erica M., the State Department, the Embassy, the Bureau of Immigration, the United States Probation, the United States Attorney's Office, the warrant, the arrest, the unproductive calls, letters, emails to multiple government agencies, the twenty-six hours of travel, the Jeepneys, the heat, the smells, the cascade of people—the craziness of this all.

A man's life is dependent upon the actions of Billy Sansone and Maria Giglio—two kids playing grownup, two lost souls who were given the grace of each other after years of searching, two kids working the steps, and with God's grace, practicing the program. I do not think about the insanity of the situation. I squeeze Maria's hand and take one step at a time.

Maria stops at the entrance to BI, and looks around. She walks over to a man serving some type of soup from a large vat. At the small plastic tables set up on the sidewalk, people are eating the soup, talking, laughing, and smiling on this Tuesday afternoon. I hang back and watch Maria as she talks with the soup man. Maria is strikingly attractive. Thirty years ago, when I met her, Maria was good-looking and so cute, guys were always after her, but now, after time has softened, polished, and refined her, she walks with an air of grace and elegance not found in most women, a modern-day Audrey Hepburn.

"Let's eat here," Maria says and motions me over. The man to whom she was talking takes two plastic bowls and sticks each one into a small plastic bag. Then, he ties the end of the bag in a knot and pours the soup into the bagged bowl, so when his patrons are finished, he pulls off the bag, and the bowl is ready to be reused—ingenious when water is at a premium.

Maria and I sit at the table nearest the soup man. The streets are loud with people and the incessant traffic, but I am at ease, and so is Maria, my Audrey Hepburn, my *Della Street*. I watch her sprinkle unknown spices from small containers into her soup. As I do with many things in my life now, I follow her lead. We begin eating in silence.

The day is hot and the air wet and sticky, but the soup is a perfect balance of spice, salt, and sweetness. I have no idea what is in the soup and I don't care. I am here, in Manila, with Maria, eating soup on the sidewalk outside of the National Bureau of Investigation and trying to help my client get out of jail. I am here now, in the present. For once, I do not have one foot in yesterday, the other in tomorrow, while pissing on today.

"This is really good," I say after half of my soup is gone.

"Isn't it? I love the spices."

"Oh my God, I am so in love with you I can't stand it!" I blurt out. Maria puts her spoon down and reaches across the table to grab my hands.

"Aw, baby, are you overwhelmed right now? I get the same feeling when I look at you. I love it, and love you."

"It's just so amazing that I don't have to worry about what I say or don't say, or do or not do when I am with you. I just am. Does that make sense?"

"Yes, that's because you are my perfect person. I mean, really, my perfect person. We are perfect for each other. This thing we have going on did not happen by accident. God put us together. He looked down and said, 'Okay, you two have had enough, so now I am going to give you each other, and you will become one, as I intended when a man and a woman come together.' And we are. We are one, and it's freakin' awesome." Maria smiles and squeezes my hands, while Manila continues to swirl around us.

Our table is right across from the entrance to BI, so Maria and I have an eye out for Chito. We finish our soups, and Maria engages in another conversation with the soup man, as I cross the sidewalk to wait for Chito.

*Maria outside the National Bureau of Investigation*

Ron told me a few months ago, at the beginning of his incarceration in Manila that he would need an BI clearance before being released. Essentially, anyone in custody in the Philippines before being released for *any* reason, must have an BI clearance, which is a background check, to ensure no open cases against the detained person exist. So even if Erica M. actually does her job and sends over a letter from the Embassy stating that Ron is no longer a fugitive, Ron still must have his BI clearance done.

"Well, there might be something," Ron said to me late one night as I sat at Maria's dining room table drinking decaf coffee. "There might be an Estafa against me. That's basically a fraud charge. Years ago, I got into an argument with a lady from whom I was renting a condo. She was gouging me because she thought I was a rich American, so I just moved out and technically broke the lease. She kept charging me for things that were her responsibility as the condo owner and threatening to evict me if I didn't pay, so just I left. If she filed an Estafa against me, then I still won't be released until *that* is cleared up."

"How would we do that?" I asked as I placed a large glob of peanut better on a Granny Smith apple.

"We would have to go to court to get it removed."

"Well, can you ask someone to find out if you have an Estafa *before* I come over to get the letter from the Embassy?"

"The government agencies here are slow and inefficient. I paid a lady I met at the jail when she came here to speak with another prisoner about his case to go to BI and check. She said I don't have an Estafa, but when I asked her for the paperwork, she said she *forgot* to get it. I can't trust her. There is so much corruption here. She likely just took my money and did nothing, because what could I do to her? I'm sitting in this shithole."

Damnit, I thought to myself. There was always something else with Ron, always one more hurdle to jump over, one more mile to run after thinking that the race was finished. When Ron was incarcerated in the Pinellas County jail, I spent more court appearances trying to get Ron approved to travel from the jail to a vein specialist, than I did working on the facts of his case.

However, I did get the approval, so Ron was transported to the vein specialist with three armed guards. I wonder what the other patients thought when this sick man was wheeled into the doctor's office in an orange jail jump suit accompanied by three armed sheriff's deputies and a criminal defense attorney. Maybe they thought that he was some Mafia don or foreign government spy? So it went with Ron, always one more thing, even before I had decided to go to Manila. I knew I would also have to deal with the BI clearance before he was ever released.

"Chito's late," Maria said as she looked at her watch.

"I know."

"What do you think we should do?"

"I texted him three times. No answer."

"I say let's go in." Of course, Maria would say that. She is a person of action, and it didn't matter that we were standing outside the National Bureau of Investigation in Manila, Philippines with no idea whom to see, or what to do, or ask, or even how to ask it. Maria was ready to go in and get this thing done.

"You lead the way, *Ms. Street.*" And she does, up to the guard station.

"My client needs a BI clearance. Where do we go to get that done?" The guard gave her directions and let us through without any questions or even searching our persons. (I need to give Della Street a raise.)

The BI building in Manila is not comparable to the FBI building in Washington DC. For example, it has no air conditioning and a large number of people seemingly wander about the halls daily. No one is wearing a coat and tie. There is no easily marked information desk so there's no need for an appointment—come as you are and when you want

The building hasn't been painted this century and in the lobby, there is no uniformity of chairs. For example, some are metal folding ones, others are plastic, and some are made of wood. Boxes, old books, and discarded furniture line the halls, as if waiting for a trash collector to come by and pick them up. The inside of the BIbuilding reminds me of ... actually it doesn't remind me of anything, except maybe a converted warehouse thrown quickly together as a field operation center, but I have never been in such a building, so the BI really doesn't remind me of that.

"Where are we headed?" I ask Maria as she confidently navigates her way through the mass of people and confusion.

"To the fourth floor to see Tess."

"You're kidding?"

"Nope," Maria responds with a smile and a quick kiss. "We are going to see Tess on the fourth floor. That's the plan."

Oh my God, I think to myself. How are we ever going to get Ron out of jail in the next seventy-two hours: Chito, Homer, Erica M., and now Tess are on the fourth floor. I have no idea how Maria knows where she is going. The building has no general layout, but it unfolds as if one is making way through a jungle, never quite sure what is around the next corner.

We jump into an elevator packed with people. The elevator jerks into motion and slowly climbs from the first floor to the second (as if a team of Filipino men located in the basement are manually pulling the elevator up by a system of cables). I think of getting out on the second floor and walking up the stairs to the fourth, but I let the doors close and wonder if I just made a life-ending mistake.

Somehow, the men in the basement complete their task and get us safely to the fourth floor. As Maria and I step out of the elevator, I see that the hallway is filled with discarded desks, boxes, tools, and other crap just laying around. Maria pauses, looks to the right and then the left, and says, "It must be this way."

Now why does she think that? What must be this way—there are no signs, no directional maps on the walls, and no arrows guiding anyone to anything. Maria is operating by some type of internal sonar that I don't have, so I must follow her, like a lost soul wandering through the jungle. I have no choice.

We come to a door at the end of the hallway, so Maria opens it and walks in. I often watch the show, *American Pickers*, and have seen a few episodes of the series, *Hoarders*, and in both shows, the viewer is taken into a world of people who have spent their entire lives collecting stuff without ever throwing anything out. The rooms that these people live in become a maze of junk through which you must navigate carefully for fear of the either getting lost or disrupting a junk tower and being buried alive, having to wait for fire and rescue to come dig you out.

Well, Tess' office in the BI building is not that bad (yet), but she and her colleagues are doing their best to appear on a special episode of *Hoarders* entitled, "Work Place Edition." The room is made up of cubicles with offices along the back wall. The walls of those cubicles are only about chest high, so we can see the works spaces of all those employed by the BI who run the clearance checks. We don't sit in the chairs that are meant for people waiting until someone is ready to address their concerns. We stand, in hopes that this will speed up the process. A woman addresses us across the short wall of her cubicle.

"May I help you?" Her workspace is a disaster, where disheveled papers are stacked three feet high.

"Yes, my client is in custody in a detention facility, and he needs an BI clearance before he can be released. He has been in custody for about five months now. He is ready to be released, and the only thing we need is a clearance check and then he can be released."

"What is his name?" I tell her Ron's name and she begins to look through a stack of disheveled papers dangerously teetering on her desk. Does she actually think Ron's paperwork is magically going to be sitting on top of the stack of papers on her desk? I'll bet half of those papers have been sitting there since before Ron was taken into custody in Florida, perhaps even longer than that.

"Can we actually speak with Tess? We were told that she is the one to whom we need to speak," I ask, hoping Tess has one of the offices that lines the back wall, and has a better filing system than *this* lady.

"I'm Tess," the lady replies as she continues her search through the detritus on her desk. Unbelievable is the only word that comes to my mind. At this rate, Ron is *never* going to get out. Yesterday, we had Erica M., and today we have Tess. Ron's freedom depends on these people ?

Months ago, Maria asked me why I couldn't get this done by phone—why would I ever think of having to go to Manila to secure Ron's release? I look over at Maria as Tess continues her search. I see on Maria's face that she understands the impending hopelessness of our current situation, and also her realization that Ron might die in this Filipino shithole, if his release is dependent upon Tess and the pile of crap on her desk.

I check my phone and see that Chito just texted me. He has been waiting at a separate entrance for over an hour. Maria calls him back, tells him where we are, and walks out of the office and into the hallway to wait for him.

I stare at Tess as she continues to "work" at finding Ron's paperwork. She abandons her sifting through the stack of papers on her desk and sits at her computer. I cannot see the screen, so I don't know what she is doing, but I know she is not looking for Ron's paperwork, since Ron's last name is long and not easily spelled, but Tess never asked me to spell his name to conduct a proper computer search. Maybe there is only one "Ron" in custody waiting for an BI clearance. I guess that is a possibility, or Tess is just wasting enough time for her to finally say, "Sorry, I cannot find your client in our system."

Chito comes in with Maria. We shake hands, and he begins to speak to Tess in Tagalog, the national language. As Chito speaks, Tess begins to lazily search back through the papers on her desk, as if magic might bring it to the top, a place where it wasn't only minutes before. As Chito continues, Tess raises her arms as if to say, "How the hell do I know where his paperwork is? Look at all this shit on my desk. I am overworked and severely underpaid, so deal with it." Tess is the first Filipino person who has not offered me a smile—a bad omen.

Chito continues to speak, as Tess keeps searching through the endless amount of crap on her desk. Then the miracle happens—Tess pulls out a piece of paper and shows it to Chito! Chito speaks to Tess, and Tess to Chito.

Then Chito says, "Bill, here is the list of people who need an BI clearance."

Chito shows me the list with Seven names are on it, with Ron's name at the top of the list. The Bureau of Immigration has asked for these men, all in custody, to have an BI clearance done to see if any outstanding charges exist against them in the Philippines. Ron told me about two months ago that he paid a woman to go by the BI and request BIclearance, because he thought he might have that Estafa. The woman actually did what she was paid to do. The request was made to the BI and now that request actually sits on Tess' desk waiting to be processed—unbelievable! Miracles do happen.

"That's fantastic. How long does it take to get clearance done?" I ask.

"That's the problem," Chito replies. *Why does there always have to be a problem?* "Tess said she cannot just clear Ron's name, but she must check *all* the men on the list, which will take about two weeks."

"Two weeks? This needs to be done in two days. Why can't she just do Ron's? How long can it take? She has a computer—right? Why can't she just run his name?"

"Bill, I asked her that, but she won't do just Ron's clearance." I run my hands through my hair and contemplate pulling some out as I do. Chito turns to Tess and begins speaking again, while I look at Maria.

"At least she has the request for Ron's clearance, and she actually found it," Maria says. She can feel my frustration, but she is correct, as usual. We *have* made progress. Tess found the request for Ron's clearance on her desk, and that is a true miracle of such an order that the Vatican could declare Tess' desk a holy site.

How long had it sat there? How many times had she moved that paper from one side of her desk to the other, while looking for other papers? What about the other men on the list? Who are they? How long have they been waiting? Is anyone fighting for them, or are they destined to languish in jail and on Tess' desk?

I smile to myself when I think back a month ago when Maria asked, "Can't you just make a call? It seemed so simple. Maria was right, in theory, but in reality, Ron would die in that Filipino jail if we had not come, and still might, but at least now he has a chance.

A thousand phone calls would not get Erica M. or Tess to do what they needed to do for Ron, or get that information to Homer, who would then get that information to the jail, who would then take Ron to the airport and see him on his way. That would never happen over the phone. Ron would have died waiting for a three-sentence letter from the United States Embassy and for Tess to conduct a BI clearance.

Chito's voice brings me back to Tess' office. "She says we can get her supervisor to order her to do just Ron's clearance, and she could do that much faster, but she needs her supervisor to draft a written order."

"Okay, where is her boss?"

"On the second floor."

"You lead the way," I command. Tess makes us a copy of the BI clearance request form and we leave Tess' office to go back into the hallway filled with furniture and broken computer parts. "Let's take the stairs," I say as Chito stops at the elevator bank. I don't want to tempt fate.

We descend to the second floor and pass people going up. No one wears "business attire," so it is impossible to know who works in this building and who is here to address some situation in their life. Come to think of it, what does the Filipino National Bureau of Investigation do to have so many people randomly walking up and down the halls, waiting in lines, and sitting patiently in the mass of chairs on the first floor? I only visited the FBI building in Washington, DC on an eighth-grade field trip, so my memory of that visit has been lost to time, but I am certain that a vast number of people were not milling about the building, wandering from floor to floor, fanning themselves due to the sticky heat and lack of air-conditioning with long-forgotten paperwork.

We arrive at the second floor and Chito leads the way to a glass window. A woman comes to the other side and Chito explains our purpose. She smiles and walks over to a large man sitting in his half-walled cubicle behind a desk that thankfully looks *nothing* like Tess' desk. However, Tess did perform a holy miracle by locating Ron's paperwork amongst the dizzying array of papers. The man looks up at us and waves us in with a smile. Erica M. could use a customer service training session from the Filipinos. We walk into his office and each takes a seat across from him.

"Good afternoon," he says with a large smile and gregarious voice. "Where are you from?" he asks looking at me, for my blonde hair is better than a t-shirt that reads, "I AM NOT FROM HERE" on the front.

"Florida." I respond. Wow! That sounds like a cliché, especially with my blonde hair and tan, which (of course) is from swimming laps in an outdoor pool during my lunch hour. I really *am* from Florida, not California, but I hope he asks me if I surf, because then I will say "No" and baffle him a bit. But he doesn't.

"Florida, wow, long way from here."

"Yes, it is. We have come a great distance to free our client," I say motioning towards Maria. His nameplate on the front of the desk informs us his name is Rolando A. "We are in the process of securing everything we need to take our client out of custody, but we need a BI clearance. The problem is that we leave on Friday, so we must make sure our client is out before then. We went upstairs and saw Tess, and she discovered the BI clearance request for my client."

I hand him the copy Tess made for us. "The problem is that my client is the last name on the list, and Tess said she cannot just clear my client's name, but must do *all* the names on the list at the same time, which will take two weeks.

"We cannot wait two weeks. We must have my client out of custody in two days. Tess said that you can create a separate order requesting an BI clearance for just my client. So that's why we are here. Can you do that?"

I sit on the edge of my seat. What I am asking is too important for me to think about what I just said. I mean, who am I to come into a government official's office at the National Bureau of Investigation in Manila, Philippines, and start making demands? I would not be surprised if Rolando laughs in my face and says, "Who are you, creepo? Who are you?"

But he doesn't. He carefully looks at the copy I hand him, and then looks up and says, "I don't think that will be a problem."

I did not realize how tense my body was until I felt myself relax. "Thank you so very much."

I look at Maria, who looks at me, and then at Chito, who looks at Maria, and then at me. I believe we are all thinking the same thing—No freakin' way!" But again, another miracle is performed, this time on the second floor of the BI building.

Rolando motions to someone across the room and says something in Tagalog. That person makes her way across the room and takes direction from him. She nods her head as he speaks. I look at Chito, who is paying close attention, for any clues as to what is going on. Chito must feel my stare, because he looks over at me, smiles, and gives me a thumbs up. The woman walks away.

Rolando turns and says, "I have always wanted to go to Disney World. Have you been there?"

I want to say, "Um, yes, I have, but before we talk about Disney World, can you tell me what you just said to your assistant so I can start breathing again?"

Instead I say, "Yes, I live about an hour from Disney World. When I was a kid, I used to go all the time, but I don't go much anymore." Though Chito gave me the thumbs up, I don't really believe that everything is working out, but I want to hear it from Rolando, so I ask, "Is everything okay? Are you going to be able to run Ron's BI clearance quickly?"

"Yes, yes, yes," he answers in rapid succession. "I have ordered a clearance just for your client. That is what we are waiting for." *Okay, now I can breathe, talk about Disney, Goofy, Mickey, Donald, Snow White, and any of the seven dwarfs.*

Maria asks Rolando a question about one of the islands of the Philippines, and I drift off. My mind is tired. I can't focus on Ron right now, or Rolando, or Chito, or Maria, or Snow White, or the beautiful beaches of the Philippines.

My mind drifts into nothingness, a kind of hibernation, a self-preservation technique I have learned in the rooms. My mind will kill me if I let it. Strange to say, but true, deadly true. I have drunk so many bottles of Gordon's gin trying to slow the incessant churning of my mind. The never-ending churning of the wheel, the worn out replay button, the catastrophizing, the sleepless nights playing out numerous hell and fire scenarios to every little molehill of a problem that I try so damn hard to make into the Himalayas. I am my own worst enemy—that I now know is true. I am working hard on ceasing to fight anyone and anything, but my most difficult adversary is myself—always has been. I had projected the problems onto others, and created an enemy on the outside, when the enemy was always within.

"Bill, what do you think?" Maria's voice hooks me by my ear and yanks me back into Rolando's office. Maria can see in my eyes, or the stare on my face, that I had left the room, the building, the city, the country, and the earth. Maria smiles and places her hand on my knee. "What do you think about Manila so far?" From the look on Maria's face, I understand that Rolando had asked me this question.

"Unbelievable." And it is in so many ways. "What stands out the most are the people. How nice and friendly everyone is. I see smiles on just about every face we pass, even on the faces of those living on the street. I feel a comfort, a familiarity to the city. It's hard to explain."

"You don't have to. I know what you mean. Filipino people are special. We have endured a lot over the years. Occupations, wars, poverty, and what holds us together is our faith in God and the knowledge that this life is but a temporary stop on our way to the eternal."

Even before Rolando spoke, I had realized that there is no separation of Church and State in Manila. Crosses and pictures of Jesus hang on the walls of government buildings. In America, we fiercely battle over whether a coach can say the word "God" before a high school football game. We spend countless hours arguing over whether teachers can teach creationism or evolution or both. Our Supreme Court wrestles with the concept of whether having a moment of "prayer" in school violates the Constitution, or should it be deemed a moment of "silence." I am sure the Filipino courts and its government fight over other things—all governments find things to fight over—but God is not one of them in the Philippines.

We continue to chat, and a woman comes over and hands Rolando a piece of paper. A smile grows across his face as he looks at it.

"See, here we go. Your client is set for a clearance." Rolando hands me the paper, and it looks the same as the one we brought down, but Ron's is the only name on it, just as Tess had requested. "This should make things go much faster."

"And when you say much faster, how fast is that?" I am leery of pushing this Filipino government official too hard, but our mission ends in seventy-two hours. One thing I am absolutely certain of—if we leave this country and Ron is still in custody, he will die in custody, and no one in the United States Embassy, the State Department, the United States Attorney's Office, the Filipino Bureau of Immigration, or the National Bureau of Investigation will care. None of my colleagues, friends, or family will care.

Why should they? A dirty old man died in jail—what is sad about that? He pled to a charge of possession of child pornography, and that scarlet letter is emblazoned upon his chest. It shines so brightly, that no one can look past it, blocking out all truth, all compassion, and all understanding. No one wants to hear that Ron was actually charged in 2015 of possessing a tape in 2008 that was made in 1995 of him having sex with a prostitute in Cuba, a woman past the age of puberty, whose age, a leading expert in the field determined, could not be ascertained with any degree of medical certainty.

For this "crime," possessing this twenty-year-old tape (he was not charged with having sex with anyone), he spent a year in the medical unit of the Pinellas County jail and has spent four months in a Filipino detention facility. In that time, he lost all his possessions and is now about to lose his life.

It does not matter that the United States government thought they had a sexual deviant in their grasp and followed him around the world for years only to find nothing, so they charged him with possessing that old decaying tape. In the minds of the American and Filipino governments, he is a child pornographer. PERIOD. So if he dies in jail, he gets what he deserves.

Everyone I told about my trip to Manila to help get my client out of jail said this to me in various ways. But Ron is not paying me—not really. He overpaid me a bit, because his case was resolved before trial, but I am not charging Ron for my time, or even my costs to come to Manila.

I am here, because he shouldn't be. I am here, because I am in disbelief that the Filipino government is holding an American citizen in custody, waiting for the United States to come pick him up, which is never going to happen, because there is no longer an arrest warrant, and the United States refuses to inform the Filipino government of this development. So Ron began to decline as my letters went unanswered, my phone calls were not returned, and Ron's paperwork collected dust on Tess' desk.

"We have computers, so it should take no time at all," Rolando replies.

So many thoughts race across my mind, so many things I want to say about the unbelievable journey my client has endured, but saying these things will not help Ron. In the past, before working my program, I would have said those things, and even though I would have felt justified in saying them, because I was "speaking on behalf of a client," I wouldn't be speaking for Ron—I would be speaking for me, for my benefit. I would have said hurtful things, angry things, ungodly things. Now, by the grace of God, I leave those hurtful things alone, knowing that if I pick them up, I will only burn myself again.

"Thank you so very much." I stand up and look at Maria and Chito. "Should we take this back up to Tess?" There is no way I am going to trust this agency to get this piece of paper from floor two to floor four and into Tess' hands. Ron might not live that long.

"Sure, you can take it up to her," Rolando says. With that, we shake hands and say our goodbyes.

"Is it okay if we come back tomorrow to see if my client's clearance has been completed?" I always seem to ask one more question—make one more demand.

"Sure, sure. Come back tomorrow. Just fine. See you tomorrow." We make our way back up to Tess' office.

My heart sinks a little when I hand the piece of paper containing Ron's request for a BI clearance to Tess. It's the same feeling I have when I hand my six-year-old daughter a bag of groceries and say, "Please don't drop this, there are eggs in there." I look at her desk: papers, folders, coffee mugs, pens, paperclips, and an empty bag of Jollibees.

"Rolando said we can come back tomorrow and see if the clearance has been done for my client," I say, not wanting to push her too hard. Ron's life depends on this frail, overworked, completely disorganized woman.

"Yes, come back tomorrow," she says as she takes the piece of paper from my hand. Maria, Chito, and I make our way out of the maze that is the BI complex.

"I think that went well," I say to Maria and Chito. "I mean it could have been a lot worse."

"I think it went great," Maria replies. "We actually found the people we needed to speak with and made some progress. The BI was much more helpful and accommodating to us than the US Embassy."

Maria is right. We did make progress, we did speak to the people who can actually help, and we didn't have to sit behind bulletproof glass.

"Promising, very promising," Chito adds as we step out of the BI complex and onto the street. Chito tells us he will give us a ride back to the Bureau of Immigration.

Just around the corner, I see the Supreme Court of the Philippines. The building is impressive, constructed with white stone. It would blend in perfectly in Washington, DC next to the United States Treasury building.

"Let me get a picture of you two," Maria says reaching into her purse for her phone.

"Sure, that would be great," Chito replies. We stand next to each other like tourists on a summer vacation. Maria tells us to smile and we do. She takes three pictures to make sure one of them comes out well. Before Maria snaps the pictures, I think of putting my arm around Chito, like I did with the barber, but I don't.

I have known him for less than a day, but there is a bond, and not just between the two of us, but between all three of us. We are on the same journey. Chito has spent time with Ron in jail. He knows about his health. He knows about the warrant being withdrawn. He knows about the problems I encountered with the United States Embassy and the State Department. He knows that getting things done quickly when interacting with a Filipino agency is just shy of impossible. He knows that we have to get this done by Friday.

Chito is a lawyer. He has clients. I can tell he is much like me, as in he also takes on his clients' problems, and does not just work to bill hours. Chito knows that I came nine thousand miles to get Ron out of jail, and while we have not spoken of that, I know that he respects that decision. I know it is a decision Chito would make if the circumstances were flipped, and his client was dying in the Pinellas County jail in Florida.

Chito knows that Maria and I arrived in Manila, a city we have never seen, in a part of the world completely foreign to us, with the elaborate and complex plan to meet him at the Bayleaf Hotel at 2:00 p.m. on Monday, and then literally see what happens next. He knows that was really not a plan at all, but a leap of desperation and faith.

Chito has faith, and he has faced desperation. I don't want to ask Chito what our chances are of getting Tess to complete the paperwork, then getting the BI clearance to Homer at BI, all while securing the letter we need from the United States Embassy, and getting that letter to Homer. Then we must have him clear Ron for release, and then have Homer coordinate with Filipino officials for Ron to be escorted by the police from the jail to the airport and placed on a plane, all within the next three business days.

I don't want to ask Chito, because I am afraid of his answer, which I am afraid will keep me from moving forward. However, that is all I can do—move forward, one step at a time, one task at a time. I cannot let my mind take over, or it will shut my body down.

We are going back to the Embassy tomorrow to get that letter, and then going to BI to speak with Homer about the letter and Ron's BI clearance. I can't control what others will do at the Embassy or BI, but I can control myself, my actions, and how I respond to the actions of others

Stay clear. Stay focused. God's will, not mine. I am not the director of this play, and I don't control the actors. I do what I can, and the hell with the rest. Simple. Simple. Stay simple.

"Nice picture," Maria says, looking at her phone. She shows it to Chito and me, and we continue walking to his car. Chito drives us back to BI.

"So we will let you know what happens tomorrow," I say with my briefcase on my lap. I am hesitant to reach for the door, as I just realized that we will not see Chito tomorrow. Maria and I are on our own.

"Please do. Call or text me if you need something."

"Thank you so much for all of your help today. We could not have done it without you," Maria says from the back seat.

Chito smiles and says, "We are a team, right?" He seems to share my hesitation, or maybe that is just me projecting my hesitation on him. I don't know. I am tired. I reach out my hand and Chito takes it.

"You are a good man," I say.

"So are you. So are you. Again, please let me know what happens tomorrow."

"Of course we will, and if we need our secret weapon to come bail us out, you'll come running—right?"

"Yes, of course, I'll be sprinting," Chito says with a smile. Maria and I get out of the car, and Chito is quickly lost in the steady stream of cars, trucks, Jeepneys, and motorcycles.

Maria and I make our way back to the BI to see Homer for the third time in two days. Maria speaks to the security guard as we enter the building. I cannot hear what she says, but the guard is nodding in agreement and understanding. He looks up at me as she speaks and nods and then waves us through without any questions or search of our bags or person.

The main floor is still jammed with people, women carrying children, other children running around the women, and men standing in groups talking amongst themselves. No one seems to be heading anywhere—not to the stairwell, not to the elevators. Maria moves quickly through the mass of people to the elevators. She pushes the button, it opens, and we step in. The door closes and the elevator jerks to a start.

"Why are we going to see Homer?" I ask, as my wits slowly return to me.

"I want to make sure there is nothing else we need in order to secure Ron's release before we plan out our day for tomorrow." The elevator doors opens and Maria steps out and makes her way down the hall. She stops outside Homer's office and waves through the glass window. Homer waves her in. I follow.

Maria takes a seat in the chair across from Homer's desk. I sit, following her lead.

"Okay, we went to the BI, and they are going to get our client's BI clearance done, hopefully tomorrow or at the latest, the next day. Tomorrow, we are going to get that letter from the United States

Embassy informing you that the warrant has been withdrawn. Other than those two things, is there anything else that we need to secure our client's release from custody?" I look from Maria to Homer and await his response.

"Jody," Homer says in a loud voice, stressing the 'y' of his assistant's name. Jody comes in, and Homer speaks to her in Tagalog. He nods in affirmation to whatever she says.

"Yes, yes," Homer says to Maria. "That is all we need."

"Can our client be out by Friday?"

"Sure, if you get me those two things, no problem."

"The BI clearance and the letter from the Embassy," Maria says confirming what those two things are.

"Yes, yes. Those are the only two things. Bring me them and I can release your client. Now he will have to leave the country, because he was placed on a blacklist when we were informed of the charge he committed in the United States, and he will not be able to return to the Philippines once he leaves, but yes, he will be out of custody."

Homer looks at Maria, who looks at him. Then he says, "I will coordinate a police escort to take your client to the airport, where he will be free to leave."

"Where does he have to go?"

"Protocol says that he must fly to the United States."

"Why?"

"Protocol."

"Who arranges that?"

"You do." And with that I could kiss Maria for dragging my tired ass back to the BI. We have to arrange Ron's flight out of the country to somewhere in the United States. BIG DETAIL one we almost missed.

"Does he need to fly to the United States proper, or can he go to a protectorate, such as Guam?" I ask.

"Guam is fine. He can go there."

"So if we book him a flight for Friday night, you think he will be able to make that flight?"

"Sure, sure—if you get me those two things."

"You will have time to arrange his transport to the airport?" I ask in seeming disbelief.

Homer begins to laugh. "Of course, no problem." When he stands, we know that our stay with him is over.

"Thank you so much for your time. We will see you tomorrow," Maria says as she stands and shakes Homer's hand.

"Yes, yes, see you both tomorrow."

"Holy crap, I'm glad you asked that," I quietly say as we make our way down the hall to the elevator. "We need to get Ron a flight to Guam as soon as possible."

"Let's take the stairs. That elevator worries me," Maria says as she passes the elevator bank.

Maria orders us coffee and I take a seat at a table in our Starbucks across the street from BI. The scene is the same as yesterday—well-dressed kids with laptops, iPhones, and earphones. They are talking, laughing, and smiling. I hope they are making the best use of their chance, the chance they have been given from their Higher Power, a chance to use a computer, to drink coffee and to talk with friends—not like so many of the children on the streets of Manila or on the streets of any city around the world.

I am not judging or criticizing, for I have failed to use the gifts God has given me to glorify and carry out His will. Rather, I have used them to further my own will, as I have tried to direct and control others for over a quarter century. I never thought I was trying to be the director of the play that is my life, but I was. When the other actors did not take my stage directions, I would become restless, irritable, and discontent. My mind would race and my anger would burn.

I am trying to clear those character defects from my life by working the program, and I have just started out on that Broad Highway, taking baby steps, while some days I take no steps at all. However, I am moving forward, and that has made all the difference.

Maria sits. We sip our coffee in silence, letting the marvelous events of the day wash over us.

# THERE ARE NO ATHEISTS IN FOXHOLES

"When I first came into these rooms, I didn't know about this God thing. There was no way in hell I was doing Step Three." Paul points to the back wall where the steps hang on a banner from the ceiling. "Made a decision to turn our will and our lives over to the care of God *as we understood him.*"

Paul smiles. "Ain't no way in hell I was going to do that. Turn my life over to some old man in the sky? Really? That's what these rooms are all about? I almost got up and left that first day, but I didn't, thanks to that old man in the sky."

Paul is a large man. His skin is weathered from years of sun, smoke, and booze. His left arm is covered in scabs and scars. Paul worked for TECO (Tampa Electric Company) for thirty years as a line mechanic. He repaired power lines, power poles, transformer boxes, and anything else that kept the power grid humming. Paul spent a lot of time in his work truck, and when he did, he always drove with the window down, his left arm resting on the doorframe.

For years, his left arm rested as he drove from job to job, the sun slowly cooking his forearm and hand. His third wife was the first to notice the spots, and when she did, so did Paul. He had them removed, and then more appeared, and when he had those removed, more came in their place. Paul used to joke that he was having his left arm amputated one small cut at a time.

He says, "I grew up in the pews of the Episcopal Church. I went to St. Stephen's Episcopal for kindergarten when I lived in Miami. After moving to Tampa, I went to St. Mary's Episcopal from first to eighth grade. I could recite the "Our Father" just about the same time I learned my A B C's. I knew when to kneel, when to stand, when to respond to the priest as a congregation, how to hold my hands during communion, and when to make the sign of the cross. I knew the stories of Jesus, the Sermon on the Mount, turning water into wine, and two fish feeding five thousand.

"Even as a child, I liked the idea that Jesus hung out with the ragamuffins, prostitutes, lowly fishermen, tax collectors, and lepers.

Since Jesus was a man, a human, he was approachable, unlike his Father, who had a long beard and sat on a gigantic throne. However, I never could conceptualize that Jesus was God, the creator of all things. Although I knew this to be true, I knew it like I knew that answer as C and not A on a standardized test. Knowing the answer does not provide much insight as to the reason behind why it was the answer.

"On Sunday mornings, I would pretend to be asleep when my mother peeked in my room and asked me if I wanted to go to church. I would lay there until she softly closed the door and made her way to church by herself, carrying with her the burdens of the family. I used to think that I went to church all week long, at school, so why should I have to go to church on Sunday—right? As if attending church was like batting practice, if you get in four sessions a week, no need for a fifth.

"There were many Sunday mornings when my mother would not let me sleep, and I reluctantly rose, put on my Sunday best, and rode to church, where I would recite the Our Father, sing "I Sing a Song of the Saints of God," kneel, stand, sit, sing, and recite some more. Mom would let my brother, sister, and me leave after communion, skipping the final song and prayer. If we were good, Mom would stop at the store and let us buy a candy before returning home, leaving God and his son alone in their house, while I went back to mine.

"In high school, I switched to a Catholic school run by the Jesuits. We had convocation in the church every morning with prayers, announcements, and more prayers. Most of my teachers were Jesuit priests or Brothers (individuals in training to become a Jesuit priest). For classes, I took Biblical Literature—Old Testament, and then Biblical Literature—New Testament. I learned more about God, his son, and the early followers. I know about Solomon, King David, and Saul, who later became Paul.

"There was a whole bunch of lying, killing, and sadness in the Bible, but that did not bother me much, for the Bible was just a book of stories, like any other book, really. When I closed the cover, the lying, killing, and sadness stopped, and so did my contact with God.

"I remember seeing my mother, late at night, sitting at her desk with her Bible open, pencil in hand, writing notes in the margins. To her, God was more than a man with a white beard sitting on a gigantic throne. Jesus was more than a man who told stories to followers. God was real. Jesus was real. They created the heavens and the earth.

"Mom talked to them, like she would talk to a friend or a neighbor. When I talked with God, I talked to him like I talked to Santa Claus, "Please bring me this, please bring me that, for I have been a good boy." For my mother, her relationship with the Lord was different, more personal, intimate and loving, but I never asked her about her faith, one of my most painful and deepest regrets."

Paul continued, "My first real conversations with God were no holds barred. I let him have it. I was a drunk. I had lost my third wife, my house, my boat, my job, and my health. Life sucked, and I wanted to know why."

He sits up and leans his elbows on his knees. "I was pissed, and I let God know it." Paul looks at the ground between his legs. "Why did you do this to me, you son of a bitch? Why!!!!"

Paul looks up at the group. "That was my first real prayer to the God of my understanding. I spoke in my own language. I spoke from the heart. It was personal, heartfelt. I prayed in desperation, in anger." Paul looks to the ceiling. "I told you I hated you, didn't I?"

Paul smiles. "And I did. I did hate Him for what He had done to me. After that prayer, I felt a sense of relief that I had never felt before. All my troubles were still there. I was still a broke, unemployed, three times divorced, bottom of the barrel drunk, but I felt a freedom I had not felt in years, and a new freedom I had never felt before.

"Since that day, the old man upstairs and I talk regularly. I still get pissed off and yell a bit, but now I know that I am the source of all my problems—not God.

"God was the one who carried me through all the shit in my life. God carried me into these rooms. God gave me my life, and saved my life, and I didn't deserve it. I am a self-centered son of a bitch, and God loves me.

"So I say to the newcomer, it doesn't matter if you believe in my God or not, but you better believe in something greater than yourself, even if it is just the fellowship of people sitting in these rooms. There is strength and hope here. I found it. I hope you do, too, and you will, if you honestly follow those steps up on that wall. That's all I have to say." Paul sits back in his chair.

"Thanks, Paul," the room collectively says.

"When I was married to my second wife, we lived in a house less than a block from our church. My mother loved that church, and on Maundy Thursday, the day before Good Friday of Easter weekend, Mom would call me to see if I wanted to go with her to see the stripping of the altar.

"Jesus was crucified on Good Friday and rose on Easter Sunday. To commemorate the crucifixion, the church strips the altar on Good Friday and tolls the bells. I would always say yes. The stripping of the altar began at 3:00 in the afternoon. Mom would come to my house at 2:45, and then we would walk over to the church together. Mom would slide into the pew, get on her knees, and pray.

"So would I, but not like her. I prayed like I sang the Star Spangled Banner before a baseball game. I said all the words, but there was no thought involved, no emotion, and no relationship. Mom talked to the Lord. I would stay on my knees next to her until she was finished, not wanting to interrupt her conversation. When she finished, we would sit in silence. I enjoyed the peaceful quiet time, but I knew there was something else going on in Mom. She had a close relationship with Jesus and was silently thanking him for giving His life for her."

"I was angry with God when I came into these rooms." Anne sits between Mark and Dianne. She wears a t-shirt given out at the last marathon she ran. Her black hair is cropped short. "Kind of like Paul, I was angry that God had done all this shit to me and had allowed me to fall so far. Step Three was hard for me. I knew I was powerless over alcohol. I knew that some power greater than me could restore me to sanity, or at least I hoped so. But Step Three, that was hard. I didn't know if I could turn my will and life over to the care of God, or even make the decision to try.

"I wanted to—I was desperate enough, but I didn't know if I could do it, I mean really do it. Sure I could fake it, but I'd been faking everything in my life for the past decade, and didn't want to do that.

"So I talked to my sponsor about it, and she told me that all I needed was the willingness to turn my life and will over to the care of God. I didn't need to figure it all out, I just needed a willingness. I could understand that.

"So I prayed, not like I used to pray, but I talked with God. I got down on my knees and literally said, 'I'm not sure where this is all going, but when I direct my life, it turns to shit. I ask you to come into my life and take over. Just take over, because I don't know what I am doing.' I cried that prayer. It was the first true prayer I ever made.

"Since that time, since that prayer, everything in my life has not been great, but it is better—a whole lot better. I am not in charge anymore. God is. I pray for wisdom. I pray for understanding. I pray for inner peace. That's all I want nowadays. I don't need anything else. I still don't have the answers, but I know now that I don't need them—just a willingness. That's all I have. Thanks for letting me share."

"Thanks, Anne," the group collective says.

"Thanks for coming with me, Bill Bill." My mom calls me Bill Bill. The stripping of the altar and the tolling of the bells lasts only fifteen minutes. Though Mom and I sat only inches apart in that pew, she was in a different world, on a different plane, experiencing something I could not yet grasp.

"I did not understand the relationship my mom had with God until I came into the rooms of Alcoholics Anonymous. I was so far adrift from any meaningful course. I was lost and didn't know that I needed to be found. Now, I wonder if my mother knew how lost I was—how spiritually bankrupt and how devoid of any real meaning and without any depth of personal understanding.

"If she did, she hid it well. She never told me how to pray, never told me how to get closer to God, and never lectured me on the wonders of giving oneself to the service of others and to God. She led by example, but I was not ready to follow her lead. She prayed for God to reveal himself to me, to open my eyes and my heart, but when the time was right for God, not for her and not for me. God answered her prayers and led me not to a grand church or a cathedral, but to a small, run down Alcoholics Anonymous meeting room in south Tampa."

"I told God to go to hell. That's how bad I was that morning. That's how low I had come." Mike has worked in the restaurant business since he was fifteen years old, bussing tables for his neighbor, who owned a small Italian place next to the Publix Supermarket. Mike is now the head chef at a Bar and Grill, just down the street from the Pinorama Bowling Alley. Mike is fifty-two years old. He has been working his program for seven years.

"Go to hell! That's what I said, because that's what I meant. Those were the first honest words I ever spoke to God, on my knees in my mother's room looking up at the cross hanging on her wall.

"And when I told God to go to hell, he wrapped his loving arms around me, and I started to cry. I cried like a teething baby. Such a big bad ass. I cried like a freakin' baby, and it felt great. It was like all the poison in me was leaking out of my eyes.

"Then my cursing turned to pleading. 'Please God, show me the way. I don't care where that way leads, just lead me out of this cesspool I am living in.' Without even thinking, I got up, took a shower, got in the car, and drove here for the first time, and I walked into these rooms, willing to do anything to stop the insanity that was my life, and that has made all the difference."

Mike sits in silence. We all sit in silence. "That's all I have to say. Thanks for letting me share."

"Thanks, Mike," we collectively say.

The room falls into silence. I let what Mike said replay through my mind. I have never spoken like that to God, and I don't mean the use of colorful language, but I have never spoken to God with complete honesty. I have never asked for help—I mean real help, the kind of life-saving help Mike asked from God.

My prayers have always been surface and shallow, selfish and self-centered. After ten years of religious schooling, and double that time spent on my knees in the pews of the Episcopal Church, I don't even know how to pray. I want to pray like Paul, Anne, Mike, and Mom. If God truly knows my every thought, then he knows I am full of shit, a phony. If I think about it too much, I should be embarrassed to come before Him.

From the time I was three years old, priests, parents, and teachers have been trying to show me how to get close to God, and at forty-six years old, I am further away from him than where I started. The only thing that gives me some comfort is that when Jesus walked on this earth, He hung out with the ragamuffins, the sinners, the prostitutes, the tax collectors. I am no better, maybe even worse, because the prostitutes at least had faith, real faith, and I don't have that. Jesus said He hung out with this crowd because like a doctor, he came to heal the sick. Well, here I am. I'm sick—spiritually, mentally, and physically—the trifecta.

"My name's Beth, I'm an alcoholic."

"Hi, Beth," the room collectively says.

Beth has been in and out of the rooms for seven years. She will put together some long stretches of sobriety, and then go back out for a while, and then come back in. She is currently living at a halfway house and waiting tables at a small restaurant not far from the club. She has straight blonde hair. She is thin and tall. She looks tired. She is attractive but wears her life struggles on her face.

Before the meetings, she sits on the back porch and smokes one cigarette after another. She rarely shares anything with the group, so I sit up a bit when I hear her voice. I am hoping to hear some experience, strength, and hope. As she begins, I say a truthful prayer, "God, thank you for putting me in this room."

"I didn't like the God thing when I came in either." Beth is wearing a white V-neck t-shirt and faded blue jeans. She has her own copy of the Big Book she keeps in her lap. "God had never done a thing for me, so why should I turn my will and life over to Him? I am supposed to be a child of God, right? Then why has He treated me like this, or let all this shit happen to me? If He is all-powerful, he could have stopped at least some of the bad stuff, right?"

Beth looks into her hands. "That's why I continue to go in and out of these rooms. I try and work the steps, but it never seems to work. Something happens, and instead of turning to God, I pick up again, and then I am off to the races for another six months until I come crawling back in here, just to start all over. I really don't know who God is, even a God of my own understanding.

"I have tried to use this group as my Higher Power, the thing greater than myself, but I have never come to believe that any power could restore me to sanity. I know drinking doesn't solve anything either. I know continuing to go back out and drink is insane. I'm tired of my life. Tired of living. I'm thirty-seven years old. I am a waitress. I live in a halfway house. I'm an alcoholic and a widow. That's about it." Beth uses her fingers to wipe the tears from her eyes.

"My God would not have taken my husband from me. He just wouldn't, but He did, and I don't give a shit about God's plan. What about my plan? My husband and I were in it for the long haul, the real deal, and then he was gone, and so was I, but I was still here. God left me here, but to do what? Wait tables, struggle with my addiction, and live in a halfway house with eight other strung-out women? Is that God's plan for me? Is that who I am supposed to give my will and life over to? Well, if it is, no thank you. But I keep coming back, like all of you tell me to do. I keep coming back, and I'm not sure why, but I do, and I will continue to come back. Thanks for letting me share."

"Thanks, Beth," the room collectively says. The room goes quiet again.

"Bill Bill," the voice says. "It's okay. It's okay."

God help me. I can't believe what I am about to do. I take a deep breath. The room is still silent. I can hear my breathing. I ask for God to hold my hand.

"My name's Bill. I'm an alcoholic."

"Hi, Bill," the room says back.

## Chapter Five

# Into the Night

MARIA AND I LEAVE STARBUCKS and drift back into the wild beauty that is Manila. The people, the traffic, the street food, the heat, the wet air, the colors of the rainbow, and the smiles, always the smiles.

Around the corner from the BI is the Plaza De Roma, which is a park located in front of a cathedral. The Plaza de Roma has been a park since 1797, the year George Washington left office. The Plaza and the cathedral are an oasis in the middle of the city, a place of quiet, a peaceful place in the middle of the chaos that is Manila.

I am trying to feel God's presence in every step I take, not just the ones I take onto manicured grounds of a beautiful cathedral. However, I don't think about this until I step into the Plaza de Roma, which means that I still have a lot of work to do.

I watch Maria as she reads about the history of the park and the cathedral on a placard posted on the grounds. She snaps photos for the travel book I know she will make when we are back in Tampa, sitting up late, drinking decaf, and listening to music.

I look around the plaza and come to the realization, or the understanding for the first time, that all these people, none of whom look anything like me, are all God's children. We are the same. There is really no difference at all. We are all standing on a tiny spec of rock delicately balancing in the middle of a galaxy, as we spin around a small star. We are but dust, mere vapor, here and gone, barely noticeable to even each other, let alone the vastness of space and time.

In the rooms, I have learned that I am not unique. I hear my story from the mouths of many people, from the construction worker, the teacher, the painter, the unemployed housekeeper, the retired boat captain. They are me, and I am them. I find comfort in this understanding of sameness. We are all sick and suffering, whether it be from alcohol or pills or codependency or food addiction or anger or depression or .... These conditions are but symptoms of a hopeless state of mind that the twelve steps have unlocked for us.

Because we are all the same, our differences are so minor, trivial, and surface that I can learn about me from that construction worker or the retired boat captain. Everyone I meet can be a teacher, my teacher—an instructor as I make my way along the Broad Highway, and I need guidance along the way, guidance with every step I take. Understanding this fact has redirected my thoughts and allowed me to surrender them to the care of God, as I understand Him. Maria walks and continues to snap photographs. I drift closely behind.

Then, back at the hotel, I ran on the treadmill and swam laps in the rooftop pool. Maria loses herself in a full body massage, twelve dollars for a full hour. We showered, dressed, and headed back out into the city

We arrive at the Ilustrado just before ten - a restaurant tucked on a side street in the center of Intramuros. Ilustrado is a small place made of brick. Plants and strings of lights fill the small courtyard. The restaurant is almost empty. A young woman shows us to a table and we collapse into our chairs. As usual, Maria and I sit next to each other. This is not a conscious decision; rather, a subconscious one, stemming from the need to be able to lean against one another at any time, and I do lean against Maria, placing my head against her arm. She strokes my head and runs her fingers through my hair.

Three men playing guitar are serenading a table across the room. I am so tired and so comfortably relaxed, Maria doesn't even ask me what I want, but orders for the both of us. She notices that our waitress sounds like she is not feeling well, sniffling, but instead of asking for another server, one who is not suffering from a head cold, Maria reaches into her purse and pulls out a small Vitamin C packet, one you can dissolve in water.

"Just pour this into a glass of warm water, stir, and drink. It will stop that sickness that is coming on." Our server takes the package and smiles.

"Just put in water and stir?" she asks looking at the packet in her hand.

"Yes, just put in water and stir." She takes our order and the Vitamin C packet and returns to the kitchen.

"That was so nice."

"What was nice?"

"You giving our server a Vitamin C packet."

"Well, she's sick, and I had one in my purse."

"I know, but most people, me included, would be thinking about asking for a new server, one whose nose is not going to run into the food, but you are thinking of making sure she is alright. That's pretty cool."

"It's nothing. I had the packet in my purse. It cost less than a dollar."

"It's not about the cost—it's about the thought. My instinct would be selfish and self-centered. I don't want her to make me sick. She needs to get away from me, so she doesn't negatively affect my trip, my plans, my health, my self-centered life. Your instinct is to take a person and try to make that person better. That's awesome, but very rare."

"No it's not, anyone would … "

"Absolutely—no one would, so don't give me that. You are one special lady, Maria Giglio. Quite amazing. I am blessed to be sitting by your side."

"Thank you, lover. That's so sweet."

"Not sweet—true." Maria hooks her arm around mine and we lean into each other. The three musicians come to our table and ask Maria what she wants to hear.

"*What a Wonderful World* by Louie Armstrong." The men begin to play and all the world seems right, even if just for this moment. My eyes grow heavy. I let the weight of our mission lift from my shoulders and out of my mind. For just this moment, I am not on a life and death errand, but sitting in a restaurant holding on to Maria. That is it. I drift with the music letting nothing else in. I cannot control tomorrow, but I can control right now, and what I choose to do, choose to think or choose not to think. Right now, I am in this moment. My breathing is slow; my limbs are heavy. I am in Manila with Maria and there is nothing else I need.

"*I see trees of green, red roses too, I see them bloom for me and you, and I think to myself ...* " It is a wonderful world, absolutely wonderful.

We finish dinner and head out into a quiet night. The roads in Intramuros are empty. The families who live on the sidewalks have settled into their makeshift living arrangements, consisting of cardboard beds and dirty blankets. I hear music drifting through the alleyways, soft and melodious. Maria and I do not speak, but are both searching for the music's origin, for the sounds are guiding us, pulling us along.

We see a church in the distance. The building is dimly lit, just the cross over the door putting forth a soft glow. A window in the building attached to the church is open, and the sounds of soft voices singing flow out into the courtyard and into the night air. No traffic, no horns, no exhaust, no bustling people, for the first time since we arrived, the streets of Manila are quiet. Only the sound of those voices clinging to the wet warm air.

I squeeze Maria's hand and want to pause, to slow or stop time, to stay right here in the now, in the place I have never been able to stay. I feel the presence of my Higher Power, the presence of God in this soft and gentle night. His presence magnified by the simplicity of the evening, just the soft light and the sounds of young voices, reminding me that He is always there, if I can just let Him in through the intervening clamor that constantly distracts me and holds my mind hostage. We stay for only a few minutes. We are tired and need rest. We slowly walk away and the sounds of those young voices follow us, growing slightly fainter with each step until the voices are no more.

I lay in bed next to Maria. We hold hands. I pray and give thanks for my health and safety and for that of others. I am thankful for the peace God has brought to me—whether I deserve it or not, I am thankful. I close my eyes and let the world slip away.

"I see trees of green, red roses too, I see them bloom for me and you, and I think to myself … "

## Chapter One

# Billy v. United States Embassy, Part II

THE ALARM AWAKENS ME from my coma, and I struggle to turn it off, not sure where I am. Maria does not move. I sit on the edge of the bed and collect my thoughts, an odd phrase, but one that is apt for this morning, for my thoughts are spread out, random, and need to be collected and assessed before I can determine what is the next step I need to take.

Since it is impossible for me to collect them all, I focus on the few I can manage and pray that the other ones leave me alone while I try and do the next right thing. I know the first thing I should do is pray, meditate, and ask for guidance, for my life run on self-will has not turned out so well.

But I don't do that, for I am jumping to the next thought, which is all the text messages, emails, and phone calls I am sure I received while I was sleeping, as my clients, thirteen hours behind me, were spinning through their own lives.

I look at my watch—6:04 a.m., Wednesday morning. That means it is 5:04 p.m., Tuesday evening in Tampa. I wince when I think of all those hours I was sleeping and during that time, my lawyer life and the clients and courts that are the fuel for that engine were going full throttle.

I pick up my phone and head to the desk in the corner of the room. I start with the emails. I delete the junk and then look at the notices sent by the court for future court dates. I put the court dates in the calendar on my phone, and then into my paper calendar, highlighting in yellow the client and what county the case is in. A yellow highlight denotes a court appearance in my high tech system of office management. Office visits and other appointments are not highlighted, for if I miss those, no arrests warrants are issued.

Then I move on to the substantive emails. Most of my clients contact me by text message, but a few email, so I begin to answer these, starting with the oldest and working towards the most recent. Wendy wants to know what is going on with her case. Because I work for myself, and I have no staff, I am tasked with every detail of my clients' cases. So even though I don't have Wendy's file, I can respond.

Wendy is charged with battery on her boyfriend, though neither she nor her boyfriend called the police. They got into a fight at a campground while trying to set up a tent at night, which did not go so well. The alcohol they had consumed while neglecting to put up the tent in the daylight hours made a simple argument grow into a large one and things got physical and someone called the police.

Wendy's boyfriend was the only one to have injuries, a few scratches on his face. In a domestic violence situation, the police always arrest the person who has no injuries, for in these types of incidents, someone is always going to jail. Arresting one of the parties involved in a domestic dispute is the easiest and most efficient way to completely diffuse the situation.

When the police tried to tell Wendy that she was being arrested for a crime, she pushed one of the officers and then was taken to the ground. So her misdemeanor battery on her boyfriend charge is now accompanied with a felony battery on a law enforcement officer.

Wendy is a sweet lady with no prior record. She is embarrassed about the situation and "cannot believe that I had to hire a criminal defense attorney."

I respond to her email that I have sent a letter to the prosecutor asking the State to drop the battery against her boyfriend (who does not want to press charges, for he said the combat was mutual) and to allow her to do a diversion program for the battery on a law enforcement officer, so the charge will be dismissed if she completes a few community service hours and takes an anger management class. I tell Wendy that I am waiting for the State's response to my letter and will keep her informed.

Paul wants to know where we stand on his DUI charge. It is his third DUI, the others are from 1995 and 1999. I write to Paul and let him know that I sent a letter to the State Attorney's Office asking them to amend the charge to a reckless driving. Paul was pulled over for running a red light. He refused to do field sobriety exercises after the police officer smelled alcohol on his breath. He also refused to provide a breath sample.

The State has very little evidence to prove that Paul was under the influence of alcohol "to the extent his normal faculties were impaired," for that is the law in the State of Florida. Drinking and then driving is not illegal. If it was there would be no parking lots at bars. Drinking to the extent that a person's normal faculties become impaired and then driving is illegal, and that is what the State must prove in Paul's case.

Rick is not happy with the diversion program and wants me to ask the State for another offer. He says he can't afford the twenty-six week batterer's intervention classes, and that all he did was grab his girlfriend's wrist, because he wanted to see her phone and who she was texting. I let Rick know I will contact the State to see if I can get an alternative offer.

Jill is charged with aggravated stalking, but she is adamant that she is the one who was being stalked by her former boyfriend. I asked her to go through her old text messages and send me the ones from her former boyfriend that will support what she is saying. Then, I will then put together a packet of information and send it to the State Attorney's Office for its consideration. She has attached photographs of numerous text messages. I thank her, tell her I am out of town, and will get to this when I return.

Matt is in big trouble. He emails me often. A few months ago, he began a sexual conversation with a fourteen-year-old girl online, and then travelled to a Steak and Shake where he was to meet her for sex. The fourteen-year-old girl was actually a thirty-seven year old police officer, so when Matt arrived at the Steak and Shake, his life turned upside down. He has a wife and two small boys. He faces eight years in prison. I have set depositions in the case, and those are to take place next week. I have no news for Matt and just tell him that we will know more after the depositions. At some point, he is going to have to say goodbye to his boys. The case against him is very strong, so the fight is just to determine how long his prison stay will be.

I start a TO DO list for things I need to get on as soon as I get back to Tampa. Having finished the emails, I next go through the text messages. Most of my clients just want an update on their case. I respond briefly but with enough detail to calm their frayed nerves.

> **Randy:** nothing new. I still have not heard from the prosecutor about the body camera video in your case. We can't proceed until we know if there is one.
>
> **Anna:** No, I can't offer the prosecutor money to drop the case. That is illegal.
>
> **Michelle:** I have not heard about your husband's transfer to a new prison closer to you.
>
> **Harry:** No, the interlock device is not a condition of probation, it is required by Department of Motor Vehicles for those with multiple DUIs.
>
> **Monica:** Even though you have a prescription for oxycodone that does not mean that you can take a bunch of them and then drive a car. The State is not going to dismiss your DUI.
>
> **Kelly:** Yes, court is mandatory for a speeding ticket when you are travelling 30 miles over the speed limit (she was travelling 103 mph in a 45 mph zone).
>
> **Randy:** It does help that you have a new job. The State will consider that when we negotiate your case.

**Bonnie:** No bond means your son cannot get out of jail. We already went to court to set a bond, but the judge denied it because your son picked up a new felony charge while on felony probation.

**Dan:** Yes, if you plea as charged, you will be placed on the Florida's sex offender registry.

I finish the last text and sit back in my chair. One day at a time. I cannot fix all of these problems today, even if I was in Tampa and not Manila. I need to focus on what I actually can do today and do it, then focus on what I can do tomorrow and do it.

I say this to myself as a form of prayer and meditation, trying to let go of all of the things I cannot change and focus on the things I can. I cannot get Bonnie's son out on a bond today. I know he has four kids under the age of eight. I know his wife is a drug addict and cannot handle them, so the kids are with Bonnie. I know her son is going to lose his job because he is in jail. I know Bonnie cannot care for those kids much longer.

I know that the Department of Children and Families will get involved soon, and likely, the department will take those kids away. I know Bonnie's son is a good man who is just struggling with a drug addiction. I know he is not a "criminal." I know he is a good dad. I know their lives are being ripped apart, and they are looking to me to hold it all together.

I also know I can't do anything for Bonnie's son today, sitting at this desk in a hotel in Manila. I want to, but I can't. I know Bonnie needs to go to work, care for her ailing mother, and for her son's kids. I know she is about to break and is reaching out to me for guidance, for support, for a lifesaving rope to grab onto as she travels out of control down a raging river towards the waterfall she knows is just around the next bend in life's river.

The text I send her is inadequate. She knows there is nothing I can do right now. I have told her this before, but she needs me to hold her hand. She needs to put her head on my shoulder and let the tears flow, but I can't do that today, not in person, and not in a text. I have no reassuring words. I need to move forward.

"God, give me the strength to accept the things I cannot change, the courage to change the things I can, and the wisdom to know the difference." We say the Serenity Prayer at the beginning of every AA meeting, but I should pray it at the beginning of every day. I am trying to use the tools I have learned in the rooms out in the world and not leave that wisdom locked up in the cabinet along with our clubs' literature and pamphlets about the program.

A couple of months ago, I got into a texting battle with Maria's ex-husband over something stupid. I wrote things I shouldn't have and so did he, but I don't control him and need only worry about my side of the street. I called my sponsor and told him what I did. He was not happy. He told me that I was not spiritually fit enough to engage with this man. I tried to change the subject, because I knew he was right. "Well, I missed you at the meeting tonight. It was a good one," I said.

"You didn't learn a damn thing at the meeting," he replied. "Don't leave the knowledge in the rooms—it is meant to be carried into the world."

"Hey, lover," Maria calls from the bed. I turn towards her and smile. "How is Sansone Law this morning?"

"I'm just glad it's late in Tampa, so people will stop pestering me," I say.

"Oh, you love it," Maria replies. I smile. Maria knows me well. "Get back in bed and cuddle with me for a few minutes." I climb back in bed, and we wrap our bodies together as I hold her tight. "Contra mundum," I say burrowing my head into her chest. "Contra mundum," she replies in a whisper.

People in Manila must not drink that much coffee. Our waiter incredulously asks, "More?" when I motion to my coffee cup for number four to be poured. The cups are small, and it is actually only about two cups worth of coffee, so I say, "Yes, please," and he fills it up and walks back to the kitchen where I imagine that he tells his buddies that the American at table six is getting high on caffeine. Maria and I finish breakfast and linger over the coffee cooling in our cups.

"Are you ready for today?" Maria asks.

"Are you?" (I'm letting Della Street do all the talking. I almost got us detained at the Embassy last time we stepped foot in there.)

"Just remember that everyone has a job to do, and … "

"But they are not doing it," I interrupt. "The US Embassy is a joke, a bunch of people trying to cover their asses, because Ron's been rotting in a Filipino jail for the past four months and they know it, and don't know what to do about it, so everyone is ducking for cover."

Maria patiently lets me finish. "I know, but yelling and throwing a childish fit is not going to help Ron. Remember this is about him. We don't have the luxury of time to get into an argument with the Embassy today. We need that letter stating Ron is no longer a fugitive and the United States is not going to pick him up. That is the only goal for today. That simply must happen. Going in there with guns blazing will not help the situation." Maria takes a sip of coffee, as I let her words burrow their way into my thick skull.

"I know. I'm just shocked, or naive, or whatever it is. I would think the United States would be falling over themselves to get Ron out of jail. He is a seventy-year-old American lawyer locked up in a shithole for no reason, and the American government has not sent a simple letter that his lawyer asked them to send four months ago. Now his lawyer is here in Manila, having traveled nine thousand miles to get that letter, and they are giving *me* shit. Really? Do they think I'm just going to shrug my shoulders, say I tried, and go visit the beaches? No one cares."

"You're right. No one gives a shit about a seventy-year-old child pornographer."

"He's not a child pornographer. That was such a bullshit charge."

"I know it, but they don't. They see that is the reason why he was on probation and they roll their eyes and think he should be in jail."

"But that's not how our system works. He has paid his debt, more than his debt. There is no reason for him to be … "

"But why should they care? Why should they care about Ron?"

"Because it's just not right."

"Yes, but that's not enough. You know that. This has nothing to do with what is right. If it did, Ron would have been out months ago, and we would not be here. You think I could have told anyone I know that I was going with you to the Philippines to get a child pornographer out of jail?"

"But that's not what this is."

"I know that, but no one else does. No one wants to hear the fact that he did not possess child pornography, but instead possessed an old tape of him having sex with a Cuban prostitute. That sounds so much better."

"But that's not a crime."

"It doesn't matter. We are not dealing with the law. We are dealing with people, and no one cares. That is why Ron is still in jail: no one cares." We sit in silence. The waiter takes our plates away. I hear the traffic rumbling by. Manila is awake, if it even went to sleep.

"I care," I softly say.

"I know you do, baby. I know you do."

We set out onto the streets of Manila for Day Three. Maria calls for a GRAB, which is the Filipino version of UBER. We jump into the back seat and tell the driver to take us to the United States Embassy. We leave the hotel, take two right turns, and are on Roxas Boulevard. The traffic is bumper to bumper, but I don't mind.

Even though we are running out of time to get Ron out of jail before we leave the country, I am in no hurry to get to the Embassy. I don't have a good feeling about this morning, I am tired and don't know if I have the spiritual strength to handle bureaucratic incompetence.

I do not claim to be the smartest man on earth or even in Hillsborough County, or even on De Leon Street where my office is located for that matter, but what happened and is happening at the Embassy is utter and sheer incompetency, no other way to describe it.

Well, Maria might describe it as selective incompetence in that why should the United States be in a hurry to get a convicted child pornographer out of jail, and Maria might just be right—no one cares. No one cares about the facts of the case. No one cares that Ron was actually charged with possessing a twenty-year old tape, a tape so old the government was afraid to let me watch it for fear the tape would disintegrate .

No one cares that a leading doctor at the University of Florida in child development said it was "impossible" to say whether the girl on the tape was under eighteen years of age.

No one cares that the United States government tracked Ron for years around the country and found NOTHING. No one cares that he pled guilty because the offer was time served and he was tired of fighting. No one cares that he was arrested in Manila on a mistaken warrant. No one cares that he is dying in that jail.

I guess Maria is right, the United States Embassy in Manila is not incompetent, just vindictive and cruel.

The GRAB driver pulls over and we step out. We see the same guard that we saw yesterday so we head towards him. He smiles as we approach.

"Good morning," I say. "We need to speak with Erica M. in American Citizen Services."

"They are in an all-day training. You cannot see her today." I almost laugh. Incompetence? Vindictiveness? Or just cruel?

"Erica M. told us to come back today. Can you send her a message that we are here?"

"No. She is in all-day training. I can't send her a message," and the guard smiles. It is not a vindictive smile. He is Filipino. He is just passing along the facts, as he was told them. Maria and I step to the side to allow the guard to speak to a family who stepped up behind us.

"Are you kidding me? She's in all-day training? An important detail she forgot to tell us, don't you think?" I am furious.

"I know."

"We don't have time to 'come back tomorrow'. We can't waste a second, let alone a full day." The heat from the day and my anger bring sweat to my brow.

"Didn't Erica say that she needed to talk to law enforcement?" Maria asks.

"Yes."

"So why are we going back to Erica at all? She's going to tell us the same thing that she needs to talk to law enforcement. Why don't we go straight to law enforcement?" (Brilliant, Della.)

"Who is the person from the Embassy listed in the Summary Deportation Order?" she asks.

I open my brief case and pull out my file. The Filipino government issued a deportation order based on information from the Diplomatic Security Service Overseas Criminal Investigations Unit Division of the United States Embassy.

I pull out the Summary Deportation Order and begin to read: "Records show that on 14 August 2017, Isaiah R. Attaché, US Department of State, Diplomatic Security Service Overseas Criminal Investigations informed BI that Ron is a fugitive from the USA for violation of probation in relation to his original charge as a sex offender." I look up.

"Let's go see Isaiah R." Maria says.

The Guard directs us to the other end of the Embassy.

"*Della*, I'm impressed," I say as we walk towards the entrance on the north side of the Embassy compound.

"Well, what was Erica M. going to do, really? She was going to sit behind that bulletproof glass, tell us that nothing was her fault, and then say she tried but has not been able to reach law enforcement, so there's nothing else she can do."

"You are so right." Before we reach the entrance on the north side, we pass a large sign that reads, "United States Embassy."

"Wait, I just have to get your picture in front of that," Maria says.

'This is not a tourist destination. I'm not sure they allow pictures."

"Well, we need one. I'll be discreet." I stand with brief case in my left hand, not sure if I should smile or look serious, but then again, the picture is for us, so why does it really matter, but it feels as if it should.

Maria holds up her phone and takes the shot, and as she does we hear someone yell at us from the direction of the Embassy compound. Maria doesn't flinch and begins to talk loudly into her phone, "Yes, I understand that, but we need to get this done now." She pauses as if the imaginary person on the other line is responding to her. "OK, I guess I can wait, but I'm not happy about that. Not happy at all. Actually, I'm furious," she says angrily. (Brilliant, Della!)

Not only did Maria immediately provide a cover to her taking a picture in a forbidden zone, but she did so in a loud and pissed off voice, and who wants to deal with a half-crazed pissed off American woman first thing in the morning—no one, and apparently not even the man who was walking towards us with a gun holstered on his side, for he stops, turns, and retreats into the compound walls. I look at Maria and smile.

"That picture will look just fine in the photo album I will make," she says sliding her phone back into her purse. I love this half-crazed, pissed-off American woman.

We enter the north side of the Embassy and step into a small waiting room. I walk up to what looks like an information desk and ask if we can speak with Isaiah R. The lady behind the desk informs us that we need to speak to the man who is sitting in a kiosk behind thick glass. Maria and I approach.

"We need to speak with Isaiah R. It's about our client, Ron." The man looks at me and then at Maria.

"I am not sure if he is available right now."

"That's okay. We travelled nine thousand miles to talk to him. We will wait. Just let him know that Ron's lawyer from America is waiting to speak with him."

"It might take a while," the man says. I look at my watch, then back at the gentleman behind the glass.

"We have all day. Just let him know we will wait all day. Thank you." And with that Maria and I take a seat in the chairs that line the wall next to the front door and wait. Maria pulls out her book, *Touch Me Not*, written by Dr. Jose Rizal, the man who set off a revolution and created the independent Philippines, as it exists today.

*Billy v. United States Embassy, Part II*

I didn't bring a book, so I am left alone with my mind—a potentially dangerous situation. Sensing the danger, I pull out my phone and click on my Bible app. I scroll through the Gospels looking for my old friend, Paul. Sometimes, I wish God would strike me blind as Saul was, before he became Paul. I need to be hit in the head with a hammer. Perhaps that's the only way I might actually wake up.

However, God doesn't work that way. Then again, maybe he is striking me blind or hitting me with a hammer, but I am so far adrift I don't even notice it. If God did choose me, as he chose Paul, would I be able to endure the hardships that Paul endured, the poverty, the prisons, the loneliness? Paul must have doubted. How could he not? He was a human being, right—a sinner?

When sitting in those jails, he must have wondered if he was doing the right thing, if this call from the Lord was real or imagined, because it landed him in prison. His faith couldn't have been that strong, that unshakable that he didn't doubt at all, doubt whether he was actually doing God's will, or doing his own will and calling it God's. How am I to know the difference? All I have is my mind, and how can I trust my mind?

I hear people say, "Trust in your Higher Power, trust in the Lord," but my mind is the thing that allows for that trust, right? And what if that same mind is sick, suffering, selfish, and self-centered? How can I rely on this mind to allow me the freedom to trust, have faith, truly believe, and to jump off that cliff knowing that I will be caught?

My mind and my life run on self-will, which is the root of all my problems, so how can I be sure that my mind is actually letting itself go to let God in? If I make a decision to turn my life and will over to the care of God as I understand him, my mind is making that decision, and my mind has an understanding of that Higher Power. A sick and suffering mind cannot heal another sick and suffering mind, so where does that leave me?

A man walks in through the door and saves me from myself. He knows the armed guard and the lady sitting behind the information desk. They begin to speak in Tagalog. From the laughter and levity of the conversation, it is clear that they are friends. Maria continues to read. My mind is thankful to have something, someone else on which to fixate. After a while, the man looks at us and asks, "Are you hungry?"

"Sure, what do you have?" Maria responds closing her book. The man has a small sandwich bag in hand, and pulls out what looks like white Playdoh covered in coconut. "What is that?" Maria asks as she stands up and steps towards the man.

"It's a little dessert I make." He explains to Maria the contents and how he makes it. I am still sitting in my chair. Maria nods and then asks questions, as if she is going to try and make the dessert tonight, and she most likely would, if we were not in Manila, but probably will try it, when we return home. The man goes through the ingredients and also explains the process of cooking the little playdoh balls. He hands her one and she takes a bite.

"Wow, that is so tasty." Maria turns and offers me some. I get up, take a piece, and eat it. Super flavorful and sweet. The man explains to Maria that his mother taught him how to make the sweet treat when he was a child. Maria and the man talk. I watch. The lady behind the desk tells Maria that her mother made the same treat. It is a Filipino favorite. The armed guard, who is also Filipino, walks up shaking his head in agreement. His mother also used to make the same treat. All Filipino mothers did and do.

Maria asks what it was like, growing up as a child in the Philippines, and they begin to answer. They speak as if they grew up on the same street, and maybe they did. However, they did not grow up living on the sidewalks, as so many children in Manila do. They had a Norman Rockwell childhood with a third-world flare. Maria asks more questions, which are greeted with smiles and cheerful answers.

For a moment, we are not in the United States Embassy in Manila waiting for the man who informed the Filipino government that they must hold Ron as a fugitive of the United States. Ron is not dying in a Filipino jail. Homer is not waiting for us to give him a document stating Ron is not a fugitive. We are not relying on Tess to complete Ron's BI clearance and get that paperwork to Rolando (who will then give it to us, to give it to Homer along with the letter from the Embassy. Then we will coordinate Ron's release from jail, and to the airport, where he will be free after languishing in an uncertain hell).

I am not thinking about all this or the forty-eight hours in which we must have it all done. If I am certain of one thing, it is this: if Ron is not released while Maria and I are in Manila, he will die in that jail.

An American lawyer being held by the Filipino government at the request of the United States government will die in jail, because the United States never informed the Filipino government that Ron was no longer a fugitive. Ron's death will not make headline news. It would not make any news at all. Who gives a damn about this child pornographer anyway? Some slimy criminal defense attorney and his girlfriend? Let the son of a bitch rot in that jail. The United States of America is too chicken shit to tell me to my face that this is the government's official position on Ron's situation—let him rot in that jail and if he dies, he dies!

About an hour and half after our arrival, a man walks into the room with an array of badges around his neck and asks, "Are you Mr. Sansone?"

"Yes," I say rising to greet him. "And this is Ms. Maria Cavallaro." Maria and the man shake hands.

"Isaiah is not here today, but I can help you. I am the one who arrested Ron." My heart does a backflip.

"Well, then, perhaps you can." The man pauses as if waiting for me to begin, but before I do, I take a quick breath and pray not to blow the situation up.

"I am Ron's lawyer from Florida. I was the one who handled his underlying case. I was the one who negotiated the plea deal that allowed him to leave the country at his choosing and come to the Philippines, even while on supervised release. His probation officer did not see that part of the order, and violated Ron for leaving the country. The Court issued an arrest warrant. You arrested Ron at his home in the Philippines.

"Two days later in Tampa, I had that same Court withdraw the arrest warrant, because Ron actually was allowed to leave the country when he did. That was in August. I have sent letters, emails, and made dozens of phone calls over the past four months asking why the Filipino government has not been informed that Ron is not a fugitive from the United States, and that the United States is not coming to pick him up.

"I did not receive any response at all. Therefore, I have travelled nine thousand miles from my home in Tampa, Florida, to Manila to see why my seventy-year-old client in frail health is still in a Filipino detention facility.

"Here I am." It is now his turn to speak. "By the way, what is your name? I did not catch it."

"I am Joel O. I am an attaché to the State Department Criminal Investigations Unit. Ron was actually my first arrest. After his arrest, I went on leave and have only been back a week or so."

I am sure Maria is on edge. Is Joel O. starting to sing the "It's not my fault" song, so Maria knows that I am about to jump out of my skin, if he hits the first note of this tune.

Joel's drivel continues. "We did inform the National Bureau of Immigration that Ron is no longer a fugitive."

I jump in, "You sent them a document to that effect?"

"No, but we did inform them … "

"When you say 'we,' to whom are you referring? You?"

"The criminal investigations unit. I was on leave."

"Then how do you know if a 'we' actually informed the Filipino government, because *we* have been to the National Bureau of Immigration a number of times since our arrival in Manila. *They* told us they have no information about the warrant being withdrawn."

"Who are *they*?" Joel asks. My blood pressure begins to rise at his mocking question.

"Homer Arellano. He is the one handling Ron's case. He is the one who has the authority to release Ron. He told me directly that he has absolutely no information from you, the United States, that Ron is no longer a fugitive."

"Well, even if I sent the letter, he would not be released without a BI clearance. You see, a BI clearance is something you might not know about. It requires ... "

"We know all about it, and I have taken care of that piece. I have been to the BI, and Ron's clearance was completed today. What we don't have is a letter from you, and by *you,* I mean the United States, stating that Ron is no longer a fugitive. As you know, Ron is in poor health. Have you seen him since you arrested him?"

"No, I have been on leave, as I just told you."

"Ah, yes, you did say that. Well, let me tell you that his health has not gotten any better living in that jail for the past four months. Did you know he is an American lawyer from Georgia?"

"No, I was not aware of that."

"Yes. He is a Georgia lawyer in a Filipino prison. I have travelled nine thousand miles because I cannot get you, the United States, to answer any of my letters or emails."

"I believe someone did answer your email."

"Oh, yes, you are right. After dozens of emails went unanswered, someone did finally reply when I demanded to speak to the Ambassador upon my arrival in Manila. So, yes, you are correct, someone *did* reply, but why did it take ... "

Maria jumps in sensing I am losing focus on what needs to be done. "What we need is just a simple letter from you, the United States, explaining that Ron is not a fugitive, and that the United States is not going to pick Ron up. You agree with the fact that Ron is no longer a fugitive, right?"

(Nice question, Della.) We wait for his response. He has no option but to agree. So he does, as he says, "Yes, I agree with that."

"Then if the Filipino government needs notification of that, because they don't remember someone calling to inform them of the situation, can you send a letter to that effect for their file, yes?" (Della is on a roll.)

"Yes, I can do that," he replies.

"Can you do that while we wait?"

"Well ... "

"We will wait all day if you are too busy. We have nothing else to do. We came nine thousand miles just to get that letter," Maria adds.

"Yes," Joel says with a bit of hesitation, "but I cannot give you a copy. I need to send it directly to the BI."

"Of course, so we will head over to the BI right now. When will the letter be there?" Maria asks.

Joel looks at his watch. "This afternoon."

"Okay. We will be at BI this afternoon and wait for its arrival. Can we please have your phone number, so we can call you if the letter does not arrive at the BI?" (Della keeps the pressure on.)

"Sure." More hesitation. Joel gives Maria his number, and I am smart enough to keep my big trap shut.

"Okay. Thank you so much, Joel. We will be at BI waiting for the letter to arrive." Maria sticks out her hand, and Joel hesitates for the third time, but this time, he takes her hand and shakes it. Then Joel and I shake hands.

"Thank you so much," I add. "We will call you later to confirm." And with that, Maria and I head out of the United States Embassy.

## Mission Accomplished!

Third Grade Teacher: **1**.

Special Attaché of the Criminal Investigation Unit of the US Embassy: **0**.

*Day 3*

Chapter Two

# Chinatown

"BINONDO IS THE DISTRICT OF MANILA referred to as Chinatown." We sit in the back seat of a cab. Maria reads from a book she bought on Manila. Since we only had a week to prepare for our trip, and most of that was spent on the logistics of getting here and situating our kids and work lives before we left, Maria is doing what I now refer to as "speed tourism."

"It is the oldest Chinatown in the world, established in 1594 by the Spaniards as a settlement for the Catholic Chinese." Maria and I are off the clock until the afternoon, when we head back to the BI to check on Ron's clearance, and then back to BI and Homer, to see if Special Attaché Joel O. followed through and sent the letter informing the Filipino government that Ron is no longer a fugitive.

Maria continues to read, and I begin to drift off as the cab winds its way through the traffic-filled streets of Manila. I hear her voice, but not the words. They do not register. I look out the window and feel tears build behind my eyes. I look to the sky hoping that the stillness of the clouds combined with the upward tilt of my head position will keep the tears from finding their way around my eyes. I search for Step Three and hold on: "Made a decision to turn my will and life over to the care of God as I understand him."

I close my eyes and I hear Roger's voice. He is sitting by the water cooler next to Pete. "My will is my thinking. My life is nothing more than my actions." He speaks slowly. He is an old timer with lots of years of sobriety. No one in AA holds any position of authority. We are a fellowship. No one is paid. There are no titles. Maybe "servant," because that is the highest pay grade in AA. Just a bunch of drunks helping out other drunks. I listen. I hear. I try and understand.

"I thought that my life was just fine but I just drank too much. Came to realize when I stopped drinking that it was my mind that was the problem—my thinking was the real problem. I had to get honest with myself, and that was a whole lot harder than putting a plug in the jug.

"You see, I was so selfish and self-centered I thought that if everyone would just leave me alone, my life would be great. It was the world's fault, not mine." Roger pauses. "Come to find out that I am the problem. That was a real eye opener.

"After I quit drinking, my life was even worse, because I had to deal with myself, and I didn't like myself very much, and no one else did either. So once I started working those steps up on that wall, my life started getting a whole lot better. I was not in control of everyone anymore. I didn't have to direct that play. Once I realized that I was not in control, my life began to get better. Once I started listening to people and letting them live their lives, my life got a whole lot easier. I don't have to run the world in order to live in it. I just had to do my part, whatever that might be, one day at a time. That's all I got. Thank you all."

Step Three: Roger, the Rooms, my Higher Power, my will, my life, my thinking, my actions, and the care of God—one day at a time.

The cab pulls over and Maria and I jump out. The clouds, the head position, Roger, and Step Three all helped keep the tears at bay and my mind relatively calm as the storm blew by.

Chinatown is even more congested than central Manila: the colors, the closeness of the people and the buildings, the smell of traffic, the garbage and the heat. You can actually smell the heat in Manila and hear the cacophony of sounds from people's voices, dogs barking, meat frying, cars moving, music playing, and church bells ringing—a reminder that God is always near—the shops selling their wares, the homeless, the school children, the professionals on lunch break, the construction workers fixing the sidewalk, the old men sitting on chairs taking in the day, the shop owners, the street food chefs, young men sitting on mopeds checking their phones, men carrying boxes, women unloading produce, cats and dogs looking for discarded scraps of food, the power lines twisting overhead in a disorganized spider web, clothes drying from balconies above—they must smell like exhaust, but then how would anyone notice? Chinatown, Manila, Philippines.

"Unbelievable," Maria says as she grabs my hand and looks around. "Where should we go?"

"I don't think it matters," I say looking from side to side. Maria smiles in agreement and starts to walk. She turns into an alley, which actually is a food bazaar. The alley is lined with small restaurants, coffee and pastry shops, food vendors selling produce, and cooking various types of meats and dishes. I feel as if I am in a tunnel with no empty space.

I look up. Wires run overhead connecting building to building, apartment to apartment. I can barely see the sky. We are in a third-world city version of Antelope Canyon. I follow Maria. She confidently strides through this utterly foreign scene.

Two days ago, I thought she was going to have a panic attack when we stepped out onto the streets on Manila. The sights, smells, and heat punched her in the stomach, making her nauseous, queasy, and sick. Now her nose guides her down the alley, stopping along the way to look at the array of foods. I walk behind her.

"Hey, lover, what about this?" Maria asks as she stops at a street vendor. There are noodles, seafood, meats of all types on sticks and in sauces, steamed greens, rice, and eggs. I never thought I would want to eat seafood cooked in a congested and dirty alleyway, but the smell of the food pushes aside the city around it.

"Looks good." And it does. I take a seat at a small white plastic table inside. The street food vendors are actually the working kitchens for these restaurants. The food is cooked in the alley, and after you order and collect your food, you step inside and sit down. So there are no menus and you don't have to ask to see the chef, because the chef is the person standing in the alley preparing the food.

Maria is smartly dressed. She stands in a crowd of people, all of whom are placing their orders. I cannot hear her over the array of sounds, but she looks confident, comfortable, as if this is her favorite alley in Manila Chinatown, after having spent years testing and trying the others.

I feel a sense of peace wash over me, as if God himself reached down and pushed aside my worries and calmed my troubled mind. I am in a foreign part of a foreign land, Manila's Chinatown, but I don't feel out of place. I don't look like a single person in this city of twelve million people. No one has light skin and Florida sun blonde hair, but I am clothed with a sense of belonging, a comfort, maybe the same comfort Maria must feel as she mixes with the locals in the alley.

People are people, right? We are all on this planet together, right? But this is not true. We, as people, as humans, divide each other based on the color of skin, the choice of religion, the imaginary boundaries we have drawn on the earth. We divide. We repress. We judge. We blame. We hate. The Bible is full of people dividing people over race, religion, geography, and stature in society.

The Bible was written thousands of years ago, but have we changed—at all? Am I any different? I would probably be the first one to cast that stone, for I do and have cast them every day—I am lying to myself if I think otherwise. Would I befriend a poor carpenter who hung out with the lepers and prostitutes and walked from city to city, depending on handouts of food and places to stay? Would I be able to see, or would I be blinded by my ego, my vanity? Unfortunately, I know the answer.

Manila Chinatown. I sit at a plastic table in a plastic chair in an alley waiting for Maria to bring our food. I want to hit the PAUSE button. I want to stop time. I don't want to go anywhere. Just sit, right here, right now, a nobody in this vast foreign land. I am comforted by my surroundings. Manila has wrapped her arms around me and told me to rest.

Maria sits down. "I got us a fish."

"I see that," I say as she places a large fish, head and all, on the table between us.

"The people here as so nice," Maria says as she pulls her chair towards the table.

"I know."

"I mean incredibly nice." Maria looks back at the alley. "I had a brain freeze about the money, and two ladies were so helpful. Crazy. I pull out this wad of colorful money. I don't even know how much it is, while I am standing in a crowded alley in Chinatown, and I don't think a thing about it. Not even a thought that someone would take it crosses my mind."

Chinatown

"I know. It's crazy."

"Could you do that In New York? I mean, am I crazy? Should I be scared? I don't know?"

Maria picks up her fork and digs out a piece of meat from the side of the fish. "Wow, that is so flavorful!" She takes another bite and continues. "I mean, everyone I know told me to be so careful when I told them I was going to Manila. That I should think twice about going, don't post on social media, and I was a little nervous, but …

" She pauses and looks around. "I don't know—there is something about this place, the people—I feel so welcome, so at home."

"And this coming from a woman who almost died of a heart attack right on the sidewalk forty-eight hours ago."

Maria laughs out loud. "I know. It's crazy."

"Now you are eating fish cooked in an alley. I am certain that this restaurant is not regulated by the health department."

"No," Maria laughs again, as she takes another bite of fish. "No one is checking the quality of the food in this place, but isn't it excellent? So fresh, so flavorful. This could be served in any high-end American restaurant, and people would pay top dollar for it. I just paid a little over five American dollars for the both of us." Maria looks back into the alley. "So much food. Food is so cheap everywhere, but people are starving right next to it, but they don't steal and barely beg. They just walk by hoping for a handout. Remarkable. Truly remarkable."

And it is. As I was waiting for Maria to pick out our lunch, a homeless man dressed in a filthy red Coca Cola t-shirt came up to a group of school girls standing in line next to Maria. The man did not say anything, but pointed to his mouth, as if he was mute, or so hungry he could not spare the energy to speak.

One of the girls held out what looked like a candied apple. The man pointed to his mouth indicating that he has no teeth so he cannot accept the generous gift. She is dressed in a linen white top with a blue pleated skirt and stands next to her friends, who are dressed in the same outfit. Their school must be close. The girl pulls out her wallet and opens it up. I could see an array of colorful bills jammed in the middle.

The starving man did not grab the wallet or the money, but patiently waited for her to find the gift amount and hand it over. After accepting the money, the man bowed slightly in thanks. He turned and walked away. The girl said something to her friend, who nodded in agreement while pointing at one of the dishes on display.

Such a simple interaction. No fear. No judgment. Just a young girl helping a poor man eat for the day. So simple, like a mother handing a few dollars to her teenage boy, so he could run to the arcade or the pizza place.

Maria and I eat in silence or rather, there is silence between us, as we listen to the sounds of Chinatown and the city moving about us.

"The food is remarkable. I think the dirt from the alley gives it the flavor." I smile and take a last bite.

"I should ask them for the recipe," Maria says, as she looks at the woman serving the food in the alley. "Tampa has a great Asian market, and I bet it sells all of the spices used in this."

"I think that's a great idea. It would be fun to try and recreate this at home." Maria sits on the edge of her seat about to hop up and step out into the alley. I wait for her decision. She is thinking.

"I can't do that," she says settling back into her chair.

"Why not?"

"Look how busy that woman is. I can't interrupt her for a recipe. I don't even have anything to write with."

"Maria, my briefcase has been an appendage to my arm since we landed in Manila." Maria laughs and places her napkin on her plate. She is not going to ask for the recipe, though I know she wants to.

My Maria would love to wake up early on a Saturday morning in Tampa, head to the YMCA for body pump, then to the Asian market where she would buy fresh fish and spend as much time as it takes hunting for the exact spices that were used on the fish in the alley in Manila. Then she would come home, take a shower, read a devotional, and spend some time quieting her mind.

When I walk through the door, she will have everything ready to start. She would not start the cooking process without me, even though I am no help. She wants us to experience this together, always together, everything together. I sit in a chair at the table just off the kitchen, and we talk as she prepares the food. "I'm not sure how much of this to use. I forgot to ask the lady, blasted."

I smile. Maria is going to go by experience and feel, which is probably better than exact amounts anyway. She talks to me about her day, as she rubs the fish with some spices. She reads a Bible verse she wants to share. Her legs are wobbly from the workout at the Y.M.C.A. Her mother's addition to her home is coming along nicely.

There is a movie playing at the Tampa Theatre, but she would rather stay home. I tell her about the new client I met at the jail. Attempted kidnapping. Then, about my swim and my afternoon meeting.

"How was the meeting?" she asks. The dinner comes along slowly, but that is just fine. This, watching Maria stand in the kitchen working wonders with the spices she picked up at the Asian market, is why I will mentally reach for the pause button, wanting to stay in that moment, to stay in the present.

"Want to get going? Let's explore Chinatown for a bit before heading back to the BI." Maria stands up and I take my cue. Maria takes one more look at the lady dishing out the food as we pass her. I know Maria wants to, but she won't. Maria thinks it would be selfish for her to stop this lady and ask her for a recipe when she is so busy trying to make a living, so Maria slowly walks by, as if the smell in the air will reveal which spices are being used.

Binondo Church is located in the heart of Chinatown. The church has been damaged by many natural disasters and was almost completely destroyed during the Second World War, leaving the Bell Tower as the only original part of the church still standing. The church was founded on the current site in 1596 and has been continuously used as a place of worship as fires, typhoons, and wars raged throughout the centuries.

We step inside. Maria walks to the left and starts down the side aisle. I head for the pews in the center. The ceiling contains separate paintings depicting the life of Christ, his birth, his teachings, and his arrest and crucifixion. I have always found comfort in contemplating the life of Christ. His selflessness, the ridicule and pain he endured, but I have always just contemplated his life and never let him in.

I have always left my God within the walls of the church and never carried Him outside. I have never put on the amour of God, only read about others who have. Jesus' life to me has been more akin to a feel-good book or movie, bringing about a warmth and a peace within the moment, but when the last page is turned or the credits begin to run, the warmth turns cold and the peace turns to discontentment.

I look around. Some people are taking pictures, some are praying on their knees, and some are sitting in the pews like me. I wonder what is running through their minds. Are they quiet and still, or spinning on that never-ending hamster wheel?

"What are you thinking about love love?" Maria sits next to me.

"Nothing."

"Now, I don't believe that for one second."

I smile. "Crazytown," I say pointing to my head. "I am living in Crazytown."

"You and me both, baby." Maria slips her arm through mine. We sit in the stillness of the church.

"Please hit the pause button," I say. Maria smiles and holds on tightly. We sit. My mind empties. Time betrays us. The pause button is always broken. It never works no matter how many times I push it. Maria leads the way out of the church and back onto the street. We wind our way among the street vendors, traffic, and people.

So much food. So much meat. So much produce. Where does it all come from? The fruits are so fresh, so plentiful, so full of color and life-giving substance. I stop at a produce vendor. She is selling green apples, oranges, blackberries, cherries, tomatoes, oranges, limes, pears, and a few things I have never seen before. I purchase three green apples. She places them in a bag. She looks at me and smiles—almost a laugh. I smile back.

"Where you from?"

"Florida," I say, confirming the stereotype.

"Ah, Florida, nice place, huh?"

"Yes, it is. Warm like here."

"Long way from here."

"Very long way."

"Enjoy your stay in Manila," she says as I hand her the money.

"Oh, I will, and am. Quite a city. The people are so sweet, so nice." She flashes a broad smile.

"We are Filipino."

"I am beginning to understand that." I take the bag and place it in my briefcase.

"God bless you, man from Florida. Be safe in your travels."

"Thank you, and God bless you, too." And I mean it, for I feel as if God is around us. He walked out of the church with me. He is on the streets. He is in this produce vendor. And maybe, just maybe, He is in me, too.

Maria and I continue our journey. We have no direction, no plan. We turn down a street if something catches our eye—a vendor, a building, a group of people, a colorful banner draped across the street. For a few moments, I forget about Ron, Homer, Tess, Rolando, Erica, Isaiah, and Joel. I forget that after two days, I still have no letter from the Embassy, no BI clearance, no plan for Ron once he is out of jail.

Before I left for Manila, some of my friends asked me what I was going to do when I got here. I told them the truth, "I'm going to Manila to pitch a fit." That was the plan. I have no power. No authority. I sent unanswered letters to the State Department and the Embassy. If the United States government does not respect me, why should the Filipino government? And my client, he's just some dirty old man, a child pornographer, so who cares if he dies in that jail, right?

We pass over the Pasig River. The water is stagnant and foul smelling. Maria puts her hand over her mouth and nose. Garbage drifts slowly on top of the water. Life is not sustainable in this water. It is thick like soup.

Apartment buildings line the river. Clothes hang from balconies, drying in the foul-smelling air. I stop atop the bridge and look out onto the water. Maria walks on. I see a young woman with a child strapped to her back walk onto the balcony. She begins to collect the clothes.

She does have a place to live, unlike other mothers with children on their backs, but this cannot be the place of her dreams. This cannot be what she envisioned for herself when she was a little girl and she thought about where her life would take her. I wonder if she smells the foulness of the river anymore, or has the stench so permeated every aspect of her life that it is just one piece making up the whole of everything around her. She does have a place to live, but no one wants to live in garbage, and that's what this river is, garbage, filth, and sewage.

This river was not always like this. Fish must have swum in these waters at some point. The water must have been safe for drinking when the first humans came upon it. Now, it is a toxic sludge. Why does the government do nothing about this?

What am I going to do? Stand on this bridge for a few more moments thinking about how sad this woman's life is, and how I would like to be the knight in shining armor riding in to save her from this life? She is almost finished collecting the clothes. I will then walk on, and she will go inside, and I will never see her again. The child will grow up on the banks of this filth. I will do nothing for her. I will do nothing for that child. Will she have dreams? Who will help make them come true? Not me. I know that. I have no armor, shining or not, no armor of God. I don't know how to put it on. I stand naked, clothed only in my selfishness. I am defenseless against myself. The mother and child walk inside. The moment is gone.

I catch up to Maria. She is at a produce stand inspecting the fruits and vegetables. I slide my hand into hers. She doesn't ask me where I was or what I was doing. She knows.

"The produce is so fresh," Maria says as she looks from side to side as if to say, "Where did all this fresh food come from amidst this congested city?"

"Maybe it was dropped from heaven," I say, responding to the words she did not say.

"Maybe you're right." I know Maria wants to buy some vegetables for the meal she is cooking in her head, but we have no place to cook, and we need to get back to Homer, and continue our journey on this life-and-death errand. She lingers over the peppers and spices. She does not want to let this go. This is her moment, and she holds on.

"Okay, lover," she says without moving her eyes from the food. "I guess we have to move on."

I look at my watch. If Joel is a man of his word, the letter from the Embassy is at the BI, somewhere in that massive maze of a building, so Maria and I need to get there to ensure the letter makes its way to Homer's desk.

"Yes, love love. We need to go." Maria turns, pulls me in close, and we walk away. Her moment is gone.

Maria peels off from me and heads towards a nice hotel across the street. She looks back. "Come on."

I do, and follow her into the lobby. The air conditioning cools the sweat on my back, bringing me to a chill. Maria sits in one of the plush chairs on the far side of the lobby.

"Let's sit for a minute, charge our phones, and figure out our next steps." I sit next to her.

"Homer—that's our next step," I say.

"I know that, silly." Maria plugs in her phone, and I sink into the chair and feel the weight of the jet lag, the walking, and the reason for our trip to Manila pushing down upon me.

# BEING CONVINCED

"Being convinced, *we were at Step Three*, which is that we decided to turn our will and our life over to God as we understood Him. Just what do we mean by that and just what do we do?" (From: The Big Book of Alcoholics Anonymous page 60.)

The Big Book continues, "The first requirement is that we have to be convinced that any life run on self-will can hardly be a success." I have a master's degree and a doctorate of laws, but these do not help me with these three seemingly simple sentences. What does *being convinced* really mean to me and for my life? Of what am I truly convinced? Anything?

Am I truly convinced that there is a Higher Power, a God of my understanding, or have I just been told Bible stories over the years, and pray to the God in that Bible when my life sucks and I need Him to do something for me? What does it really mean that "any life run on self-will can hardly be a success?" Wasn't I taught that if I put my mind to something, my will, my power to it, I could do anything? Just pull myself up by my bootstraps? Make my own destiny? Make my own tomorrow? Self-will is now a bad thing?

My life has run on self-will in that I have willed myself, my ways, my needs into each and every situation I have ever faced. I have lived my life like the stage actor trying to run the whole show, and if each person would just stand on their mark and do and say as I wished, then life would be great.

It's not that I have bad intentions, I actually have good ones, but the problem is I don't control other people, no matter how hard I try. The harder I try, the more those people control me. I am just beginning to understand this, but it does not come easily. Old habits are hard to break. How about trying to break a way of thinking, a way of conceiving the world and all the people in it that has been with me, directing my every thought, my every interaction since I was a child? My "habits" are ten inches of solid concrete. Try breaking that.

Mike sits in the corner by the water cooler. "I'm convinced that I'm an alcoholic. That was an easy one. I'm also convinced that when

I work the steps and the twelve principles that go along with each one, my life gets better, and when I don't, my life sucks." The twelve principles that correlate with the twelve steps are: 1) honesty, 2) hope, 3) faith, 4) courage, 5) integrity, 6) willingness, 7) humility, 8) brotherly love, 9) justice, 10) perseverance, 11) spirituality, and 12) service.

"If I live by these principles, I don't have to drink anymore. I don't have to fight nobody anymore. I don't have to fight myself anymore. I can find some peace for my weary old mind. You see, I'm a big sissy. I don't like pain. I don't like lying in bed awake at night worrying about things and people I can't control. I need to let that shit go.

"When I first came into these rooms and people started talking about God and Higher Powers, I was thinking, *You people are a bunch of religious crackpots.* But I came to understand that I am not in control of the world. He is."

Mike motions to the ceiling. "Whoever that might be for me. I don't have to try and control everyone anymore. That's not my job, and I'm not that smart. I just have to live my life by those steps and those principles up on that wall. I am convinced that when I don't, my life sucks, and I don't want to live like that, not anymore.

"So I had to get honest with myself. I had to realize that the world was not my problem. I was my problem. I had to start listening to you people, the people in these rooms, because I wanted what you had—freedom. Freedom from a sick and suffering mind. One day at a time, that's all I can do. That's all I have. Thank you all."

"Thanks, Mike."

"My name's Mary and I'm an alcoholic."

"Hi, Mary."

"I was convinced that I hated everyone, and everyone one else in the world was a raving lunatic." Mary sits between John and Suzie. She is a retired schoolteacher and wears rings on every finger. "I was also convinced that my life was out of control, and that I was never happy.

"When I came into these rooms, I just wanted to figure out how to drink less, not completely stop. But when I came in here, I did stop drinking, and then I realized that drinking was not my problem. My problem was all the other stuff that I was masking by my drinking. Like Mike said, my problem was me."

I turned in my chair to face Mary. Mike and Mary are completely different people. They inhabit separate worlds, run their lives on separate planes, work in separate socio-economic circles. Mike wears faded jeans, a ripped t-shirt, and a faded baseball cap. It is his uniform. Mary wears a full-length summer dress. Her toenails are painted hot pink. Her hair is salon perfect.

But inside these rooms they are the same—sick and suffering, trying to change their way of life. Inside these rooms, they have a common identity, a common bond, which is stronger than any club either one might be a part of outside of these rooms. Inside these rooms, they are on a life-and-death errand. Inside these rooms, they have ceased fighting everyone and everything. Inside these rooms, they don't just tolerate each other, or even just respect each other. They completely rely on each other for experience, strength, and hope. Inside these rooms, these two people share common goals—not to die an alcoholic death, not to live with a hopeless state of mind, and to be relieved from the bondage of self.

Inside these rooms I am beginning to listen to others for the first time. I listen to Mike. I listen to Mary. Inside these rooms I attempt to smash and re-smash my ego, so myself will not run riot. Inside these rooms I pray for the first time. Inside these rooms, I am trying to become convinced.

"I am also convinced," Mary continues, "that I was not a nice person." I love my son unconditionally, but others, I love with a long list of conditions. I don't want to live that way anymore. I want to love people unconditionally, and that is hard for me, but I am trying. Thanks for letting me share."

"Thanks Mary."

Pedro raises his hand to speak. "My name's Pedro and I'm an alcoholic."

"Hi, Pedro."

"I first came to one of these meetings in the penitentiary. I was a bad ass suffering from a bad state of mind. But I learned something in there. It took a while, but I learned something." Pedro wears a gray tank top, jeans with paint and dirt clinging to them, and brown work boots. His hands are thick, toughened by years of hard work. The muscles in his arms are chiseled and his veins lay atop his forearms like ropes on a ship's deck. He sits in one of the chairs along the back wall.

"I didn't know anything about the God thing. I was born in New York, and I grew up on the streets, and I had to rely on myself, trust myself, take what I could get, because no one was going to look out for me, you know. So I came into these rooms and people were talking about God and a Higher Power and giving up control to him or it or whatever. I thought to myself, *I ain't giving control up of my life to no one or no thing. I'm a bad ass mother fucker and I'm in control.* That's what I thought."

Pedro looks at the ceiling then to his hands. "For some reason, I kept going to those meetings, and I started thinking to myself, *If you're such a bad ass mother fucker, what are you doing in the God damn penitentiary, dumb ass.* I started thinking that I've been in control of my own life since I was ten years old, and since I took control of my life, I was in juvie twice, county jail four times, and now the pen. Things weren't going real good.

"So at those meetings, I started listening. I wanted what the other guys in the rooms had. They had freedom. Even though they were still locked up in the pen—they had a freedom. I wanted that shit. I wanted it real bad.

"Now I'm out, but I'm still here, in these rooms. I clean bars for a living now. I used to drive a Porsche, but now I push a mop, but it's all good. I got freedom now. Just today this guy was asking me to start another job, and I looked at my watch and it was 5:11. I plan my day around this 5:45 meeting, and I told him that I got to go. This room is my church, my gym, my home. I come here to recharge. I am convinced of that. That's all I have. Thanks for letting me share."

"Thanks, Pedro."

Mike, Mary, Pedro. I am convinced that I want what they have. I am convinced that I am not there yet. Why not? Why is this so hard? I am convinced that my life and my manner of thinking are unmanageable. Am I convinced that a power greater than me can restore me to sanity, or am I still trying to do it myself?

"I want to be convinced like Mike that when I follow the steps and the principles up on the wall, my life will get better and when I don't follow those spiritual principles, my life will suck. I want to be convinced that pushing a mop is better than driving a Porsche as long as I have these rooms. I want to be convinced that a life run by SELF-propulsion will only put me on a collision course with somebody. I want to be convinced that I don't have to run the whole show. I want to be convinced that I cannot wrest satisfaction and happiness out of this world as long as I try to control it. I want to be convinced that my troubles are of my own making, and it's only by surrendering control to my Higher Power that I can get out of this hopeless way of life. I want to be convinced that my self-will is not helping me, not protecting me—rather, it is killing me. I want to be convinced that my sick and suffering mind cannot heal my sick and suffering mind. I have always asked God to speak to me, and never thought He has. Maybe, just maybe, God gave me Mike, Mary, and Pedro. Billy, get out of your own way. Start by being convinced of the need for that."

### Day 3

## Chapter Three

# Jodieeeeee

MARIA IS IN CHARGE OF THE LOGISTICS of our trip. I made the final decision to travel to Manila nine days before we were to land. We knew nothing about the country, the city, where to stay, where to eat, or what to do. The plan was to meet Chito at the Bayleaf Intramuros Hotel at 2 p.m. on Monday, December 4. That was all we had.

Maria booked our flights that took us from Tampa, to New York, to Taipei, to Manila. She found a hotel near the Embassy, which is not far from Intramuros. She made sure the hotel had a gym and a rooftop lap pool, so she didn't have to watch me slowly drift into madness because I was unable to work out—one addiction for another.

She ordered a street map of Manila, Dr. Rizal's book *Touch Me Not*—which started a revolution, a Tagalog phrase book, Filipino money, and an AT&T plan that would allow me to operate Sansone Law from Asia with no additional charges. She got an immunization shot and told me where to go to get one, but I never did.

She also had to plan for her own departure from the Western world. She lined up a substitute teacher, made lessons plans for the entire time she would be gone (those kids were not going to coast while she was away), arranged with her ex-husband to take care of their son, and many other things I am sure, but I was not focused on her.

I was focused on me—selfishness and self-centeredness are my expertise—I am a true master. I work in self-centeredness as other masters work with oils or clay. Maria arranged for the hotel to send a driver to the airport to pick us up, so we didn't have to deal with public transportation at one o'clock in the morning in a foreign city in a foreign land.

We left Tampa on December 2. Manila is thirteen hours ahead, so with the length of travel time and the flipping of the clock, we were scheduled to arrive in the early morning hours of December 4. Where did that leave December 3—my birthday? We were to cross so many time zones, when would it be December 3?

We flew EVA Air from New York to Taiwan. The flight attendants wore lime green uniforms and looked like porcelain dolls, their skin flawless, ink black hair perfectly placed.

The quickest way from New York to Taiwan is north over the top of the world, so that is how we flew. Our plane took off and headed up over the Artic Circle, down over Siberia, the Koreas, and then on to Taipei .

Somewhere north of Alaska, four flight attendants came to our row. They had a small cake and card. They wished me happy birthday, and giggled as I sang, "Happy Birthday to me." All the flight attendants had signed the card, for they all knew me. I was the crazy American who was doing yoga next to the bathroom in the rear of the plane. They had to step over me when I was doing push-ups and downward dog next to the drink cart—one addiction for another. Maria, thankfully, handled all of the logistics. We celebrated my birthday at 37,000 feet. Outside air temperature was -47 degrees Fahrenheit.

"I think we can get a cab outside. A GRAB car will take too long. They must not want to drive into Chinatown. Maybe it's too congested, and that's saying a lot for this city," Maria says, not looking up from her phone.

Though the hour is getting late and we need to head back to the BI to see Homer, neither one of us moves, content to sit in the plush chairs, with the air conditioning, the clean bathrooms, and the smell of lavender, which is being pumped into the air through unseen air vents.

Maria continues to work on her phone. I continue to do nothing, content to let the world spin around without me for a bit. I close my eyes and ask God to take over. This is part of working my program, realizing that a life run on self-will, but without a Higher Power, is a life bound for both personal destruction and destruction of those in my path, like a tornado ripping through a midwestern town.

How does a sick mind heal a sick mind? It can't. That's why I have to be willing to turn my life, my thoughts, my actions over to the care of God, not just for a few minutes in the morning or when I am tired in bed and about to go to sleep at night.

I need to turn my life, my will, my thinking, and ALL of my actions over to the care of God. PERIOD. Only then will I be free from the burden of the self. Only by completely surrendering will I gain freedom. I can no longer try and be the director of the play, because no one is listening. So why should they?

They are too busy trying to direct their own play, in which I am just one of the actors, but I am not listening, for I am trying to direct them. So what we have is a bunch of directors running around trying to control the actions of other directors who are trying to control the actions of those directors. No wonder the play never comes off well. No wonder a life lived trying to be the director of others quickly ensues into chaos.

But I have been trying to be the director for forty-five years, the director of my chaotic play, so it's hard to give up control, even if I never actually had control, and I didn't and don't, but I continue on – "Please exit stage left! You with the flowers in your hair, aren't you listening to me? Exit stage left!"

The woman with the flowers in her hair does not hear me because she is yelling at me, "You with the blonde hair, stand on the X next to the bed, not next to the dresser. Don't you hear me??!!!" Chaos. Madness. A life run on self-will.

We step out of the hotel and back into the wonderfully dizzying world that is Manila Chinatown. Maria leads. I follow. She heads back to the main artery that runs through Chinatown. Cars, buses, trucks, motorbikes, Jeepneys. Where are the cabs? A Jeepney in Chinatown will not drive to Intramuros. Jeepneys are kind of like trolleys in that they don't venture out of their neighborhood. Maria flags a cab that stops. She walks up to the window and says something to the driver, and then steps back and the driver takes off.

"What was that?" I ask.

"He won't drive to Intramuros." I stand on the curb blissfully helpless as Maria tries to secure our transportation. The stream of traffic continues its journey through Chinatown, and no cab in sight. Then, a cab pulls off to the side of the road in front of us, and Maria walks up. She speaks though the open window. She turns and heads back towards me.

"What happened there?" I ask.

"He's having lunch." We wait. We watch as cars, buses, trucks, motorbikes, and Jeepneys pass us by. I look at my watch. Time is ticking. Time is not our friend. A cab mercifully pulls up just before my mind begins to slip out of control. Maria negotiates. She speaks and then listens. Speaks and then listens. Speaks again and then listens again. What in God's green earth are they talking about? Maria then motions for me to come.

"Let's go," she says. I slide into the backseat next to her.

"What was all that high level discussion about?"

"He normally does not leave Chinatown to drive to Intramuros, so I said I would pay extra, and here we are."

(Della Street to the rescue.) The cab takes off. I settle into the seat as the cab heads over the bridge, turns a corner, and then pulls over.

"What are you stopping for?" Maria asks.

"Bureau of Immigration is right over there," the cab driver points to his left. We were in the cab for less than two minutes. Maria and I look at each other and laugh, both realizing that we would have saved

# 5 DAYS IN MANILA

time, and money if we had just walked. I grab my briefcase and step out. Maria follows.

I smile as I head across the street towards the Bureau of Immigration. It's crazy that this Filipino government building is now familiar to me, as if I am walking into the Hillsborough County Courthouse in Tampa. Maria leads the way into the building. She speaks to security, secures our passes, and we head to the second floor to see Homer.

As we exit the stairwell and turn the corner, we see that there is a line in the hallway, a swarm of people waiting to see Homer. We settle at the back of the line. I look at my watch. 2:47 p.m. We have nothing to do the rest of the day but make sure that Special Attaché Joel sent that letter over to Homer. Then what? In the next two days are we really going to get Homer to give the order to release Ron from jail? And then what? How does that happen? Where will Ron go?

The Deportation Order said that Ron is not only a fugitive, but is a danger to the Filipino people, because of the underlying charge. He is to be placed on the government's blacklist and never allowed to return to the Philippines once he is released.

I have selectively overlooked this major detail, because my focus, and Ron's has been to get him out of that shithole at all costs. But where will he go? Can we get him off the blacklist? How does that all work? I try not to focus on things that will only happen after the miracle does—Ron's release from jail.

The line inches forward. I helplessly look at my watch. Maria is not as patient. She walks up to Homer's glass door and peers in. She waits until someone sees her through the glass, and then Maria waives and mouths something I cannot understand. Who is she waving at? What is she saying? She can't possibility be … And with that, Maria motions for me to come to the front of the line. She opens the door and we step into Jodie's office.

Jodie is Homer's assistant. She is pretty, petite, with porcelain skin and ink black hair, which she wears pulled back in a ponytail. Her office is so jammed with stacks of paper, files, and random boxes that it looks like she is in the beginning stages of packing up her office to move to another location. But she is not—this is how the office looked on Monday, and nothing noticeable has changed today. I am sure if we come back in a year, discerning even the movement of one item in that office will be an impossible task. Jodie motions us to walk to Homer's office, and we do.

"Hello, my friends. Back so soon," Homer says with a big smile. "Are you enjoying Manila? I hope you have had some time to take in the sights."

"The food is amazing. It is absolutely everywhere," Maria says.

Homer laughs. "Food is very important to the Filipino people."

"I just don't understand why there are so many starving people, right on the streets," Maria adds. I cringe. Will Homer take this as an insult to his country, his city, from a "rich" American?

"Yes, that is one of our city's most pressing problems." Homer looks at a file on his desk. "So big, it is hard to know where to start." From the manner and the feeling in which Homer said this, I can tell he has thought about the problem, had discussions about how to fix it, maybe even made some steps in that direction, but the problem is still there right outside his office window. It is there when he leaves work and walks to his car. It is there when he returns in the morning. It is as plentiful and ubiquitous as the street food itself.

"But we are not here to speak of Manila's problems, but your client's, correct?"

"Yes," Maria responds. This is her meeting. "We went to the US Embassy this morning and secured the letter that you need. They said they would fax it to you this afternoon."

"Jodieeee," Homer says in a loud voice. Jodie immediately appears at Homer's door. "Has a fax come through from the United States Embassy concerning their client?"

"No faxes from the Embassy," she replies.

Homer looks at Maria. "Who were they going to fax it to?

Maria looks at me.

"Not sure. Let me give him a call," I reply. "Special Attaché Joel gave me his direct line." I pull out my phone and dial the number. I place the call on speaker.

"Special Agent Joel," the man answers.

"Hello, this is Bill Sansone. I represent Ron. Maria and I were at the Embassy this morning, and you said that you were going to fax a letter stating that my client was no longer a fugitive, and — "

"I did," Joel interrupts.

"Well, I am in Mr. Homer's office, and he does not have a copy of that letter."

"Who is Homer? I don't think you are even in the right place," Joel responds in such a perfectly condescending asshole manner that he must have spent years perfecting it, honing his craft.

"No, I am in the right place. Mr. Homer is the one who is handling Ron's case." I feel my blood pressure rise. "Have you ever even been to BI?" Maria shoots me a quick look that says, 'Shut up. Don't piss him off. We need that letter.' As I speak, Homer says, "Jodieeee," and she appears at the door. He says something to her in Tagolog, and she disappears.

"Listen, I faxed the letter to the proper authorities. I'm not sure who you have been talking to, and I don't know who Homer is. I want you to know … " I see Jodie appear in the doorway with a letter in her hand.

"Ok, thanks, we got it. Good bye," I say and abruptly hang up. Special Attaché Joel is a disrespectful, lazy, and self-centered asshole. I can only pray he finds his way to a twelve-step program, for he desperately needs one. Jodie hands the letter to Homer. He reads it slowly. Maria and I are sitting on the edge of the cliff. If this is not the right letter, or does not say the right thing, I am going to jump off that cliff and end this maddening paper chase through the streets of Manila. Homer looks up. Maria and I hold our collective breath.

"Okay. This is fine. This is what I need." I exhale, not sure what to say.

"So, what does that mean?" Maria asks.

"It means I will release your client from custody." Homer hands me a copy of the letter. It reads as follows:

> Dear Commissioner Morente:
>
> The US Department of State, Diplomatic Security Service, Office of the Overseas Criminal Investigations (OCI) at US Embassy Manila would like to inform the Bureau of Immigration that the Warrant of Arrest for Ron for the violation of supervised release has been withdrawn on August 31, 2017 by the United States District Court Middle District of Florida, Tampa Division.
>
> In that regard, Ron has no outstanding warrants in the United States and does not require a law enforcement escort for his travel back the US.
>
> OCI appreciates your timely action on this matter. Should you have any questions, please contact Criminal Fraud Investigation.
>
> Respectfully,
>
> Joel O.

The letter is dated December 6. I successfully convinced the Court to withdraw the warrant, the entire basis for Ron's incarceration, on August 31. I am elated, stunned, and unbelievably pissed off. I got the warrant withdrawn in August, over three months have passed, and the United States Embassy only sent this letter informing the Filipino government that Ron is not a fugitive on December 6, and only after his lawyer flew nine thousand miles to pitch a fit in the lobby of the Embassy. Who is accountable to Ron? What about all the time he spent in that shit hole for nothing? What about the deterioration of his health? His mind? His sanity? Who pays for that? Who cares about that? I know the answer, not the "US Department of State, Diplomatic Security Service, Office of the Overseas Criminal Investigations (OCI) at US Embassy Manila" or whatever their bullshit title is.

I finish reading the letter and look at Homer. "So what now?" As I say this, Jodie walks in and hands Homer another sheet of paper. He laughs. He turns the piece of paper towards Maria and me so we can see it. It is a copy of the request for Ron's BI clearance along with all the others on the list. The one Tess said would take weeks to process. "It's done. He's clear."

"His BI check is done?" Maria asks.

"Yes. Done," Homer replies with a laugh as if acknowledging the craziness of our efforts to secure Ron's BI clearance, when it only took a few hours to perform.

"So you have all the paperwork you need?" I ask.

"Yes, we are all set," Homer says as he places the copy in Ron's file. I take a deep breath and look to the ceiling. Ron has been in custody for almost four months. All those unanswered phone calls, emails, and letters. Months of banging my head against the walls of the United States Embassy, the State Department, United States Probation, the United States Attorney's Office, and Maria's kitchen table. And there it is—two pieces of paper in Homer's hand. That's all I needed.

"So what happens now?" Maria asks.

"You just need to get me Ron's passport and a flight to the United States, and I will arrange transport to the airport."

"Okay, I can go to the jail tomorrow and pick up his passport. Why does he need to fly to the United States? Can't he just go anywhere?" I ask.

"Well, he has been placed on the blacklist, because of the American charge, and since he was to be deported, he must fly to somewhere in the United States. To allow anything else would require more

225

paperwork, and I am sure you don't want to deal with getting that accomplished before you leave."

"No way," Maria adds.

"Does he have to fly to the United States, or can he fly to a US protectorate, such as Guam?" Ron will have apoplexy if he has to go to the country responsible for his needless prosecution and incarceration in two countries.

"Guam is fine," Homer replies.

*Bill, Maria, and Homer at the Bureau of Immigration*

"Does he have to stay there, or … "

"Once he is on a plane for Guam, I do not care where he goes or what he does, as long as he does not come back to the Philippines, unless you want to get him removed from the blacklist, but that is more paperwork." Homer smiles. I smile back.

"We will deal with removing Ron from the blacklist later," I say as I sit back down in the chair. Maria looks at me as if to say, "Don't get comfortable, he's got a line of people out there. Let's go."

I stand up as if commanded. "Well, we shall see you tomorrow with Ron's passport and a copy of his flight itinerary to Guam." I reach out my hand and Homer takes it.

"That will make three days in a row that we have visited you. Aren't you excited?" Maria says as she takes Homer's hand. He laughs.

"No problem. No problem," he adds. Maria and I walk out of his office, through the chaos of Jodie's and out into the hallway. As Maria closes the door, we hear Homer yell, "Jodieee." We laugh.

Maria and I spill out of the BI onto the streets of Manila. We are holding hands and almost skipping as we cross the street to our Starbucks. I sit at an outside table. Maria goes in and orders. I think to myself, 'Our neighborhood Starbucks in Manila, Philippines? What the hell am I doing here?' I laugh out loud and sit back in my chair, close my eyes, and take in the sounds and smells of the glorious city around me.

Chapter Four

# Daddy's Little Girl

BACK AT THE HOTEL, I head straight for the gym for a run on the treadmill and a swim in the rooftop pool. "It's your number one priority," says Maria.

"What is?" I ask.

"Working out," she answers.

"Number one priority—what does that mean?" I ask.

"It means it's your number one priority."

"Over you and the kids?"

"Baby, it's okay. It's your number one priority."

"It is the only thing that keeps me sane."

"Lover, it's not a bad thing. You are just taking care of what you need to take care of. You must take care of yourself, and that is how you do it. I love that you have that outlet."

"Number one priority, huh?"

"Number one priority."

After I take care of my number one priority, I return to the room. Maria is still at the spa—eleven dollars for an hour-long massage. She can't believe the price, so she returns each day to make sure that the price is for real. Upon daily confirmation, she hands over her money and lets the women in the spa work their magic.

I lay on the bed. Five days without an AA meeting? I have the schedule of all of the meetings in Manila some of which are close to the hotel, but I have not yet made the decision to attend one.

Alcoholic Anonymous was started by two men who realized that the only way to stay sober is for one alcoholic to talk to another—no medications, no doctors, no counseling, and no religion. One alcoholic talking to another alcoholic. Twelve Steps. One book. No leaders. No dues.

There are now AA meetings in 174 countries. The only requirement for membership is a desire to stop drinking. PERIOD. AA does not affiliate with any outside organization, and there are no dues and no leaders, so money, power, and public controversy do not enter the rooms. AA is a truly altruistic fellowship. People helping people. PERIOD.

The world has never seen, and never will, a sex or money scandal in the rooms of AA or a power struggle. Alcoholics Anonymous is run by a bunch of drunks and has helped millions and millions of people all over the world. Its purpose is singular. There are no distractions and no interference.

While not a religious program, it is a spiritual one. I spent ten years attending religious schools and devoted my life in the pews of the church, but I found God in the rooms of Alcoholics Anonymous. I do believe that a power greater than myself can restore me to sanity, and that power is God. But for another person, that Higher Power might be something or someone else. Some believe that the AA fellowship is the power greater than themselves, and that is just fine.

There are no rules in AA, only twelve steps, and you follow them as best as you can with the help of a sponsor and the AA fellowship. A bunch of drunks, a room, a book, and twelve steps.

Maria returns rested and glowing.

"How was the massage?"

"Best eleven dollars I ever spent."

"You said that yesterday."

"And I will say it again tomorrow." Maria showers, dresses quickly, and we head out into the city. On the way back to the hotel, Maria spotted an interesting-looking local bar. The sign out front said that it has live music every night.

Even though I no longer partake in alcohol, I have no problem being around those who do, so we elect to see how the locals relax after the daily grind. The bar is not far from the hotel, so we decide to walk.

We pass the family who runs the small newspaper cart on the sidewalk just down from the hotel. The man is pulling a tarp over the cart. His wife is unfolding a large piece of cardboard and places it next to the cart. She then reaches for a thin rolled mat. She unrolls it and places it on the cardboard. The young child gets out of the chair and onto the mat. They are preparing for bed. This family will spend the night on the sidewalk. Where will they bathe? Brush their teeth? Go to the bathroom in the middle of the night?

When morning comes, they will get up. The man will remove the tarp and open for business. The woman will roll up the mat and fold the cardboard. The child will not go to school, but will learn only that which can be gleaned from the street. No reading, writing, or arithmetic—all the subjects that I complained about, but led me down the path of financial independence and physical comfort.

Where would I be if I grew up on the sidewalk next to my father's newspaper cart? Where will this child be in ten years, twenty? I have been given so much in life: shelter, food, clothing, money, cars, education, health care, soccer games, baseball practices, trips to North Carolina in the summer, Disney World over Spring Break, birthday cakes, bicycles, basketballs, money for prom night, tutors to help me along the way, and I ended up a selfish and self-centered alcoholic.

I would not last a week on the sidewalk next to this newspaper stand, and neither would the rest of the neighborhood, since my yelling and complaining would be so loud and so constant that the poor people would pass a hat, take up a collection, and put me on a bus to the south side of the city. Maria and I walk on.

The Diamond Hotel could be on Fifth Avenue in New York or on Michigan Avenue in Chicago. The building reaches high into the Manila sky. A guard out front is passing a mirror underneath the cars, checking for bombs. The man at the door wears a neatly pressed uniform. He greets us warmly and opens the door. The main entrance is filled with lights, glass, marble, and Christmas trees.

"I just want to look around for a minute," Maria says, as she steps towards a grand staircase that leads to the second floor and a better view of the scene around us. I follow. I reach the top of the staircase winded, my body telling me it is tired of moving.

I lean on the railing that overlooks the restaurant and bar below. The buffet has meats and lobster tails so large I can see them at this distance with my bad eyes—also, fruits, cheeses, covered dishes, cakes, and other sweets. The bar is next to the buffet line.

The usual suspects are all gathered on a glass shelf behind the bar: Jack, Johnnie, Jose, Jameson, and the Captain—my old friends are always there to welcome me back and refund my misery at any time.

On Fifth or Michigan Avenues, the excess of such a place would not be as palpable, but in Manila, having just stepped off the street, the extravagant display of concentrated wealth is on full display. I sit down in a plush chair next to the balcony rail.

"I'm just going to walk around a bit," Maria says and I smile to let her know that I heard her. A man walks by in a tuxedo, a glamorous woman on his arm. Her jewels are so large that they appear to be weighing her down, but I don't judge. How can I? Here is a trustworthy saying: of all of the sinners in this room, I am the worst, and I know that, and for me, this is progress. The chair is comfortable and so is the air-conditioning, the smell of Christmas trees, and spiced candles burning somewhere close. I close my eyes and begin to drift.

"Let's go," Maria says, bringing me back to the lobby of the Diamond Hotel. "Nothing special here, just another fancy hotel." I smile, stand, and follow Maria down the staircase, past the grand

Christmas tree in the lobby's entrance. A man holds the door for us and asks if we need a car.

"No. We'll walk," Maria says.

"As you wish," he replies. And with that, we are back on the streets of Manila, New York, and Chicago, behind the golden door.

The bar is just down the street on the corner next to a money-changing business, and across from a 7-11. Maria walks in as I hold the door. A line of young women greet us as we step inside. They are scantily dressed, have broad smiles, and are paying attention to me, not Maria.

"Do you need a table? A drink? Some food? Want to play pool? Want to hear the band upstairs? Are you having a nice night? Where are you from?" These questions come in overlapping succession from the line of women as I pass. I follow Maria to a table top on the other side of the bar.

"How many hostesses can one place have?" I ask, taking a seat next to her.

"Those aren't hostesses," Maria laughs.

She can see by my face that I am lost in confusion. "They're hookers."

My head snaps back to see the women I just passed. "Billy, don't be so obvious." I hear Maria's advice, but I still stare and count. One, two, three, four, five, six, seven hostesses are scantily dressed—it is possible, right? I mean, Hooters built an empire on boobs and wings, and in that order.

"Look around this place," Maria says, and I do. Hostesses seem to be everywhere, talking mostly to Western-looking men.

"Maybe this is just the most friendly bar on the planet," I say, finally realizing that Maria is right. "The owners want to make sure every male in the place is well attended."

Maria laughs. We take a seat, as I continue to survey the place.

"Billy," Maria says in teacher voice just loud enough for only me to hear.

"Okay, okay." I was staring a little too long, a little too obvious. A waitress comes to our table. She is wearing a t-shirt with the name of the bar on the front. She is clearly not one of the 'hostesses.'

"What will you have?" she asks.

"Vodka and soda," Maria says and the waitress looks to me.

"Water," I say.

"How do you want that?" the waitress smiles.

"In a glass," I reply. And with that, the waitress returns to the bar, passing hostess after hostess as she does.

A man is at the table next to ours, who looks American, perhaps in his mid-sixties. He is frowning—actually, more like pouting. His hair is dyed black, which is noticeable even in the poor light in the bar. He is overweight, wearing a shirt two sizes too small that wraps tightly to the fat rolls around his stomach.

He is nursing a drink and scowling at the room. He sits at the high-rise table by himself, and therein lies the problem. In a room full of hostesses, he sits alone, with money trying to jump out of his pocket, but no hostess takes an interest.

The Big Book and the Bible tell me not to judge others, but I still do. I am human. I am a sinner. So I sit at the table across from Maria and judge the man at the table next to us. I create his entire life in my head. He is a plumber from New Jersey. He roots for the New York Giants, and not the Jets. He has never been married, a fact that still pains his mother, who lives with him and cooks for him every night—her baby.

He comes to the Philippines every other year, telling his mother that he likes the beaches, but when he comes, he sits in smoky bars and waits for a hostess to approach him. He learned about Asian sex vacations on line. He does a lot of things online and one day will be raided by the police for distributing child pornography.

His mother never thinks to ask him why he returns from the Philippines paler then when he left, having spent a week at the beach. He drinks too much, eats too much, and smokes too much. He is a walking appetite, devouring everything in his way. He is slothful, lazy, judgmental, and self-centered to the core and holds people emotionally hostage. He is a liar, boastful and angry.

He and I are a lot alike. The only difference is that I have been blessed to have stumbled into the rooms of Alcoholic Anonymous, found my Higher Power, and am on the long road to recovery.

One of the hostesses walks up to his table, and I cringe. She is just a sweet little thing, like a little girl playing dress up. Her hair is ink black and comes to the middle of her back. Her eyes are brown, her skin flawless—and yes, I am staring that close and that long.

My stomach turns. Please don't, baby girl. There must be some other way. There must be something else you can do.

But is there? Was she a child of the street, snapped up, cleaned off, and placed in this bar to work? Where is her father? Mother? Do they know? If they did, do they pray at night? Pray she will return, but return to what? What do they have to offer her? A cardboard bed on the sidewalk next to the newspaper cart?

What do I offer? Prayer? Judgment? Pity? Who am I? What value do I add? How am I any different than the plumber from New Jersey? I have been given everything I have in this life — everything! What have I done, what am I going to do, and where will I aim for what I thirst?

The girl sits down next to the man.

"Baby, that's enough. Look at me for a minute." Maria says as she gently reaches for my hand.

"But … "

"I know, sweetheart. There's nothing you can do right now." Maria's voice is soft and tender, like a mother's trying to soothe a child.

"I know, but ... "

"Let it go, sweetheart." Maria grabs both of my hands as in prayer. I feel helpless, slothful, lazy.

Maria and I finish our drinks and head across the bar to the front door. She senses my discomfort. This is not a place to just hang out in and absorb the atmosphere.

I don't look at the table next to us as I walk by. I can't. The hostesses tell me goodbye and to come back anytime. They don't acknowledge Maria.

The night air is warm and thick with moisture. Maria and I hold hands. In the past, I have had girlfriends and wives, but never held hands. Maybe I was too self-absorbed to think about it, and maybe I just never had the right hand to hold.

When my hand is free and I walk next to Maria, I slide it into hers without a thought—like putting my hand into my pocket. I find security in the warmth of her hand. Comfort. Stability.

The Big Book and the Bible tell me that I cannot put too much faith, too much trust, and too much need in any one person, for that person is just that, a person, a sinner, flawed like the rest of us. Ultimate faith, trust, and need must remain in God, for He will never let me down, never judge, never walk away, and never let go of my hand. I know this. I understand this as a concept, but I am human, and I need another human. So rightly or wrongly, I squeeze Maria's hand in both hope and prayer and walk this earth holding on tightly, maybe too tightly, but I am not about to let go.

The streets are alive with people, and Maria and I slip into the moving stream. "The Korean place is only three blocks from here," Maria says as she leads me down the street. Maria has assumed the responsibility of planning all our meals, especially dinners. I guess she doesn't want to sit in the hotel room eating peanut butter on Granny Smith apples.

We walk. I hold her tightly. Before we left for Manila, many people warned us of the danger of coming to this country and questioned our need to actually come here, with talk of violence, kidnappings, drugs, and gangs.

Since the moment we landed and stood in line at immigration, we have been greeted with smiles not guns, laughter not yelling, street food not street drugs, and packs of children not packs of gang members. There is a warmth to the city that comes not from the sun, but from the people. It is palpable, and everywhere I go, I feel as if I am returning—returning to a place I once knew, although this place is completely foreign.

When I sit in a plastic chair next to a street vendor, it is as if I am waiting to hear, "Mr. Bill, welcome back. How have you been? Please sit. Tell me about your travels." There is a small feel to this massively large city.

But there is the other side, the side we were warned about. So as not to see it, I focus on Maria's hand as we walk towards the Korean restaurant just three blocks away. But I do see it. Actually, I hear it first. "Hey Mister, want to come in?" "Want a date?" "Come here and talk to me."

The girls stand on the sidewalk out in front of the businesses. They are dressed in the same fashion as the hostesses at the bar we just left, so similar that there must be only one store in all of Manila that sells such clothing. I wonder what that store is be called? Red Light Lingerie?

Maria steals a quick look at the girls on the sidewalk. There is no judgment. I know Maria. Just like the children who are playing with garbage in the middle of the day rather than being in school, Maria is searching for a solution—how to fix this unfixable situation.

"Hey, Blondie," a girl yells out to me. "Be my daddy." Oh, I wish I could be, sweet baby girl. I wish I could be.

Chapter Five

# God Have Mercy on Me

MARIA AND I WALK OUT of the Korean restaurant and into the night. I am full, a feeling I do not often allow myself the pleasure of experiencing. I have lost control in so many areas of my life, so I try to gain balance by controlling others. This is not a healthy way to try to balance one's life, just an illusion really, a semblance of control, kind of like making sure your seatbelt is tightly fastened before the plane crashes into a mountain side. But I am human, a flawed sinner, and still taking baby steps in my walk with my Higher Power, so I don't belabor the fact that I under-eat for the illusion of control. I know I do, but admitting this to myself is progress, a step forward on my new path.

We hold hands. "I don't feel like going back to the hotel just yet. Let's get a drink and play some pool," Maria says.

"Absolutely!" We stroll down the sidewalk, passing the same hostesses standing on the same sidewalk. They don't yell out to me as I pass. Maybe they see the peace and love on my face and know that the woman next to me is my world, and no one, no temptation, will take me away from her. Or maybe they just remember that I ignored them about an hour and a half ago and don't want to waste their breath.

As we cross the street at the end of the block, I notice a boy, maybe twelve or thirteen, following us. In Manila, it is easy to follow someone without being noticed. The city is jammed with people at all times of the day, but this boy is not trying to be secretive or stealthy.

No, he just crossed the street, got behind us, and started to close the gap.

Maria glances at me with a worried look on her face. She too has noticed our young shadow. I release Maria's hand, step off the sidewalk and into the street, slowing down a bit to see what reaction this instills in the boy. He does not look at me but closes the gap on Maria.

He must say something I do not hear, because Maria turns and sternly says, "No!" He has one hand up under his shirt as if holding a weapon. Maria quickens her pace and so does the shadow. I speed up getting behind them.

"Hey, you need to walk elsewhere my friend," I say.

The shadow does not acknowledge me, sticking close to Maria, so close he is about to touch her. My heart rate accelerates, so does Maria's pace.

"Get away," she says.

"Hey!" I yell.

With that the shadow slows down and Maria quickly crosses the street. I follow her. As I do, I feel the shadow slide in behind me. I turn. His hand is clearly holding something under his shirt. A knife? Gun? A vile of acid to throw on me?

My heart is pounding. Maria is walking ahead and not looking back. I feel the shadow upon me. I don't turn. I keep walking. He is so close I can smell him. Heart pounding. Sweat pouring. Breath quickening. The shadow's hand slides into my back pocket as he bumps into me.

I violently turn. My fist clenches. The shadow does not flinch. I turn and walk on. The shadow stays close. "You need to get out of here," I say in desperation.

The shadow bumps me again, his hand slipping into my pocket. I spin, fist held high. The shadow's expression does not change. His eyes are dull and lifeless. Is he a pathological killer? I lunge towards him as if I am about to strike. "Get out of here!" I scream, and with that, the shadow retreats.

My heart is about to explode in my chest. As I watch him turn and walk towards the sidewalk, I notice how thin his legs are, so thin they must have trouble carrying him around the city. He removes his hand from under his shirt. No knife, no gun, no vial of acid. He walks wearily as if worn out by the effort it took to keep up with me. He reaches the sidewalk and sits on the curb. He is not a danger, this shadow, but just a young boy.

I notice that he wears no shoes, and his feet are blackened with dirt and filth. He can't be more than twelve or thirteen years old. This boy is not a greedy dangerous thief. This boy is starving to death. He was not holding a weapon under his shirt, but his distended stomach, bloated from days upon days with no food.

I unclench my fist. This boy is dying a slow and painful death, surrounded at every corner by that which will bring him life—food, but no way to get it.

I come to a stop. Maria is already around the corner. The boy sits and stares blankly at the street. I almost punched that starving boy in the face. Just a boy. How did I not see that? How did I not notice that his thin legs could barely keep him upright?

Who do I think I am? A man of God? Is that how Jesus interacted with the sick and suffering? With a clenched fist protecting the earthly treasures in my pocket? I have always wondered what I would have done in Biblical times, if Jesus had told me to leave everything I had behind and to follow him. I like to think I would have followed, but who am I kidding—only myself of course. I would have clenched my fist, raised my voice, and yelled for that crazy carpenter to get out of my sight.

I walk on. I don't go up to the boy, reach out my hand, and offer anything to help him live one more day. No, I walk on. I give him nothing. I am just one more violent interaction in his sad and violent life.

That boy is a child of God. He reached out to me for help, and I turned in anger, leaving him to die slowly on the street. He is the first starving boy I have ever encountered in my life. On my couch at home, drinking coffee early in the morning, if the question entered my crazy mind as to what I would do if I ever encountered a starving child on the street, I would come up with all of these grand gestures of kindness, which would earn me accolades, maybe a spot in the paper or on television, maybe an award of some kind celebrating my generosity. But I don't do any of the grand gestures. I leave the boy on the side of the street, catch up with Maria, hold her hand, and offer a pathetic apology to God for my pitiful actions and inaction.

# I'M NOT MUCH, BUT I'M ALL I THINK ABOUT

Jim usually sits next to Michael in the corner of the room, next to the water cooler. He says, "I'm an egomaniac with an inferiority complex." Jim was in and out of the rooms for years, and now has over two decades of solid sobriety. He is suffering from the same thing Michael is suffering from, and Roger next to him, and Dave, Stu, Mike, Alan, Peggy, Paula, Ed, and Angela. We suffer from a hopeless state of mind, and alcohol is but a symptom.

The real problem is our thinking—not just our drinking. Drinking is *not* our problem, but being sober IS. In the Twelve Steps of Alcoholics Anonymous, alcohol is only mentioned in the first step: "We admitted we were powerless over alcohol—that our lives had become unmanageable."

Step One is a conclusion of the mind that allows us to continue on to Steps Two and Three, and there we find a solution—one that is based on turning our will and our thinking over to the care of God as we understand Him. From then, *we* must take action.

We must make a fearless and moral inventory of ourselves (Step Four) and admit the exact nature of our wrongs to God and to another human being (Step Five). We must be ready and willing to have God remove our character defects (Step Six) and humbly ask Him to do so (Step Seven). We must make a list of all persons we have harmed (Step Eight) and make direct amends to them all, unless doing so would injure them or others (Step Nine). We must continue to take a *daily* personal inventory, and when we are wrong, promptly admit it (Step Ten). We must through prayer and meditation improve our conscious contact with our Higher Power, praying only for HIS WILL and the power to carry that out (Step Eleven). And if we make it this far, we have had a spiritual awakening, and we must carry this message to other alcoholics, others who are suffering from a hopeless state of mind, and practice these principles in all of our affairs (Step Twelve). These are the Twelve Steps. A simple program, simple steps, and a simple way of life, but alcoholics love to complicate things.

Roger once said, quitting drinking was the easy part. Changing his thinking, recovering from his hopeless state of mind, living his life on life's terms, and having compassion and understanding for others at all times and in all situations—these were the hard parts. However, this freedom, this new way of living, comes from working the program. Alcoholics Anonymous is not a religious program, but it damn sure is a spiritual one, for it is only through a spiritual awakening that we recover from the obsessions of the mind. The program is not a thinking program, but an action program. The steps are not to be memorized, but worked and lived.

Jim says, "I'm a tough son of a bitch, but my troubles have been from the misuse of willpower." He must be over seventy years old. He wears a Budweiser t-shirt—one that doesn't just look retro—it *is* retro. When he purchased his shirt, the emblem was not faded and the edges around the collar were not frayed. "You see, I used to use all my energy trying to control everyone and everything around me, never realizing that I was the one out of control."

Jim leans forward, taking the position a father would take before confiding in his son the secret to a successful life. The room is quiet. Some lean back in their chairs. Some lean forward. Some sit with their eyes closed, as in prayer. Some eyes are wide open.

I sit between Joe and Dave. I feel at peace, even if just for this hour, for I know a peace that has eluded me for over twenty-five years. I have come to love and tremendously rely on the advice I get in the rooms. I have a bachelor's degree, a master's degree in English literature, and a law degree. I studied comparative criminal law at St. Edmund Hall in Oxford, England. I practice criminal law in front of numerous federal and state court judges. I have been lectured by brilliantly trained minds, but I await what Jim has to say as if my life depends on it—because it does.

"My life was going to continue to spiral out of control, until I stopped trying to bend the world to the shape I wanted it—stopped trying to bend people into the mold that I wanted them to fit. I had to let go and realize that I am not in control of everything and every person around me. Thinking that way leads only to frustration, anger, rage, then hopelessness, despair, and then to the well-worn seat at the end of the bar, where the bartender would be happy to refund my misery one drink at a time.

"I have been working since I was twelve years old. I spent two combat tours in Vietnam and have the shrapnel scars to prove it. I worked construction in the hot blazing sun for over thirty years. I have had three wives, five children, twelve grandchildren, and a great one on the way. I was a mean son of a bitch, a man who would get into a bar fight if someone just looked at me the wrong way. I kept the emergency room at Tampa General Hospital busy every Friday and Saturday night for a quarter of a century."

Jim sits straight up in his chair. "I am a man, right? A real man, right? Right!?" He leans forward again. "I was a goddamn child. A little infant baby, crying out because someone knocked over my milk. I threw more temper tantrums than all my grandchildren put together. It was all about me. What I wanted, when I wanted, how I wanted, and mainly, how much I wanted.

"This program has taught me to stop thinking like a child, and I'm working at it, and I'm getting better." Jim looks down at his hand as if in prayer. "I thank God for this program. I thank God for these steps, my sponsor, and every single person sitting in this room tonight. I love every single one of you. I would have died a miserable death many years ago without these steps and without my brothers and sisters in this room. I'm going to keep chugging on. As the Big Book says, "We are not saints, and I am striving only for spiritual progress, not perfection, but at least I'm not the devil himself anymore." Jim looks up. "That's all I have. Thanks for letting me share."

"Thanks, Jim."

The room hangs in silence, taking in all that Jim said. We are brothers and sisters. We can all relate to Jim's story—perhaps not the details, but the mental obsessions, the selfishness, and the unease that leads to anger and rage. We all have these character defects in varying degrees. Jim isn't an Oxford don or a professor of constitutional law, but he is a teacher, and I hold on to his message of hope and strength.

Mike is running the meeting. He breaks the silence. "I'm not much, but I'm all I think about." A few laughs ripple through the room. We understand. We come from various backgrounds, educational, societal, socioeconomic situations, but we are one at this moment, right now, united in strength, hope, and a unified love for one another. I don't want this moment to end, and know that I somehow must try to carry this feeling into the world outside these rooms. The meeting comes to a close. Chad does the chips. Our club has a colorful chip system denoting lengths of time in sobriety, but the most important is the white chip. Chad holds one up.

"The white chip is for anyone who wants to surrender and join this way of life, give up the high cost of low living." Chad looks around the room. Angelo in the corner raises his hand. This is his first AA meeting. The room erupts into applause. Angelo gets up and walks over to Chad who hugs him. "Keep coming back," Michael yells from the corner.

Janice is celebrating five years of sobriety. She is a cardiac care nurse at Tampa General. The room erupts as she stands up, takes her five-year chip and a hug from Chad. "How did you do it?" Roger yells, who is sitting next to Michael.

"By giving up control to my Higher Power, daily prayer and meditation, and coming to meetings with a bunch of drunks like you guys." The room explodes into laughter and applause. We then move into announcements. Dave announces that there is a beginners meeting every Saturday night at 5:45 p.m. focusing on Steps One, Two, and Three. Mary announces that after the Friday night meeting, there is bingo.

"Okay, if there are no further announcements, we have a great way of closing here at New Beginnings," Mike says. "We stand and form a circle around the table and clasp hands." Mike continues, "Janice, will you take us out?"

"Sure," she replies. "Who keeps us sober?"

"Our Father, who art in Heaven, hallowed be thy name. Thy kingdom come, thy will be done, on Earth as it is in Heaven ... " The group speaks in unison, holding on to one another, each one asking for guidance and strength from God, or whatever Higher Power or concept of God they might have.

When we finish the prayer, people begin to filter out of the room. Michael and Tony are talking to Angelo, making sure he feels comfortable and that he has a sponsor, with a phone number to call if he needs to reach out. Angelo is smiling. Michael hands him a copy of the Big Book, just as Dave did to me at my first meeting. Janice is talking to Barbara and Steve. I begin to pick up the copies of the big book left on the table. We just had the last meeting of the day. I stack the books and place them in the closet with all the other AA literature.

As I pick up a few styrofoam coffee cups on the table and put them in the garbage, Wayne comes over to me and says, "One hell of a meeting."

"Yes, it was. You doing okay?" I ask. Wayne just came back into the rooms after a five-year relapse. A couple of nights ago he shared that he just stopped working the program. He thought he was strong enough to handle things on his own without the steps and without the help and support of a bunch of drunks, but he was wrong.

Wayne is a welder. He tells me that he got his job back and has an apartment just around the corner, so he can walk to meetings. His kids are older, grown up, and he has started talking to them again. Wayne is working the program again, for without it, his life became unmanageable. "Alcohol wasn't really the problem. It was my character defects. I never got a handle on those. I thought I could go it alone. Well, I'm back," and he smiles.

I place my hand on his shoulder. "So wonderful to have you back," I say.

Most of the people have drifted outside, some to their cars, others to the back porch to sit, smoke, and trade stories. Wayne says he has to get going, as he's meeting a friend for dinner and he walks out.

I am left in the room by myself. I linger, taking a paper towel and slowing wiping down the table. I empty the coffee pot and throw the grounds in the trash. I bag up the trash and turn out the light. Ken and some other old timers are playing cards at a table in the next room. I say my hellos and ask where the trash goes.

I walk outside with trash in one hand and my Big Book in the other. I throw the trash away. The stars are out. The breeze is light and cool. I can hear people on the back porch. I think about going back there, just to hold onto this peace and fellowship for a little longer, but I know I must learn how to take this peace with me into the world outside the rooms. I get in my car and I place my Big Book on the passenger seat and pray for the courage and strength to get out of my *own* way.

### Day 3

## Chapter Six

# I'm Not Judging Anybody But …

**MARIA SAYS** as I catch up to her, "That was crazy."

"Yes, it certainly was." I decide not to get into what is going through my mind, of how pissed off I am at myself for almost punching that starving boy in the face. However, I don't want to talk about myself, even in the context of offering an apology for my actions. I want to hide from myself.

We are on our way to a bar, and I know I will not drink. I don't need to or want to, as the mental obsession has been removed, but I still need to escape from my most devious and unforgiving problem—myself.

In 1997, my first wife told me she wanted me to have an alcohol assessment. So to appease her, I went to the main hospital in Portland, Oregon, where we were living together, yet separate, at the time. I don't remember the assessment, but I am sure I lied or convinced myself what I was saying to the drug and alcohol counselor was the truth.

I don't remember what the counselor told me, but I do remember when my wife came home that night, I was sitting on the couch drinking a beer. She stared at me in disbelief. "I don't have a problem," I said as she walked out of the room without saying a word. "That's what the doctor said."

*What the hell?* I thought to myself. She's the one with the problem—not me—an attitude problem. I settled in to watch a baseball game without a care in the world for just as long as that comfortable buzz would last. I had found my Higher Power.

Maria steps through the front door of the bar and I follow. The place is packed. The music is loud. The light is low. Hostesses are everywhere. Drinks are flowing. People are laughing. Maria seems like she knows where she is going, so I continue to follow.

*How can she know that when we're in a bar in Manila?* When she heads towards the staircase and ascends, I follow. People pass me on their way down. Drunk. Laughing. This bar is just like any other bar I have been in, except for all the hostesses, and no one has blonde hair.

The people are just like all people in the bars all over the world. I don't know why I am surprised, but somehow I thought being on the other side of the world in a foreign land that everything would be different, but it is not, because the people are not. Not these people at least, who are hanging out at a bar on a Wednesday night. Aren't all the people who get drunk at a bar on Wednesday night the same? Okay, this is a gross generalization, but I don't care, and it's true. From Portland, Maine, to Portland, Oregon, to an island in the South China Sea—all the same.

"Love Love. What's the matter?" Maria asks as she puts her arm around me at the top of the staircase.

"Nothing."

"Lover?" she says with a knowing smile.

"Okay, just a little bit of crazy town, but I'm fine." Crazy town is how I refer to my thinking when it's out of control, spinning from subject to subject, scenario to scenario. Maria and I take a seat at a high top table next to the bar.

A live band is playing on stage—three women and one man. The lead singer is Filipino. She is small, very attractive, and has a booming voice. Maria orders a beer and I order tonic water with lime.

When I was drinking, I loved going to bars. I loved the physical bar itself, and I usually sought out an establishment with a long wooden top with heavy bar stools. I enjoyed sitting across from the colorful bottles filled with various types of spirits all meant to do the same thing, suppress my character defects, numb my spiritual malady, interfere with my connection to my Higher Power, damage my liver, dry out my body, thin my wallet, and steal the hours I have on this earth. Yes, indeed, alcohol was my master, and I gladly gave my life, my time, my thoughts, my actions, my relationships, and anything else of value over to it. A reasonable trade, right?

The music is loud—too loud. I am certain I am the only one in this bar drinking tonic water and hoping that someone will turn the music down. I scan the room. People are leaning into one another, laughing, dancing, drinking, and eating. I am annoyed with the place, the people, the excess, and the waste. I know I shouldn't think this way, for some people drink normally. Just to have a good time. A few drinks to enhance the situation, not escape from it.

My sponsor reminds me to only focus on my part, and not on anyone else's. I can only control myself and keep my side of the street clean, but I love crossing that street with clipboard in hand, taking notes about all of the scraps of paper rolling about, nitpicking, meticulously detailing every candy wrapper, bottle top, cigarette butt, but not looking behind me at the avalanche of discarded material clogging my side of the street. My side of the street makes a New York City landfill look like a nature preserve.

After a while, Maria asks, "Want to play some pool?"

"Yes, please," I say, looking forward to distracting crazy town for a while. Maria and I have been playing pool together for almost thirty years. Back when we were young at Florida State University, all the bars had pool tables. Now all the bars are really just dance clubs, which happen to have a bar in them.

My favorite bar in Tallahassee was a place called the Warehouse. This place was more of a pool hall that happened to have a bar in it. Maria and I never dated in college and never dated until God graciously put us together after years of turmoil. However, Maria and I often hung out, and that would sometimes mean we would end up at the Warehouse to shoot some pool after a long night of drinking.

Back then, I would play pool with a cigarette in my mouth. I took great pride in the fact I could steady myself for a combination shot with cigarette smoke drifting into my eyes and never blink. What a marvelous accomplishment. Such talent. Such determination. Over the years, I lost my interest in pool and concentrated solely on the drink in my hand—not wanting anything to come between me and the calming elixir.

Now all these years later, Maria and I play pool again. This time, I play with no drink in my hand and no cigarette in my mouth. Maria is an interesting pool player, actually two entirely separate players. With one shot, she will hammer the ball into the side pocket and with the next, she will completely miss the ball.

I look at Maria as she racks the balls. Maria Giglio and Billy Sansone are playing pool in a bar in Manila, Philippines on a mission to get someone out of jail? Are you serious? So much for planning out one's life.

Five years ago, I was living in a beautiful home in the most exclusive part of Tampa. I had a beach house in Sarasota, Florida. My son was four, my daughter, one. My wife was on her way to becoming a federal judge—the ultimate power couple. I was on the vestry of the church. I could see my church from my bedroom window, so we could walk as a family to pray on Sunday mornings. A Norman Rockwell painting come to life.

With pen in hand, I could have easily have scripted out where I would be in five years. I would be in essentially the same place, kids five years older, more money in the bank, more clients on the ledger, more suits in the closet, more awards to my name, more, more, MORE!

But here I am in a bar with Maria Giglio in Manila with no beach house, the same suits, gone from the church, in AA, no awards, a Norman Rockwell painting gone awry, but … happy, truly happy, or at least getting there on the road of life climbing the ladder to heaven—not the career one. I don't think even my creative writing background could have aided me in penning this pathway.

Maria is on fire tonight. She makes three shots in a row. She is solids, and the striped balls are all over the table. The volume coming from the band is much lower in the poolroom, so the old man is happy.

"Where are you guys from?"—the voice sounds familiar, but foreign in this context, a southern drawl, maybe from southern Alabama or rural Georgia.

I look up. The man who owns the voice has multiple tattoos on each arm, hair cropped short, and a bit of a belly, but is powerful looking. His shirt has an American Flag on the front and says something about heroes.

"Tampa," I say knowing that I do not need to add Florida, because he will know where Tampa is.

"Macon, Georgia," he says while he chalks his pool cue.

"What are you doing here?" Maria asks the obvious question that he will certainly ask us. Manila is not high on the bucket list of places to visit for any world traveler.

"My wife is Filipino. I was stationed at the Embassy for a couple of years and came to love the place, fell in love, married, retired, moved back home to Georgia, but now thinking of moving back here." I notice the woman with whom he is playing pool. She continues to play, but not introducing herself or even looking in our direction.

"How long did you live here?" Maria asks.

"Four years. I was a guard at the Embassy. At first, I didn't know what to make of Manila, but came to love the place, the people, and the food."

"Us, too," Maria adds. "We have only been here a couple days, and the city is growing on us by the day. Right when we got here, I couldn't handle the smell, the poverty, but … "

"There's something about Manila, isn't there?" he adds.

"Yes," Maria agrees. The woman is still playing by herself. She is randomly hitting the balls, not even using the cue ball.

"We live in Georgia, but I am about to retire from the military, and we think we are going to move here. Her family lives in a town about two hours south of here. She doesn't like Manila all that much, so I decided to come for the week by myself, and she stayed back with the family."

Okay, so who is the girl playing pool—a girlfriend, friend, date, hostess? The man keeps talking to Maria, but I tune him out. I can hear Maria saying something about Ron and getting him out of jail, but I am focused on the woman.

She has stopped playing pool. She sits on a chair on the far side of the room. Why does she not come up to us? It is as if Mr. Georgia has told her to be seen, not heard, and maybe, not even seen. She picks at her fingernails, perhaps deciding if she needs a manicure. She is dressed like a hostess, but who am I? Half of the undergraduates at Florida State University go out on Friday night dressed like hostesses.

I don't try and hide my stare, which is easy, because she does not look over at me. I pay close attention to the ring finger on her left hand. Maybe she is the wife and Mr. Georgia is just controlling, or she is shy, but Mr. Georgia said he came to Manila without her, so …

"I used to come to this bar a lot when I worked at the Embassy. Love the music and the pool. Place is always packed with hookers," he says motioning with his head back to the main part of the bar. "We are just playing pool." He motions to the hostess on the stool picking at her fingers. "I like her because she is older, so I can talk to her a bit. A lot of the hookers here are just so young. Can't talk to them about anything."

He says this as if we will understand and nod our heads in agreement. However, I don't understand or nod my head, for when I am on a family vacation with my wife to see her family, I do not go to another city for the week and play pool with a hooker. I have many character defects and spiritual maladies, but hanging out with hookers on family vacations is not one of them.

Mr. Georgia drones on, and Maria listens—or I assume she does. The girl is still fixated on her ring finger. I want to leave. The bar, the booze, the noise, the hostesses, and Mr. Georgia are not a healthy combination for me. I put up my pool stick and sit in a chair on the other side of the pool table. I look at my fingernails and smile, because now the older hostess and I are relegated to the same role in a sense, picking our fingernails and waiting for something else to happen.

"Hey, Love Love, you ready?" Maria grabs my hand knowing that the answer is yes. Mr. Georgia wishes us good luck on getting our client out of jail, and we leave him to finish his family vacation without interruption.

We spill out onto the streets. Only three days have passed, but the streets of Manila are becoming very familiar, and so is the heat, smell, filth, and poverty. We do not make it ten yards from the front door of the bar before the crushing poverty sets in.

A family is sleeping on a flattened cardboard box on the sidewalk. The child, maybe two years old, is snuggled in between his parents. The child has no blanket, pillow, or stuffed animal—let alone a bed, a bedroom, a toilet, or a shower. Will this child grow up to be a hostess? A mother on the street raising her child on a cardboard bed? A starving teenager on the streets getting yelled at by a rich American whose belly is as full as his is distended with malnutrition?

I walk by. I stare. The family is asleep. Does God visit them at night, in their dreams? What are their dreams? Who is their God? A loving God, one of compassion, mercy, and grace? Would I be trying to strengthen my relationship with my Higher Power if I slept on that cardboard bed? Would I know a God, and if I did, what would I think of Him as I lay on the sidewalks?

I have the luxury of spending time in a program designed to rid me of my character defects and help me build a relationship with my Higher Power, and I still bitch and moan that life is so hard, unfair, as I tuck myself in between my clean sheets after turning down the air conditioner to make my selfish and self-centered ass more comfortable as I continue to bitch and moan.

We walk by. The family does not move. They are used to people walking by. Everyone walks by. To them, I am no different than Mr. Georgia who is still playing pool with a hooker, as his wife is eating dinner with her parents in another city.

I am just another person walking by, not stopping to care, only long enough to get a good look to later tell my friends about how bad the poverty is in Manila. I offer no help, not even a prayer. I hold Maria's hand, but to this family she could be holding Mr. Georgia's hand, and it would not change a damn thing.

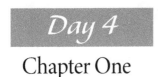

## Chapter One

# Live from Manila, It's Dead Air Sansone!

**MORNING COMES QUICKLY.** I rise from bed, trying not to disturb Maria. I look at my watch—6 a.m., so it's 5 p.m., Wednesday evening in Tampa. I sit at the desk, download my emails, and begin to scroll through them. The usual suspects appear.

The ones I answer first are the new client referrals from Dominic. When people are arrested for a crime and reach out to a lawyer, they don't wait a whole lot of time before moving on to another lawyer, if you take too long to answer. They are in crisis and need to talk to someone immediately about the case.

I send a few quick emails saying that I am in Manila for business and can speak with them when I get back next week. If that is too long, I can speak with them later tonight and move on to my current clients. Most are replying to emails I sent asking them to review documents from the State Attorney's Office about a piece of evidence in their case or they are sending back paperwork that needed a signature. Some clients are just asking what it going on with their case.

I send responses to them all before I check my text messages. This is the preferred method of communication with almost all my clients. I respond quickly to each inquiry:

- I'm in Manila. I will check the file when I get back in town next week.

- I spoke with the prosecutor and she is thinking about amending your charge to a reckless driving.
- The detective has not called me back. I will ping him again today.
- Sure you can come to the office for a meeting. I'll be back in town next week.
- No bond means your son does not have a bond on the charge, so you cannot bail him out of jail.
- I understand that you think the cop is lying, but I can't just say that to the prosecutor to get him to drop the case. We actually have to show he really is lying.
- "No file" means the State has chosen not to file charges against you.
- Your son has a twenty-year minimum mandatory on the charge. That means if he is convicted, he will be sentenced to at least twenty years in prison. I will call you next week to discuss in detail.
- Yes, I heard that Bobby is in jail again. His girlfriend called me last week. And, yes, I know she is pregnant.

I make some notes on my legal pad of the things I must do when I get back to the office and then I look at my watch. My clients will be eating dinner soon, so then hopefully, they will be going to bed and staying out of trouble.

Then the activity on my phone will calm down and let me focus on what I need to focus on—Ron. Today, we head to the jail, or detention camp, or wherever Ron has been for the last four months. It is Thursday. We leave Saturday morning. Time is running out.

I am trying to check in with God first thing in the morning, to set my mind straight and to remind me of the path I am on. Staying on that path is my number one priority, from which everything else hangs. The capstone, the keystone, the fulcrum. All apply.

I put my pen down, turn my phone over so as not to be distracted by any new messages and place my head in my hands. At forty-six years old, after ten years spent in religious schools and countless more in the pews of the Episcopal Church, I am just now learning how to pray. My prayers are no longer formalistic or ritualistic. They are simple, personal, conversational.

*Jesus, can you help me out today? I am sick of dwelling in my own mind. I want to do your will, but don't know where to look or how to find it. I try and open my eyes, my ears, my heart to you, but I don't know if I know how. I am lost within. Guide me. Guide me today. I am tired of how I interact with the world. I know I cannot change the world or others, but I can change how I react to the world and others. I need your help. My way sucks. My way leads to destruction and ruin for me and all of those around me. Guide me today. I don't want to have a way anymore—just your way. I pray. I beg. Please.*

I sit in silence, not wanting the day to begin. Maria is sleeping. Manila is not. Time is not. Maria brought her Bible and it rests on the edge of the desk. I should read something—get myself immersed in God's word.

I have read passages in the Bible many times over many years. I have read and heard God's word, but I have never listened. I have always sought out what God's word would do for me and how I might benefit. How does God's word help me? The Bible, however, is not a self-help book even though I have always treated it as such. *Becoming The Best Person You Can Be*, by God, forward by Jesus.

God calls for us to surrender our will to Him, and it is only through surrender, complete surrender, that we gain complete freedom. God calls us to be his servants. He is our employer. We work for him. The self is gone—smashed into tiny little pieces. The Bible is not a self-help book, but a self-smashing book. It is only by smashing and re-smashing the self-will, the Ego, that we gain clarity and freedom. For me, for this alcoholic, for this sick and suffering individual, smashing the Ego is not like smashing a light bulb, because if it was, the light bulb would be miraculously put back together in just hours, or even minutes after the smashing. I must smash, re-smash, and re-re-smash—a never-ending process.

Maria begins to stir. I look at the time. The poet Robert Frost comes to mind:

> *The woods are lovely, dark and deep,*
> *But I have promises to keep,*
> *And miles to go before I sleep,*
> *And miles to go before I sleep.*

"Hey, lover. You sleep okay?" I ask as Maria sits up.

"Like a banshee."

"And how do banshees sleep?"

"Like a rock."

"And how do rocks sleep?"

"Like banshees." I laugh and get into bed next to her. She is warm. I am not.

"Get your freezing hands off of me!" Maria cries as she shrinks from my touch.

"But, lover … "

"Don't, but lover me. Keep your love hands to yourself until they get warm." I pull Maria in and wrap her around me like a shield, a shield from the world. I don't want to move. I don't want to get dressed, brush my teeth, eat breakfast, step out into the streets of Manila, go to the jail, see Ron, go back to BI, or see Homer. I just want to lay with Maria in my arms and lay behind my shield. I am supposed to put on the armor of God before I step out into the world, but I am not sure how to do that yet, so I lay with Maria, keep her close to me, and wait.

I hold on and wait until she says, "Lover, we have to get going." She sits up. The armor is gone. I am alone.

Breakfast comes with our room and is served in the main restaurant of the hotel. I order coffee and Maria heads to the buffet. The buffet is the same every morning, but that is just fine, because the array of foods offered is so numerous and diverse: eggs, fruit, bacon, fish, lechon (pork), rice, potatoes, and vegetables. Breakfast, lunch, and dinner all served at the same time. I drink coffee and smile at Maria as she turns and looks back towards me.

"More coffee?" the waiter asks, not waiting for me to say yes. He knows I want more coffee. He has waited on us every morning, and I am not sure which he finds more fascinating—my blonde hair or the amount of coffee I drink. Maria sits down. She has an array of food, a bit of breakfast, a bit of lunch, a bit of dinner.

"You love this breakfast, don't you?" I ask.

"Yes," Maria smiles. Maria eats and I drink my coffee, trying to stall the start to the day, like a child pulling the covers over his head and telling his mother that he is sick and can't go to school. I don't want to go to school today, but I must, so I stand up, head to the buffet to get a little breakfast, a little lunch, a little dinner, and sit back down next to Maria.

"Today is a big day," she says.

"Yes, it is."

"I'm a little nervous."

"Why?"

"Ummm, because we are going to a prison in Manila. Not something a third grade teacher from Tampa, Florida, does every day," and she smiles.

"Not something a criminal defense attorney from Tampa, Florida, does every day either," I smile back.

We finish breakfast, and Maria orders a GRAB (the same company that runs Uber). Outside the hotel, the day seems the same as the day before, and the day before that, and the day before that. The air is wet and warm, filled with exhaust and stale urine. The roads are jammed with trucks, cars, Jeepneys, mopeds, and bikes.

I sit on the curb while Maria is on her phone. I no longer feel like a foreign man in a foreign land. Even though we have only been in Manila for four days, I feel a sense of comfort on these streets, a sense of belonging and of familiarity.

Perhaps it is because Maria and I are not tourists hitting the most visited sites, wondering where we should eat lunch and where to take a stroll or whether to take a nap or pose for pictures. Maria and I dress each morning in business attire. We have a business plan. We eat where we find ourselves near food. We don't stroll, but step with purpose from one government agency to the next. We don't visit sights, but we walk past them or through them, as we talk about Ron, Homer, Jodie, Tess, Joel, BI, and the BI. The Starbucks outside the BI in Intramuros is our post work hangout—a place not to take a seat and plan the next excursion, but to decompress from a long day at the office. I feel more at home in Manila, Philippines than I do in Miami, Florida, the city where I was born. The GRAB pulls up, so I open the door for Maria. She gets in and slides to the other side. I follow her and we are off.

Camp Bagong Diwa, Bicutan, Taguig City, where Ron is jailed, is south of Manila, so with the never-ending congestion on the roads, Maria and I settle into the back seat of our car. Maria pulls out her phone and takes some videos of the streets.

"I will never be able to describe this place. I must show it to people."

I sink into the seat. Maria is right. Today is a big day. In one sense, the errand seems simple enough. We need to pick up Ron's passport, talk to the warden about coordinating Ron's release, and plan his transportation to the airport. Then we need to book Ron a ticket to Guam, head back to Homer's office to hand him the passport, and print the ticket confirmation. Only then can we head to our Starbucks and sip on a cup of decaf. Simple.

However, the same trip can also be described another way. We are going to a Filipino jail, but I have no credentials to enter it and Maria has less than none. I have no legal authority to speak to Ron. Even if Ron has his passport on him, the guards might not allow me to take it or anything else, out of the prison. The warden might not be there, but if he is, he might refuse to speak to me. If he does speak to me, he might laugh when I talk about transporting Ron to the airport TOMORROW, as I might not be able to get a flight to Guam or Homer might be out of the office when we return—yes, a very simple plan.

I look at my watch. 9:04 a.m. Back in Tampa, a Christmas party is in full swing at my office. Dominic and I host a Christmas party every year for our clients, friends, judges, prosecutors, and other criminal defense attorneys. This year my brother, John, is catering the party. He owns a Spanish restaurant in downtown Tampa. Dominic's law firm and my law firm are located in a one-hundred-year-old historic house. We put a tent up over the parking lot. We have a band, a magician, a full bar, great food, and Mr. and Mrs. Clause will be there sitting for pictures. Dom is going to broadcast his radio show live from the front porch.

*THE ASK THE DOM SHOW* is a legal call-in show. I co-host it about once a month. We field questions from callers about their legal queries and problems. While we give serious advice, the show can take on a non-serious tone when we playfully engage with our caller and listeners.

Dom calls me, "Dead Air Sansone," a name that has stuck with the listeners. He came by the name naturally. When I first began to appear on the radio and either Dom or a caller would ask me a question, I would take a few moments to collect my thoughts before speaking.

As a trial lawyer, I have been trained to collect my thoughts before speaking, even a few seconds of pause can be just enough to make sure I am not only answering the question, but composed in doing so. On live radio, taking a few seconds for such composure is called "dead air." In the early years of my speaking on Dom's show, I would consistently compose myself and collect my thoughts before speaking. In those few seconds, Dom would laugh and say, "That ladies and gentlemen is what we in the radio business refer to as – Dead Air. And thus, "Dead Air Sansone" was naturally born.

9:04 a.m. Thursday in Manila is 8:04 p.m. Wednesday evening in Tampa. Dom is on the air. Before I left, Dom told me call in, so I could broadcast live from Manila. I dial the number.

"Ladies and gentleman, we have a special caller," I hear Dom say on the other line. "Dead Air Sansone is somewhere in Asia. Where the hell are you, Bill?"

"Manila."

"Dead Air Sansone is in Manila, wherever the hell that is, live on air right now. So Dead Air, how are you? And have you tasted fried dog yet?" I hear his panel of guests laugh. I hear music in the background.

"Fried dog, no. Fried cat, yes."

"Oh, I love it!" I can tell that Dom does. He is in his normal form, which is rare form for most people.

"Tell the listeners what you are doing in Manila."

"Well, my client was on probation in the United States. He left for his home in the Philippines, and his probation officer violated him for leaving the country even though the court had allowed him to leave. The court issued a federal warrant for his arrest by mistake. He was arrested and jailed in Manila. I had the warrant removed but had such trouble getting him out of jail, so Maria and I had to come all the way to Manila to secure his release."

"You see, ladies and gentleman, when you hire Dead Air Sansone, he will literally go to the ends of the earth to represent you. I don't even think Manila is on the earth, is it?" Dom's laugh is infectious, loud, and cackling.

"How is lovely Maria?"

"Lovely as ever."

"Where actually are you right now?"

"We are in a cab on the way to visit my client in jail."

"You are going to enter a jail in Manila? What if they don't let you out?"

"If you don't hear from me in twenty-four hours, book a flight to Manila." Dom laughs. Everyone laughs.

"Well, we miss you, buddy. The food is great. Your brother is doing a fantastic job. Your dad is here hitting on all the cocktail waitresses." Dom cackles again.

"No, he is holding court, telling all the young attorneys how to really practice law. Dead Air, we are going to have to go. The connection is not that great. We love you. We love Maria. Be safe and bring home some fried dog for me, would ya?" Laughter erupts.

"See you, Dom."

"Take care, Bill. Dead Air Sansone, live from Manila, wherever the hell that is, signing off." The line goes silent. I smile at Maria who is holding my hand.

## Chapter Two

# Camp Bagong Diwa, Bicutan, Taguig City

OUR GRAB DRIVER PULLS UP to the gate of Camp Bagong. The gate to the camp is impressive, a massive stone archway with a large metal gate that pulls back if the armed guard at the front allows a car to enter.

The armed guard comes up to the car, and the driver points to me in the back seat. I have no idea if this guard will let me in. I hand him my passport and my Florida Bar card, which to me seems a bit silly. I fully expect him to laugh or look confused and then tell me to get the hell out of there.

I tell him I am here to see my client, and an attorney at the Bureau of Immigration told me to come over to retrieve some documents from him. The guard looks at my documents, and then at me. He hands them back and waves us through. That simple. That fast. He doesn't even look at Maria or question her presence.

The metal gate is pulled back and the GRAB driver pulls forward into the camp. Unbelievable. We are in. What in the hell are Maria Giglio and Billy Sansone doing at Camp Bagong Diwa, Bicutan in Taguig City, Philippines? Playing grown up? Playing international lawyer?

Camp Bagong is not really a camp at all—at least, not in the colloquial use of the word. It is a sprawling complex made up of multiple structures lining various winding roads. Ron is being held here in the Bureau of Immigration Protection Unit, but there is no information center and no street signs, so I tell the driver to pull over.

Maria and I get out and I hand the driver his fare, and he drives off, so we are on our own. I look around, but can see no signs or information center—not even a Welcome to Camp Bagong kiosk. Where do we go? I look to the left and I look to the right, but each way looks the same. The sun is pounding. Sweat is dripping.

I have been lost in many places in many cities in my life: Tampa, Miami, Atlanta, Chicago, New York, Portland, Seattle, San Francisco, Phoenix, Las Vegas, London, Oxford, Rome, Florence, Amsterdam, Heidelberg, Nuremburg, Prague, San Jose, and Honolulu, but being lost here, in this prison in Taguig City is a different kind of lost.

I am not looking for a restaurant or a hotel or a museum or the train station. I am looking for my client, a convicted felon mistakenly being held under order of the United States for deportation back to the United States to face charges of violating supervised release. I have no official documents, and neither does Maria.

If we somehow anger any of the guards or any prison officials or if we wander into a restricted area and are ourselves detained, no one would know where we are. We could not count on the officials at the United States Embassy to help secure our release, that's for damn sure! This prospect did not seem to faze Maria or even occur to her, for she just walks straight up to the first official looking person we see and begins asking questions—what questions I don't know, because I hang back.

She tells me, "He said we need to go up two streets, and then it's about a five-minute walk from over there on the right side."

Maria takes off in the direction the man in the uniform said to go, so I follow. It takes her asking two more people, on three different streets, but we finally arrive at the Bureau of Immigration Protection Unit building.

Even though it is early December, the air is hot, and we are both sweating. However, the hopes of finding any type of respite from the heat in the Bureau of Immigration Protection Unit is slightly above nil, or maybe not even that.

A guard station is out front, which consists of two guys sitting at a folding table. Above them are the rules for all visitors. The dress code prohibits the following: "Sexy short pants, mini skirts, backless shirts, revealing dress showing cleavage, or hanging shirts revealing navel."

There must be busloads of female visitors coming to visit this part of the camp, because all the restrictions are aimed at female attire. I suppose I can wear a wife beater, a thong, and flip-flops and walk right in. There are visitation hours for regular visits and conjugal visits. The only day and time for a conjugal visit is Sunday from 10 a.m. to 12 p.m.

PRAISE THE LORD! There are "No Children Allowed" for conjugal visitations. I am not quite sure to what this is referring, and you would think that posting the prohibition of children at conjugal visitations would be unnecessary, but we are in Manila, not Miami.

We are briefly searched and taken through the gate that leads into the Bureau of Immigration section of the jail. The first thing I see is a group of men behind bars. We are outside, and they are also outside. It is as if we are at the zoo, and passing by the lion cages, but these men are the ones on display

Do they live outside? In the heat? With the bugs? And rain? That can't be, but there they are. All the men have on very little clothing, for the air seems even hotter within these walls. The air is still, stagnant, and stifling. To the right is a door that leads into a small building, so Maria and I walk in.

"I am here to see my client Ron," I say to a small man sitting behind a desk.

"Sure. No problem. I will get him. He has been expecting you. You can have a seat over there and wait please." Even in the jail, the Filipino people are pleasant to be around.

About two months ago, Ron called me from this place. I was drinking decaf and reading a book in bed. He told me that he was bribing a guard $4,000 US dollars a month to live in a small room in the infirmary. He told me there was no way he would survive the conditions the other men had to live in, but now I understand. Ron is seventy years old and in bad health. His health was failing even before he was arrested and sent to this hell hole. Ron is amazingly resourceful, but now I understand the full extent of his resourcefulness after seeing where he has been living for the past four months. I would be curled up in the corner crying like a baby. Ron is in his private room with a computer, internet access, a cell phone, and his American lawyer, me, travelling from Tampa to Manila to arrange his release. Not bad under the horrid conditions and circumstances.

The door opens and the small man holds it as Ron comes in with his walker. He looks fairly good. He has a healthy weight. As I stand, Ron smiles.

"What the hell am I doing in a Filipino prison?" I say returning the smile.

"I have been asking myself that same question every day for the past four months." We laugh and embrace.

"Ron, I would like you to meet Maria."

"I have heard so many nice things about you," Ron says as they embrace.

"Me, too," Maria replies.

"It's nice to finally meet the brains of the operation," Ron adds.

"You're right about that," I laugh. The mood feels slightly festive—not at all what I expected. We are in a jail in the outskirts of Manila. Ron has mistakenly been here for over four months. Every effort I have made to secure his release before traveling to Manila has failed: calls, letters, emails, faxes—all ignored.

And here we are, Maria and Billy, Plant High Class of 1990, in Camp Bagong Diwa, Bicutan, Taguig City, Philippines. My program teaches me to live one day at a time—not to plan too far into the future. The God of my understanding teaches me the same thing, not to worry about tomorrow, because tomorrow will have enough trouble of its own.

Two years ago, I would never would have imagined in a thousand lifetimes that I would be standing in a Filipino prison with Maria Giglio trying to secure the release of my client, but here I am, and so is Maria, and so is Ron.

"Let me show you my digs, and we can talk." Ron's walker leads the way out the door across a small quad. Ron pauses outside the door that leads into his room. He points to a hole in the cement, which exposes a pipe.

"Remember Ralph?" Ron asks. On Thanksgiving Day, Ron texted me a picture of a large rat. His caption read "Thanksgiving Dinner – you have to get me out of here!"

"Yes, I remember Ralph."

"That's his home, just outside of mine. Sometimes he comes in for a visit—never as an invited guest though." Ron opens the door and in we go. The room is about ten feet by fifteen feet, not much bigger than any normal prison cell. This is Ron's world now. There are piles of paper stacked on a shelf, clothes, a computer, and small packets of food everywhere. His bed sheets have a floral pattern that my daughter would like.

"I paid three hundred US dollars for those sheets," Ron says as he notices me looking at them. "You can get anything in here, but it will cost you." Ron looks at Maria. "I am so glad you finally got here. I can no longer afford the rent."

We all laugh. The room has a small air conditioner up in the window above the door that makes a lot of racket and spits out only a small amount of air. As I take in the room, Ron begins to tell Maria how people bribe guards to escape from this place. The going rate is twenty thousand US dollars, or one million pesos.

A tiny bathroom is attached to this small room that has a sink, a toilet, and a spigot on the wall, so Ron can fill up a red plastic bucket and sponge bathe himself. He is only allotted one bucket of water a day, so he has to put in measured thought and planning prior to using even one drop.

The more I look at Ron, the more I see that he is not well. He is wearing plastic flip flops, and I see that his feet are a deep purple color and appear to be turning black. He has open sores on his ankles, and these are just the maladies that I can see pushing their way to the surface. What other maladies lie within? Underneath the skin? His heart? His blood? His mind?

I have been living Ron's horror from the outside, as an observer, and mostly a passive one at that. Ron spent over eighteen months in the Pinellas County jail, and now four months in this Manila shithole. If Maria and I had not come to Manila, Ron would die in this place. I am certain of that, and what would the United States government do?

If the US Embassy was advised of Ron's passing, which could be any day, would they offer an apology to Ron, to his family, to his friends, to me? I would not bet the bucket of water on the floor of Ron's filthy bathroom that the United States would do more than quietly remove Ron's body from this jail and quickly dispose of it after making a cursory effort to find the next of kin.

After a few more minutes in Ron's room, we head back outside. Ron wants to talk to the warden. Maria returns to the main entrance, and Ron and I seek out the warden to discuss Ron's impending departure. The air feels hotter, wetter, and more stagnant behind these walls. Men walk around scantily clothed, probably due to the heat, or maybe because they don't have anything more to put on.

## 5 DAYS IN MANILA

Ron is wearing an army green shirt and camouflage shorts. The sweat has collected under his arms, on his chest, and along his back. He lumbers forward with his walker in a place not designed for people with disabilities. Ron opens the door to the warden's office and speaks with someone on the inside. The warden is busy and will be with us shortly. We wait in the heat, humidity, and stench.

Construction is going on behind the warden's office. Ron tells me that members of the Korean mafia are housed in this facility and are building themselves a kitchen and larger living quarters. Apparently everything is available for enough money—even your own kitchen.

One of the Koreans is sitting on a bench with a nicely dressed young female. The first thing I notice about the woman is her feet. She is wearing gold-colored sandals. Her toenails are painted and her feet are clean. She cannot have been in this place long; because nothing can stay clean here. Ron tells me that she is a hooker and that the Koreans have women brought into them all the time.

I ask Ron if these Koreans have so much money and so much pull within the jail, why can't they bribe themselves out of jail. Ron tells me that they have been sentenced to death in Korea, so these mafia men are bribing the Filipino government to let them stay in this jail, sheltered from the death sentence that awaits them outside of these walls. So here in this jail, these mafia men make their home. They have all the food they want, large rooms, their own kitchen, and hookers—what else would a mafia man need?

We wait for the warden. Manila is about waiting—waiting for customs, waiting for a taxi or a Jeepney, waiting for traffic, waiting for officials at the United States Embassy, waiting for officials at the Bureau of Immigration, waiting for officials at the National Bureau of Investigation, and waiting for the warden. I sit on the bench next to the Korean mafia man and his hooker. They are not talking to each other, just sitting, quietly sitting. I wonder if this man just wants some company, not sex—just a female companion to help him adjust to his new life, his life within these walls. Perhaps he misses his wife, or mother, or daughter. Maybe he was unjustly sentenced to death.

Ron was unjustly charged, so maybe this man was, too, and now he is here, waiting, waiting for his kitchen to be built, waiting for his new life to begin or for it to end. The kitchen will not help things, not really, and this man knows that, but the concrete blocks are being laid. Wood is being cut. He knows that the kitchen is just like the girl sitting next to him, something to fill the void, the hole, the black hole that can never be satisfied. The black hole eats and eats and eats, as he dumps and dumps and dumps things in—alcohol, cigarettes, food, pills, women, and even a kitchen. Nothing is ever enough.

He smokes and sits. She smokes and sits. We are all waiting, waiting for something. The four of us sit and wait. It is hot, and we wait.

A man comes out and informs us that our wait is over, and we can see the warden now. I follow Ron as he slowly, painfully, makes his way towards the warden's office, leaning heavily on his walker. I pass the Korean mafia man. I nod. He nods. We are different men, yet the same. The void within us is the same—only how we chose to fill it differs.

The warden sits behind his desk, leans back, and clasps his hands behind his neck as he says, "What can I do for you?"

Ron takes the lead. "I am supposed to be released tomorrow. This is my lawyer from the United States, who came here and has secured my release."

"Good lawyer," the warden smiles. "You are a lucky man, Mr. Ron."

"When the papers for my release are signed, I will need transportation to the airport. Will you be able to provide that?"

"Of course, no problem."

"You can arrange that tomorrow?"

"Yes, no problem. If I receive the papers for your release, I will see that you arrive at the airport and are on your way tomorrow." There must be some catch, some trap that I am not seeing, a trap that the warden is setting. "Of course, no problem."

That's it? What about the months of wrangling through bureaucratic bullshit, the waiting for meetings with various government officials, the traveling from one government agency to the next, just to be told I was in the wrong place and needed to speak with someone else, the doors slammed in my face, the letters not responded to, the phone calls never returned? "Of course, no problem." I wish the warden would repeat that again, because I cannot believe my ears.

"Okay then, the Bureau of Immigration sends you the paperwork, and you will bring Ron to the airport?" I ask.

"Yes."

"Even if his flight is tomorrow?"

"Yes."

I look at Ron. Ron looks at me. We are not sure what to say or what to do. We are lawyers. We expect confrontation at every turn, argument in every conversation, but here we sit, both of us speechless for once. The warden has figured out a way to shut up two American lawyers with four simple words, "Of course, no problem."

Do I say thank you? I appreciate that? Anything else you need from me? Very nice to meet you? Wow, the weather is hot? Do you know that a Korean Mafia man and a hooker are sitting right outside of your door? I come up with something brilliant, a response worthy of the international criminal defense attorney that I am.

"Thanks. That's great news."

Ron and I head back to the main building to get Maria. We pass all the men behind the bars, sweating, thin, tired, sitting, standing, walking in circles. They are waiting, too—like I am waiting, like Ron is waiting, and like everyone is waiting.

What are they waiting for? Do they have something in mind, a goal, something to sustain them through these languid, endless, monotonous days behind these walls and bars? Do they have a Higher Power, something, anything, greater than themselves that they can turn to when one day rolls into the next, and then to another, as they wake to find that it was not a nightmare, but real, and they are here in Camp Bagong? What sustains these men? What gets them up in the morning? Some of them look at me, smile, and nod as I pass. What did they do to get here, or not do, but are accused of? Is anyone helping them? Are there public defenders in the Philippines? Are they guaranteed representation? A voice?

As I look around and think about what it took to get to this point, I am reminded again that Ron would have died here had Maria and I not travelled nine thousand miles to make sure a letter was written, a clearance was done, and those papers handed to the right person. Will these men die here? If they do, will they die nameless? Faceless? Do they even exist?

If I had not yelled at the top of my lungs to United States personnel at the Embassy, Ron would not exist. I had to fight for his existence, wait for it, be patient, persistent, and now Ron does exist. He is right in front of me, dragging his legs behind his walker, the sweat spreading across the back of his shirt as he labors forward, and in twenty-four hours, God willing, he will no longer be an inmate in Camp Bagong.

# AS BILL SEES IT ...

... would have been the title of my autobiography, if I had never gotten sober, never worked the Twelve Steps, never came face to face with my character defects, never admitted those defects to myself and to another person, never strove on a daily basis to have a spiritual awakening, and never admitted my shortcomings to myself and to my God. But I have done these things, as painful as they were, and I continue to do these things in the face of that pain; for my character defects, my shortcomings, lurk just beneath the surface like an alligator cruising slowly in a murky lake waiting for the right moment to pounce. And pounce I still do, at people, at situations, but at least now I have Step 10, and I continue to take a personal inventory, and when I am wrong, I promptly admit it.

*As Bill Sees It* is the title of a book, and every recovering alcoholic or anyone working a Twelve Step program knows of it. The book is a collection of writings that the co-founder of Alcoholics Anonymous, Bill W., wrote throughout the years. I have the book on my nightstand, though there are periods when the cover becomes covered in dust. However, when that happens, unless I have been reading the Bible or the other book Bill W. wrote, *The Big Book of Alcoholics Anonymous*, my life starts to drift as I move from the middle of the boat to the edge and my life, my decisions, my emotions, my reactions begin to become unstable. I do so many things in life alcoholically, and by this, I mean excessively, whether it be losing myself in alcohol, work, exercise, or relationships. If I ever took up quilting instead of working my program, every home in south Tampa would have a new quilt before the fall air hits the city.

Before I got sober, I could have written a book called <u>As Bill Sees It</u>, because I had a vision, a grand vision, of how life was supposed to be, and how each person should play their part in the world according to Bill Sansone. So my grand vision of course revolved around me, my needs, my desires, my wants, my lusts. I would be at the top of the legal field, one of the finest criminal defense attorneys in the land, respected through the city and state. I would stand on top of the podium after the Florida Ironman, people marveling at my strength, speed, and agility.

I was on my way to fulfilling these selfish endeavors, too. Out of law school, I was a law clerk to two federal judges. I then made a lot of money working for a high-powered law firm. I then went to the State Attorney's office as a prosecutor to hone my trial skills and become versed in criminal law. Then onto my own law practice.

I had a house with a wraparound porch in the best neighborhood in town. I had a beach house on Lido Key, Florida. I had a successful wife in the legal profession: the power couple. Two great kids. Money in the bank. Cars in the driveway. Antiques in the house. Although I didn't have it all yet, I was still young, still accumulating material and worldly treasures. Maybe by the time I reached fifty years old, I would have it all—all that I ever wanted, needed, yearned or lusted for.

That's how this Bill saw life. And then it happened. My second wife threw me out of the house, and I landed back at my parents' house, in my sister's old bedroom. I would lie awake at night wondering what happened. Why was I so viciously attacked, seemingly without provocation. I didn't understand. What did I do to deserve being thrown out? I didn't do anything. I was wronged. I am the victim. Does anybody hear me? I AM A VICTIM!

My sister's room had not changed at all since she left for college in 1992. Cabbage Patch Kids still lined the shelves above the dresser. They would stare at me at night, in judgment, eyes wide open, looking down upon me. If I spoke about my troubles, about how I had been wronged, wronged by my wife, my family, my clients, my kids, or my in-laws, the Cabbage Patch Kids didn't seem to listen or care. They would just sit there looking down at me as if to say, "You are so full of shit, Bill." And I was, and still am, but at least I know I am now, a slight shift in my perception that has made a seismic difference.

My whole conception of how this Bill sees it had been derailed. A bomb had gone off, blowing apart my master plan. The house would soon be gone and so would the beach house, the antiques, the neighborhood, the wife, the family unit, and the power couple. I would lie awake in my sister's bedroom late at night, tears running down my face, soaking the pillow beneath my head. I was alone—completely alone. I would lie there in my "I am such a victim" state and weep until sleep mercifully came.

As I was venting to Dave on the phone one night, unloading all my troubles to the only ear that would listen, he told me, "You need to start doing some work on your knees."

"What?" I replied through my tears, anger, and pride.

"You need to get down on your knees and pray. Pray for your wife that she be granted all the happiness in life that you wish for yourself."

"Are you kidding me?"

"No, brother. Forgiving and praying for others is the only path to true freedom. It is only by completely surrendering ourselves, humbling ourselves before others and our Higher Power that we gain strength—the only strength in life that really matters."

"You're serious?"

"I have bet my life on exactly what I just told you." And so began my new journey, a slow and painful one at the start. I had no idea what to do, so I decided just to listen to what someone else in the rooms did and do what that person said to do, without thinking why, or what the purpose was, or how this would actually work. I just did it. I just followed someone else's directions.

I had run my entire life on self-will, and I had ended up in my sister's bedroom being judged by a jury of Cabbage Patch Kids, and they found me guilty by unanimous decision. Guilty as charged. So I began to walk, ever so slowly, gently, and timidly down that new road. I was afraid that I would fall off at first, lose my way, but Dave told me to keep going one day at a time.

I had a decision to make. I could: 1) Get control of my life by giving up control and giving my will over to my Higher Power or 2) Drink myself and my life away. Insanely, this was not an easy decision for me, but one that the Cabbage Patch jury forced me to make. When confronted with the two choices, should I get spiritual help and live a free life or die an alcoholic death, only the alcoholic stops to actually ponder this question. Exactly how bad is an alcoholic death?

I now walk in the middle of the road. I try not to veer too far to the left or right, but stay in the middle. I have no grand vision for myself, and if I had, it would never have included Maria Giglio and a Manila jail. I take life as it comes and deal with it as it is. I do a lot of work on my knees. I have moved out of my sister's room, so I am no longer under the constant surveillance and judgment of the Cabbage Patch jury, but even if I was, I think they would approve.

I don't own anything anymore. I rent a small place for my kids and me. I love them, Maria, my work, and the fellowship of Alcoholics Anonymous. Life is still a struggle, and I try to remain free from myself on a daily basis, but I have a life now, one worth living. I try to live humbly and by the grace of God. I have no plans, no way, only God's plan and His way for me. I am nobody, yet one of God's precious children. I don't need to control the world and those around me anymore. I keep the people within my small circle close. I keep my head in the Word and my eyes on the road before me one day at a time, one step at a time. I sit in the middle of the boat and will not fall out, even when the waters rage around me. That's how this Bill sees it now.

## Chapter Three

# Two Suitcases, Two Cabs, and One Fight

MARIA IS STILL SITTING in the front building of the jail, doing what we have become experts in—waiting.

"We are all set," I say with a smile. Ron is next to me leaning heavily on his walker.

"What does that mean?" Maria asks. That is a good question, since we have not been *all set* since we stepped foot in Manila four days ago.

"The warden said he will transport Ron to the airport tomorrow, once he gets the release papers."

"So where does that leave us now—back to Homer to get the release papers?"

"Well, we have to go back to BI to give Homer Ron's passport, and then we will ask him what else needs to be done."

"And we will get this done today, and they will take him to the airport tomorrow?" Maria asks, highlighting the unlikely timeline.

"That's the plan," I respond with a smile that says, 'What the hell else are we going to do?'

"Sounds crazy, I know," Ron adds, "but what you and Bill have done to this point is nothing short of miraculous."

"Ron is right. Maria and I have secured the release of an American citizen from a jail in Manila by hounding all the government agencies, both Filipino and American, all across the city."

Ron says, "I have two bags that I would like for you to ship to a hotel in Thailand for me. I would do it myself, but" and he looks down at his walker. "I don't think that I can manage them."

Ron has decided to go to Thailand. He does not want to go back to the United States at this time and, under the circumstances, I would also be wary. So far he has spent eighteen months in the Pinellas County jail, and now four months in a Manila jail, because of the United States government. If he travels back to the United States, he will be placed back on supervised release and will have to comply with all of the requirements attached to his supervision.

Ron does not trust the United States government and thinks someone will violate him for something. Then he will be back in jail, and Maria and I will be battling again to gain his freedom. Ron cannot take that risk, not in his declining state of health. So he has decided to go to Bangkok, Thailand, via Guam, to rest, get his head screwed on straight after this four-month ordeal, and think about what to do next.

Ron also needs to be removed from the Filipino Blacklist. His banishment from the country is based on his "fugitive" status, even though he was never actually a fugitive. Another agency battle awaits—one we do not have time for now—so Ron will depart for Guam. Then, he will move on to Bangkok tomorrow night at 10:30 p.m., if Maria and I can get his passport to Homer, his transport arranged from the jail to the airport, and nothing else screws up—oh, and yeah, the bags—ship his enormous bags to a hotel in Thailand.

We head back across the brutally hot quad into Ron's ten foot by fifteen foot rented room. The men watch us as we pass. They watch Maria. Will they die here? Does anyone care? Loved ones? Lawyers? Citizen watch groups? Anyone at all? Here they sit or stand, waiting in the heat for time to pass, and it does, slowly, languidly, like the air moving through the jail with just enough speed that you know it is there, but not enough to provide any relief.

"Here they are," Ron says as we step into his suite at Chez Camp Bagong. I had not noticed the bags before because they were covered with clothes and papers.

"They are huge," I say.

"Now you see why I want you to ship them," Ron responds.

I literally feel the weight of another task being thrust upon us. So Maria and I are to get these two colossal suitcases to a shipping facility, and send them to Thailand, where Ron is going to stay until Maria and I figure out a way to get him off of the Blacklist, make it to BI and Homer's office in enough time to drop off Ron's passport and secure Ron's transport from the jail to the airport all before 5:30 p.m. today? I look at my watch—it's 12:43 p.m. Nothing happens quickly in Manila, but we will need it to now. I stand in silence. Ron feels my hesitation.

"I know it's a lot, but I don't have another choice. As you know, because of my fugitive status, I have been blacklisted from the country, so I have to leave it until we figure out a way to have me removed from that list. These are my only possessions," Ron motions to the suitcases. "I paid someone to go to my place in Angeles City and bring them here. They are all I have." His voice cracks. The months of living in subhuman standards have broken his body, his mind, his soul, and now his voice.

"Sure we can do this, right, *Della*?"

"Sure," but I can sense Maria's own hesitation. She knows the task, or multiple tasks ahead. "Well, let's get going." The bags are heavy, very heavy.

"What the hell do you have in here?" I say struggling to get one of the bags out the door.

"My whole life," Ron responds.

Maria and I wrestle the bags out of Ron's room into the main area of the jail. Did I mention that it is hot, brutally hot? Did I mention the humidity? That the air is wet? Did I mention the smell? The place stinks. Did I mention the bags? The weight of the bags? And, oh yeah, it's really hot.

Maria and Ron go over the flight details. She bought Ron a flight from Manila to Guam, and then Guam to Thailand. Ron writes down the flight numbers and airline on a notepad. How many third grade teachers from Tampa have ever stood in a Manila jail coordinating a release of a prisoner out of the country?

"Love, can you call us a GRAB?" I ask as I see Maria and Ron finish.

"Will they let a GRAB come into the prison?"

"Good question, *Della*."

"Visitors come and go in GRABs all the time. The guards will let them in." Ron is lunging forward in front of us. I nod to Maria.

"Well, let's get these bags out front, and I'll call a car," Maria says. The men in the quad watch Maria and me struggle with the bags. Guards pass by and say nothing.

Do they know what is in the bags? We don't. The thought occurs to me that I have no idea what is in these two oversized suitcases either. They are heavy enough to be filled with bricks, but could contain anything: body parts, drugs, guns, money, books, photographs, high school yearbooks, baseball gloves, hockey pucks, swimming trophies, magazines commemorating the death of Princess Diana.

However, whatever is in these massive suitcases, Maria and I are taking them out of this Manila jail and sending them to a hotel in Bangkok. The guards do not seem to care. They are not worried. Should I care? Should I be worried? I can picture the following exchange before some official at the United States Embassy, as I sit before that official in handcuffs:

"Mr. Sansone, are you saying that you were not aware of the contents of the two suitcases."

"That is correct."

"You never looked inside?"

"No, sir, I did not."

"You took two seventy-pound suitcases cases out of a Manila jail, the personal property of your client, a federally convicted felon, and sent those suitcases overseas, specifically to a hotel in Bangkok, Thailand, and you are telling me that you had absolutely no idea of the contents of those suitcases?"

"Yes, that's about right."

"You're a smart man, Mr. Sansone, a trained criminal defense lawyer. You want me to believe … " And it would all slide down the proverbial hill from there.

"Okay," I say as we stand outside the Bureau of Immigration section of the jail compound. I place my suitcase next to the one Maria is pulling. "You wait here for the car, and I will square things away with Ron."

"Got it," Maria says as she pulls out her phone and orders a car. I fall back to the conversation with the US official who is grilling me while I am detained for transporting the suitcases:

"So your girlfriend, a third grade teacher, just ordered a cab, had that cab come to the jail, the cab driver then put those suitcases into the trunk, and you just drove away from the jail, no questions asked?"

"That's correct, sir."

"Not one guard, not one prison official, asked you any questions?"

"No, sir, they did not."

"No money exchanged hands?"

"Only with the cab driver," I say. The government official smiles.

"I mean no money exchanged between you and a prison official," he clarifies.

"No, sir."

"So you are telling me, your girlfriend just ordered a cab, the cab came, you put the suitcases into the trunk, and you rode out of the jail and into the sunset?"

"It wasn't sunset, but yes."

"Don't play games with me, Mr. Sansone." As a criminal defense attorney, I have become painfully aware that sometimes the truth sounds more unrealistic than even the most wildly spun tall tale. Even though I would tell that US official the complete and honest truth, he would not believe me, and no reasonable jury would either.

Ron is sitting in the main waiting room at a table in the corner. He is sitting next to an American-looking man. The lines on this man's face are deep, carved with worry, time, stress, and sickness.

Ron says, "Bill, this is Mike." We shake hands. "Mike is from New Jersey. He has been here for four years and was recently diagnosed with stage four cancer." I look at Mike. His eyes are vacant, distant. He is broken, dying, and spending his remaining days here in this filthy jail just outside of Manila.

"Hi, Mike." My response strikes me as painfully superficial. What else can I say? "How ya' doin'?" That would go over like a lead zeppelin. I could ask why is he here? Who is looking to free him? Anyone? Is he jealous that Ron has an attorney who came from the United States to free him from this cesspool? Can I help? Will he miss Ron, his only American friend? Will Ron's absence be the thing that pushes him over the edge? Who will Mike sit at this table with when Ron is gone? Share cups of cold coffee and bad food?

Ron and Mike talk, but I don't hear what they say. I have retreated into my own world, my mind, my bubble. It is a place I go to often in times of stress and turbulence. My mind is both a place of refuge, a safe harbor in stormy times, and also a place fraught with immense danger, a land with mines strewn all about. These two places co-exist, not peacefully, but in conflict, in war, and these two battle lines continually clash. Sometimes the safe harbor takes control, and at other times, the land mines explode all about. The battle is real, constant, and vicious, and I am not the only one held emotionally hostage by the war within.

Ron and Mike talk, and I wish I could listen, so their conversation could be part of this book, but I can't. My mind has had enough. It is tired, and so is my body. I want to sit down in the chair next to Mike and put my head on the table. I have only been in this jail for two and a half hours, but I feel broken. Mike has been here for four years. I am thankful that God did not put Mike's ordeal upon *my* shoulders, for they are not broad enough to carry such an oppressive weight.

"Hey, Ron," I finally break in. "Maria is outside getting a cab. We will drop the bags off, then head to BI with your passport, give it to Homer, and make sure you will be transferred to the airport tomorrow." I pause. "That's about it."

Ron struggles to stand. Tears gather in the corners of his eyes. "Thanks for coming all this way, Bill. I don't even know what to say, if you can believe that." Ron and I embrace. We hold each other for only a few seconds, but within the brief moment of time, I feel as men must feel who are departing a war zone after having spent months next to each other on the battlefield—a bond created and forged by the fire of life. The feelings between us are as real as the tears in Ron's eyes. I place my hands on his shoulders and say goodbye, and with that I turn and leave.

And so the saga with Ron's suitcases begins, so where should I begin? I could start at the end of our battle with Ron's bags: "I don't even want to talk to you!"

Maria yells at me. "Good! I don't want to talk to you either!" I yell back at her.

But I think it better to move forward from the beginning. So Maria is standing in front the of the Bureau of Immigration section of the Manila jail with Ron's two suitcases waiting for a cab.

"No cab yet?" I say stating the painfully obvious, because Maria is standing alone next to the two hulking suitcases, in the extreme heat.

"Nope," and sweat is bleeding through the back of Maria's shirt. There is no shade, no refuge from the cruel and relentless sun. The bags are half the size of Maria and twice as heavy. We stand guard as we watch a platoon of soldiers march by in step with rifles slung over their shoulders. No one asks us any questions, and I look foreign, very foreign and out of place, yet prison officials and guards pass me as if I am supposed to be here. Blonde-headed, fair-skinned lawyers from Florida often come to this shithole to visit their American clients, right? Or maybe they think I am with a religious affiliation and these bags are filled with Bibles and Christian self-help books. I am just another missionary offering these broken men some hope of salvation.

Speaking of God, I almost drop to my knees to thank Him as the cab pulls up. Maria and I let the driver struggle with the bags, and we jump into the back seat, taking refuge in the AIRCON, as the Filipino people call air conditioning.

"Can you take us to the mall that is located somewhere near here?" Maria says.

"The mall?"

"Yes, the mall. Do you know where the mall is around here?"

"Yes, ma'am. I know. I will take you." Ron told Maria that there is a shipping company in a store located in the mall that can ship his bags to the hotel in Thailand. Maria and I sink into the backseat and enjoy our rescue from the relentless heat.

The mall is just that—a mall, which I hate and so does Maria. We wrestle the bags out of the trunk and walk into the worst of all imported ideas from first-world countries—a mall. This one is no different than all the others, with no individuality, no culture, and nothing unique. The sameness, the blandness, the lack of originality or culture are ubiquitous in Western malls, but this is where Maria and I are, as we pull Ron's enormous suitcases into the front entrance. The mall does have AIRCON, and I will give Western advancement credit where it is due—in this heat, AIRCON is a welcome reminder of my dependence on first-world convenience.

"Where in the hell ... "

"I have no idea," Maria responds before I finish. So we begin. We wander the floors looking for a directory. We pass Starbucks and the Gap and a bunch of other stores selling the same crap that is sold in Tampa, and from Portland, Maine, to Portland, Oregon. The clock is ticking. We need to get to BI, hand Ron's passport and flight itinerary to Homer, and still have enough time for Homer to arrange Ron's transportation to the airport and his flight to Guam tomorrow night.

"What are we doing messing around with these bags anyway?" I ask as annoyance has spread throughout my body, bubbling up through the skin and leaking out of my mouth in extremely venomous speech. "I mean, this is the dumbest idea that I have ever ... "

"Well, what do you want to do now ... leave Ron's bags out here in the middle of the mall? These are his only possessions. We are where we are, so let's get these bags shipped to Bangkok, so we can hurry back to the BI. Don't think beyond that."

Maria is right. Complaining only aggravates an already tense situation, but I am a master at complaining, a real artist. I have carefully and maliciously honed my craft over the past three decades, and find myself at times reluctant to let this skill set go. Maria finds the shipping company. I don't know how she did, for I regulated myself to simply following her lead, sulking as I sometimes do. The lines are long, so we sit in the AIRCON and watch the clock: tick, tock, tick, tock. We finally make it to the front. The man weighs each bag and tells me the price.

"Thirty-seven thousand pesos, please."

"Holy smoke, how much is that?" I take out my conversion chart. "That's almost $700 US dollars." The man on the other side of the counter smiles. I pull out my law firm credit card and slide it across the table.

"We are cash only, sir."

"Cash only?" I respond in disbelief. "I don't have Thirty-seven thousand pesos pesos on me. What kind of international shipping company only takes cash?" I look at Maria in disbelief. "I mean, what kind of business is this? Is there someone to whom I can talk." The man does not move.

"Sorry, sir. Cash only."

"It would be nice if you had a sign in the window. A sign that said something like, 'This is the only cash shipping company in the world.' I mean ... " Maria puts her hand on my shoulder. I can see in her face what she does not say. We are wasting time. The clock is ticking. Maria is right. She is not always right, but she is mostly right, and she is right now. We leave without me giving another snide remark. The man behind the counter was very nice. It is not his business. He is just trying to make a living, trying to stay off the streets in this third-world city.

"Cash only? Are you freaking kidding me?" We head outside. Rain begins to fall. Maria does not seem to be listening to me, understandably since I'm not really saying anything she doesn't already know and nothing she has not already thought to herself.

We wait in a cab line outside of the mall. We do not have umbrellas. Steam begins to rise from the pavement as the rain comes down. We are in a sauna, slowly cooking, standing outside a Manila mall, home to the world's only "cash only" international shipping company with Ron's two monstrous suitcases, filled with clothes, drugs, and body parts, for all we know.

I look at my watch—it's 3:17 p.m. We need to get to the BI no later than 4:30 p.m. to make sure we have enough time to see Homer and get Ron situated for his flight out the next day. The traffic is horrendous as it always is. Over two million people live in this city. It is a third-world country, so extremely poor. It has no subway system and no light rail. These millions of people get around the city in cars, buses, cabs, Jeepneys and, oh yes, mopeds and motorcycles.

I try not to look at my watch. There is nothing that I can do. I must accept the situation and move forward, but accepting the situation for what it is, accepting that I am *not* in control, accepting that I am *not* the director, and that every person around me is *not* an actor in my play is surprisingly hard for me. If everyone would just leave me alone, and do what I say then my life would be great.

But that does not happen, cannot happen, should not happen, and I am left to deal with growing pains. At forty-five years of age, I am having the most painful growing pains in my life, but it does mean that I am growing—right? I can only pray that it does.

I sit back in the seat. Maria tells the cab driver that he simply MUST get us to the BI, by 4:30 p.m. As Maria says that, our cab is driving three miles per hour next to a truck crammed with pigs. The pigs are so jammed into their cages in the back that they can't move. They are stuck in whatever position they were in when the man at the farm jammed them into the back of this truck.

I close my eyes. There is nothing I can do but wait. I hate those damn bags! We wind through the streets of Manila, much the same way lava slowly winds its way across landscape—slowly. I close my eyes. I am not in control.

The cab driver pulls into the front of the BI at 4:47 p.m. I let the cab driver wrestle the two monstrosities from the trunk. The wheels on the suitcase I am pulling are broken, so I drag the suitcase in through the front doors and up to the security desk. Maria handles the guards up front.

"May we leave these suitcases over here?" Maria asks as she points to the side of the security desk. "We just need to drop some information off to Mr. Homer."

"Yes, ma'am. You can leave them right there." We park the suitcases and walk to the elevators only to read a handwritten sign stuck to the front of one stating, BROKEN.

"Want to try the other one?" I ask.

"No way," Maria says as she heads to the stairs and begins to climb to Homer's office on the fourth floor. When we reach the floor, Maria does not wait for me, the hotshot international criminal defense attorney, to take the lead. She heads down the hallway to Homer's office.

Once outside his office window, Maria waives to Jodie, Homer's secretary. Jodie puts up her finger indicating that Homer is in his office and will be with us in a minute, so Maria and I resume our most common role during our five-day journey—we wait.

Just before 5 p.m., Jodi waives us in. Maria and I walk through the tight confines of Jodie's office and into Homer's. He is seated at his desk going through some papers.

"Hey, it's my two favorite Americans. So how are you?"

"Fine," I say as I hand over Ron's passport. "Here is his passport and flight itinerary." Homer takes the items from my hand.

"So he's going to Guam tomorrow night at 10:30 p.m." Silence ensues.

"Is there a problem with that?" Maria asks.

"No problem. No problem at all."

"So you will be able to arrange his transportation to the airport?" Maria adds.

"Sure. Sure. No problem."

"So that's it?" I ask incredulously.

"Yes, that's it." Homer laughs. "This must be an important client. Remember that your client has been placed on the country's Blacklist for being an undesirable based on his fugitive status, but we can work on having him removed from the Blacklist at another time." Homer smiles.

"So I guess you two will be back." Homer laughs. Maria and I laugh. I am still nervous, on edge. There must be something more, a catch, a detail that we have missed or have yet to be advised of.

"So that's it?" I ask with nervousness and hesitation.

Homer's smile grows broadly across his face. "Yes, that's it, unless you have another client in custody in Manila."

"Can we get a picture with you?" Maria asks.

"Of course. Jodie!" Homer yells. Jodie comes into Homer's office.

"Take a picture of us," Homer tells Jodie as Maria hands Jodie her phone. Maria and I step to the other side of Homer's desk. We huddle together, smile, and then CLICK. Jodie hands the phone back to Maria. Maria is talking, saying something to Jodie or Homer. They are smiling.

Is it done? Did we do it? Is Ron going to get out? I feel like a person who just finished a marathon but did not see the finish line. Is the race over? Did I finish? Can I stop smiling now? Maria is still talking to Homer and Jodie.

I hear her say, "So we wait in the line just to find out that they only accept cash. Isn't that crazy—an international shipping company that only accepts cash? So we have Ron's bags downstairs and we need to ship them to a hotel in Bangkok. Do you know of a shipping company that takes credit cards?"

"Yes, of course. There is one right around the corner," Homer says.

"Perfect," Maria replies. Jodie gets a piece of a paper and Homer begins to write the address and location for Maria. Yes, we still have to deal with those monstrosities sitting at the guard desk downstairs. There is always one more thing to do, one more detail to take care of, one more mile to go, one more step to take, one more, one more, one more … .

We say our goodbyes to Homer and head downstairs. The bags are where we left them, next to the guard desk. It was not the guards who protected the bags from being stolen while we were gone, but the bags themselves—the size, the weight, and the broken wheels, so the bags can only be dragged and not rolled. No one wants them.

Maria and I get the bags and drag them outside. It is hot. I am tired. Our mission is seemingly complete. I have been working on Ron's case for over two years. My work started in the Pinellas County jail in Clearwater, Florida. Now I am in Intramuros, Manila, dragging a figurative dresser down the street. I am done, mentally, physically, emotionally. H.A.LT. equals Hungry, Angry, Lonely, and Tired. When I am in H.A.L.T. mode, I need to be careful, as I am aware that my character defects are bubbling to the surface, metastasizing like a cancer growing within.

"I don't see a shipping place. Do you?" Maria does not turn when she speaks but keeps her focus on the buildings. She looks down at the piece of paper that Jodie handed her. If the marathon is finished, why am I am still running?

"Do you see the shipping place?"

"No," I say, but I have not been looking.

"What do you think we should do?"

"Go to the hotel and worry about it tomorrow."

"Okay. I'll grab a cab." Maria is done, too—also tired of running. Maria leaves the bag she has been dragging next to me and walks halfway into the street looking for a cab. A Jeepney won't work. Too many people, and I'm not sure I could lift the bags into the back, even if the Jeepney were empty. A motorcycle with a sidecar, my favorite mode of transportation in Manila will not work. So we must wait for a cab, and wait we do. Wait. Wait. Wait. The late afternoon sun is still blazing hot. I close my eyes. When I open them, Maria is talking to a cab driver—thank the Lord Almighty. We are almost home.

The cab speedily pulls away, as it races its engine. "What happened? I yell."

"He wanted too much money."

"How much was he asking for?"

"Four hundred pesos. The cabs from here to the hotel are usually three hundred pesos."

"One hundred pesos is only two dollars."

"Two dollars!" I feel my inside temperature match the outside temperature.

"Two dollars." I leave the bags on the side of the road and head into the street. "After a day like today, you leave us standing on the side of the road in this crazy heat for two dollars? I would pay twenty extra dollars to be in a cab right now on the way back to the hotel. Two dollars!"

Maria's face shows her shock at my rage, but I unleash it, unable to reign it in. "What's wrong with you?" she asks. "I'll get the cab if another one ever comes by. Get out of the street and stand with the bags."

People in the street hear me yell. A blonde American is yelling at this pretty lady in the streets of Manila, berating her in the middle of the street. No one does anything. They stare and walk by.

I have thrown my program out the window and left all my tools in the toolbox in the shed with a padlock on the door. I let rage and anger take over. What the hell was she thinking? TWO DOLLARS! I don't think about my part, only hers. She is the crazy one. She deserves to be yelled at. I didn't do a damn thing. If only Maria had … then everything would be all right.

If she would only have taken direction from me, the director of this play, then all would be right in the world. I know this is not true. I have learned this in the rooms, but I am not in the rooms now. I am on the street, a crushingly hot street in Intramuros, Manila, trying to hail a cab, which is not coming. I have slipped backwards, emotionally relapsed.

A cab finally comes. Maria and I struggle with the bags, and then the cab driver puts them into the trunk. I plop down on the front seat, while Maria sits in the back. The cab driver gets in and then we are off.

I turn to speak to Maria, "I can't believe that you would … "

"Don't talk to me," she spits out. "I don't want to even talk to you!" she yells.

"Yeah?"

"Yeah!"

"Well, good! I don't want to talk to you either."

My anger boils, but not at Maria ... at myself. *Where is your program, Bill?* I ask myself. *Two dollars? You yelled at the top of your lungs at the woman you adore, your closest and best friend over two dollars. STOP!! I tell myself.*

I don't want to hear myself say that it wasn't about the two dollars, but that it was about the fact that I am tired and we waited for so long to get a cab, in the heat, in the stickiness, and about my thirst and my hunger, and if she had only ... .

*That's all bullshit. I hear my sponsor's voice in my head. "I don't give a shit what she did, what was your part? What did you do? What did you say? Did you work the steps? Rely on your Higher Power? Or did you do things like you have always done them?*

*And how has that worked out for you? Did you let your Ego get in the way and try and control the situation yourself? Did you try and hold that poor girl emotionally hostage, as you have selfishly done with so many women in the past? Where are all those women? Gone Bill. All gone. Who would want to live with that? Live with you?"*

My sponsor's voice is clear. He is right. What gave me the right to yell at Maria? I was standing on the side of the road with my thumb up my ass, and she was taking control of the situation, and I didn't like how she was doing things, even though I was doing nothing.

*Then do it yourself you, idiot, you selfish idiot.* I sit in the front seat of the cab alone. Alone as I should be. Alone because I push away those around me, always have, but always pushing. I want to change, find a new path, but I seem to find myself trudging the same sad and dreary path that leads to the place I have been going to for thirty years, a place I never want to see again, but where I continually return.

My anger at Maria is gone. It never should have come. I am disappointed in myself, in who I am what I do, and how I act. I so quickly return to the space that I have desperately tried to rid from my life. I immediately forget my program, forget the steps, forget my Higher Power, and forget to PAUSE when life meets me on life's terms.

I am a spiritual infant masquerading as a wise man. I am a phony, a fake, a sick and suffering human being. At the next light, Maria should just jump out of the back seat and run, run as fast as she can with all her might and never to look back, never to return to the quicksand that is my life, for she might just get stuck, and it could take her years to get out.

The cab pulls up at the hotel. I sit in the passenger seat. I don't want to get out, for then I will have to face myself, and I am afraid of what I will see, because I know what I will see. I have seen it all before.

# CONTEMPT PRIOR TO INVESTIGATION

This also could have been the title of my autobiography before I entered the rooms of Alcoholics Anonymous. "Contempt Prior to Investigation: The Chaotic Life of a Selfish and Self-Centered Know It All," by William F. Sansone.

When I first came into the rooms of Alcoholics Anonymous, I heard someone use this phrase, but like most other things I heard in those first days, I didn't know what it meant or was still not listening. However, after having worked the steps, continually talking with my sponsor, going to meetings, and doing my best to connect with my Higher Power, I understand that this phrase defines my entire interaction with the world and all of the people in it for the past four decades.

"When someone talked about Alcoholics Anonymous, I thought to myself, that's just some crazy cult. They are brainwashing people."

Roger sat next to the water cooler as he always did during the 5:45 Monday night Big Book study. "You people were a bunch of freaks who couldn't think for yourselves. I didn't need anything from you or this place or some Big Book. A crazy cult." Roger is a retired air conditioning repairman by trade, but I quickly learned that when this man opened his mouth, something very close to the absolute truth was about to come out, and I had better shut down my brain for once and listen.

"You see, I knew it all, and I wasn't about to let anybody tell me what to do, and that's what this place was all about—right? Someone was going to tell me to stop drinking, tell me to do them damn steps, tell me to make amends, tell me to pray to a Higher Power, tell me to get rid of my Ego, and to get rid of myself.

If I got rid of myself, who would I be? If I got rid of all my resentments, I would simply disappear, because those resentments constituted everything that was me. So when I first came into these rooms, I didn't listen. Nothing was going to penetrate the thick filter I had over my ears. I only let in what I wanted to let in. I was all about me, but in this place, I was supposed to get rid of me.

I had you people pegged, all figured out, even before I met a single one of you. I had this program figured out before I even stepped through the door. Contempt prior to investigation. That is how I lived my life."

Roger spoke slowly, deliberately, "And I walked out of these rooms with myself and my Ego and stayed out for over nine years. In that time, I lost my wife, my house, and my health. When I came back into these rooms, I weighed ninety-two pounds. I didn't eat anymore. My stomach couldn't take it. My liver was shot. My life was in shambles.

So I came back in and sat in this same seat by the water cooler, and I shut my mouth and opened my mind. I didn't think about whether those steps hanging on the wall over there were horseshit or not, I just started doing them, doing the steps, and listening. After a while, I realized that I needed to be honest with myself, and that's when things started to change.

This place taught me that I didn't have to be in control anymore, control over everyone and everything. That's not my job, and when I realized that, my life got a whole lot simpler. I also realized that no one was telling me what to do, but only sharing their experience, strength, and hope. If I found something in that message great, but if not, that's okay too.

I realized that this place is not a cult, because if it was, it would be the worst cult ever. There are no dues, no leaders, no requirements for joining, and you can leave anytime, come back anytime, say anything you want, and express yourself in any way you want—some cult." A ripple of laughter flowed across the room.

"I realized that when I started working those steps and those principles, my life got better. I understood that I was wrong about a whole lot of things and that I had been lying for years—not just to my family, my boss, my friends, the electric company, the cable company, my landlord, the bartender, and anyone else who crossed my path, but I was also lying to myself. I was a liar and a thief. I didn't steal from stores, but I collected a paycheck for forty hours a week when I only put in twenty. I was stealing from my boss, so until I could get honest with myself, I was going to remain a miserable and lost person. By working those steps up there on the wall, I began to get my life back, my sanity back." Roger paused as if to let the weight of his words sink in on me, a newcomer, a boy, a mere child masquerading as a man.

"I know a bar right down the street that will refund all my misery, but I don't need that anymore. I was spiritually sick and, if left to my own devices, I was going to kill myself. But this program taught me that I don't have to be left to my own devices, but I can rely on you people. I can rely on my sponsor. I can rely on those steps and principles up there. I can rely on my Higher Power. I can rely on the instructions in the Big Book.

In these rooms, I found honesty, honesty within myself, and that's when my life really started to change. I had a lot of ideas about a lot of things, but most all of them were wrong. I know that now, and that knowledge has given me a freedom beyond anything I could have ever imagined. Thank you, that's all I got."

"Thanks, Roger," the room collectively said.

Jan sat at the end of the table next to Amanda. She said, "I like the way Roger put it, 'contempt prior to investigation.' I didn't know that's how I was living my life, but that's exactly what I was doing." Jan sipped from her coffee cup that bore her sobriety date on it.

"Before I came into these rooms, I lied to everyone about everything, but most importantly, I lied to myself. I even lied to myself about things I didn't know the first thing about. I came into these rooms about three years ago with a friend.

The first person who shared was talking about God and their Higher Power and giving up the self and doing God's will. Then I saw Step Three, 'Made a decision to turn our lives and will over to the care of God as we understood him.' I stopped listening right there. I knew exactly who you people were and what you people were all about, and I didn't want any part of it. I had been a part of the Catholic church for years and it didn't do a damn thing for me, and the last thing I am going to do is sit in a room with a bunch of alcoholics and profess a belief in God, and give my will over to that God. You people were pathetic. So I left that meeting and stayed out for three more years.

Those were the most miserable three years of my life. I came back into the rooms, because it was the last house on the block, the only place that I could go. I walked in, sat down, shut my mouth, and tried to open my mind." Jan took a sip of coffee. She looked at her hands as she spoke, as if looking up might distract her, break her concentration.

"Step One, I had no problem with. I was clearly powerless over alcohol and my life was completely unmanageable. Step Two, I did come to believe that a power greater than myself could restore me to sanity. And then there was Step Three, Made a decision to turn our lives and will over to the care of God as we understood him.

Could I make this decision? What would this look like? Who was God, even a God of my understanding? If I didn't understand anything, who was the God of my understanding? I decided that I would turn my life and will over to you, this group, for you people were sober and I was a drunk, and that's the best I could do.

So I sat in these rooms and listened, and as you all shared your experience, strength, and hope, I began to find the God of my understanding, for my God looked a lot like your God. The more days of sobriety I got under my belt, the more understanding and clarity I had. The understanding and clarity came slowly, though almost imperceptibly, but one day I shared what I was thinking in these rooms.

After the meeting, a woman came up to me and told me that she really liked what I shared. She was thinking and feeling the same thing herself, but just didn't know it. What I said helped her and made her understanding of God clearer." Jan paused. Her face reddened. She clasped her hands tightly together. "I actually helped somebody." Jan's voice broke. "I helped someone draw closer to God. Me? Really? That was the most beautiful moment of my life. I love each and every person in this room. Thanks for letting me share."

"Thanks, Jan."

Chapter Four

# I Came to Believe

WE HEAD UP TO THE ROOM in silence. We leave Ron's bags at the front desk to deal with later. I walk three steps behind Maria, but the distance of the South China Sea is between us. Maria opens the door to the room and heads straight to the shower. I sit down on the bed, alone with myself, the last person I want to be with.

Today should be a day of triumph, a celebration of a remarkable journey. Maria and I did it. We travelled from Tampa to Manila not knowing what to expect with one goal in mind—get Ron out of that Manila jail before he dies. We did that, the schoolteacher and the lawyer!

On the eve of our triumph, after a long week of successfully working with government officials from the United States and the Philippines, I sit on the bed—alone. Maria is in the shower—alone. We are in the same room, but apart.

We are not planning a celebration nor patting each other on the back. There are no calls to the United States telling others of our unbelievable journey and our ultimate success.

I do not feel like a success, but rather, a failure—a worthless and utter failure in the most important area of my life. I have been here so many times before, sitting on the edge of the bed alone. It does not matter whether I am in Manila, Tampa, Tallahassee, Portland, or Pittsburgh—alone is alone. It feels the same, because it is the same. I didn't have to travel nine thousand miles to come to the realization that wherever I go - there I am. However, I just did, and here I am again, alone on the edge of the bed, and it doesn't matter where the bed is. It is always in the same place.

Maria comes out of the bathroom with her hair tied up in a towel.

"What do you want to do tonight?" she asks.

I want to say, "I don't want to do this, feel like this, act like this, or be like this. I love you, need you, want you, can't live without you and want to be one with you—I am so sorry for how I acted. Please forgive me for I truly and sincerely apologize."

In the past, I have never said such things in the grips of my anger, because my mind was cluttered with self-justification for the way I acted. Now sitting on the edge of the bed, I hear my sponsor's voice, "If nothing changes, nothing changes." So I take a deep breath, and I think, here it goes:

"I don't want to do this, feel like this, act like this, or be like this. I love you, need you, want you, can't live without you, and want to be one with you. I am so sorry for how I acted—please forgive me, I truly and sincerely apologize."

"Baby, I don't want to be like this either." Maria sits down on the bed next to me and we hug. The South China Sea is gone—a thousand-mile distance vanishes in seconds. No need for more apologies, no need for further explanations, and no need to say why we said what we did, why we acted like we did, no justifications, and no expectations of the other person—just honesty, simple honesty, the most difficult and elusive trait for me to acquire.

Step Two states: "Came to believe that a Power greater than ourselves could restore us to sanity," and I believe this, and I must in order to move forward. My Higher Power helped me speak those words to Maria that erased the South China Sea. Left to my own will, I would still be adrift, listing in the middle of the raging sea, certain of only one thing—other people's culpability for my life being the way it is, and there I would list until I drowned.

"Let's get dressed, go out, and have fun tonight. We did it, baby. Ron is out." Maria is right. We hug again. If nothing changes, nothing changes. I smile. I stand up and notice that the room is filled with love.

Adriadico Street runs through Malate and is known for popular restaurants and bars. At the center is Remedios Circle, a literal circle surrounded with bars, shops, and restaurants where people drink coffee, practice night yoga, and relax as the city swirls around. The circle is paved in different colored bricks with a fountain at its center. We arrive at Remedios Circle and see huge lights, police blocking traffic, and people standing around as if waiting for something to begin. Maria and I stop in the crowd.

"What's going on?" Maria asks a diminutive man standing next to her.

"Steven Segal movie," he replies. Maria turns to me.

"They are filming a movie. How fitting, since we are actually living a movie." I laugh and hold Maria's hand. I feel peace. My burden is light. We watch as the director sets the scene, a truck and a motorcycle head towards each other shooting as they pass by. The scene is filmed, reset, and filmed again.

We watch the scene play out four times and then head into a restaurant on the circle. Maria orders a wine for her, and a water for me. We sit in silence again, but the silence holds a different texture, a true peace that passes my understanding. I feel as if I have been living under water and someone just brought me to the surface and said, "See, this is what it is like to breathe."

Wow, it is much easier to breathe when you are not underwater.

Maria orders hummus and vegetables. She suggests that we should eat an appetizer here, and then head to a Korean restaurant that she read about, which is just down the street.

"So this is Manila," I say. Maria laughs.

"I know. We have been so busy, most of the time, it felt just like another work day."

"Can you believe it?"

"No, I can't."

"Did you think we could … "

"No, I didn't."

"What do you think about what's happened this week?"

"I don't know. I will have to process it. So much. It seems like we have been here a month."

"Are you glad you came? I mean not much of a vacation. We have worked our asses off and sweated through it the entire time. Not many girlfriends would have done this. Manila is not a vacation destination."

"So I'm just your girlfriend? Don't like the sound of that." Maria smiles and looks into her drink.

"Okay, how about lover, agape lover, best friend, half of my heart, and the air I breathe? How is that?"

"Better. You're getting there." Maria and I talk. We laugh. The stress and weight of our mission is lifting, though it still lingers, tugging at me. For Ron is not free, and until he is on the plane, we have done nothing, accomplished nothing.

I do not let my mind wander to the What Ifs, which have been my security blanket since I used to sleep with a security blanket. Over the years, I have reached for them at all times, in all situations, good and bad. But instead of cloaking me in security, they wrapped around my neck until my vision is clouded and my thoughts are jumbled. I have spent half my life lying in bed playing out wild scenarios of events that never occur.

Example: the wife and I have a fight. I have been drinking. The fight is over some trivial resentment that has mushroomed into a dark and ominous cloud, because I failed to communicate, but rather internalized what I was thinking and feeling, so I walk away.

Okay, that is it, I think to myself. Fine, I will just have to live my own life within this marriage. That's fine, I will live my own life, and if that doesn't work, we will divorce. I suppose she will get the house and the kids. Kids are fine, resilient. I'll just get a little place, so I can be by myself.

I'm by myself already, and she, she never listens, always picking on me to do this, to do that. If she would just leave me alone for one second, I would have peace, but I will find that peace. I will find it alone. I can find it even if I live here, with her, in this marriage. I just need some space, need to be left alone. I need to soak. Gently soak in my gin.

I can find a moment of peace there, but then she comes storming in, and there goes my peace. I can live alone in this marriage. I already do. I can't live like this. I can't take all the nagging or the interference. I'll just do my part with the kids, and then do my own thing. I will be fine. Life will be good. Peace. I will finally have peace. Peace is all I am looking for, and I will find it, if everyone would just leave me alone.

Of course, I never found peace. Who finds peace with a mindset like that? I tried to find peace within myself. The problem was that I kept showing up to wherever I was going, and whether alone, with my kids, or anyone else, peace never came.

"Came to believe that a Power greater than ourselves could restore us to sanity" Step Two. I have come to believe this, or at least I have the willingness to believe this, for I was insane, still am, but I now recognize my insanity, doing the same thing over and over and over knowing the result will be an absolute disaster, but doing it anyway.

This is how I have lived my life and would have continued to live it until my final days, walking this earth alone, looking for peace, but never finding it, running my life on self-will. A life run on self-will is a life that leads to a collision with someone or something. The collision always occurs, and I stand at the edge of the wreckage wondering what happened. Only God can direct without the collision, but only if I let Him. I am in Manila, sitting across the table from my best friend and lover, and I have come to believe.

We drift out of the restaurant and back onto Remedios Circle. I say "drift," because that is what it is. I am drifting, floating just about the ground, on a higher plane than when I came in. I have found a peace, and I am blessed. I am not going to think about how long it might last, something I would have done in the past, quickly crushing the fragile peace. Instead I let it be, just for today, just for tonight, just for this walk from Remedios Circle to the Korean restaurant three blocks away.

## PAUSE

I want to hit the Pause button, to linger in this time. I am in Malate, Manila, with Maria Giglio, my best friend and lover. I have found my Higher Power in the rooms of Alcoholic Anonymous and am working on that relationship. It is one I never took the time to cultivate and nurture, but I was hoping it would somehow just materialize. I am sober. I am healthy. My mind is clear. Just for today. Just for tonight. Just for the next step. I came to believe …

Chapter One

# The Bags – Part Two

I WAKE TO THE MORNING LIGHT slowing creeping into the room. Maria is still asleep. I don't look at my phone. My watch reads 6:47 a.m. It is Friday morning, so it is 6:47 p.m. Thursday night in Tampa.

While I slept, my criminal life in Tampa churned away. Results from court hearings I had other attorneys cover while I am in Manila, calls from clients, bondsmen, prosecutors, judicial assistants, worried parents, drug rehab facilities, and emails from all of these people and more.

I don't want to look at my phone for I know where it will lead me, and I am not ready go there yet. I am peaceful, and my peace is so fragile and newly acquired that I must be careful with it, careful with me.

I have learned that being careful with myself is not selfish and self-centered, but vital to me being a vessel, an instrument for my Higher Power, but I am still a child on this road and have much to learn. I sit in the chair at the desk, with my calendar and legal pad next to my computer.

I want time to stop, for I am not ready for the day. I am not ready to deal with clients, court personnel, concerned loved ones, emails, phone calls, and Ron's bags, sitting at the front desk of the hotel.

Maybe I am still selfish and self-centered. Maybe I am still thinking of myself first, MY will, not HIS. I don't know. I am still a child on this journey, so I sit and try and quiet my mind, for my mind has always been my most destructive problem.

When I was a child and spending the night at a friend's house, I would get anxious when the sun would go down and bedtime would come. I would worry that I would lie awake all night, unable to sleep, and then would not be able to play when the sun came back up, for I would be too tired from my restless night.

Because I worried about this, my worry became a reality, and I spent many sleepless nights at friends' houses, suffering silently as the time slowly ticked away. My mind has been my problem long before I had my first drink of alcohol.

As Roger has said many times in the rooms, "I suffer from a hopeless state of mind, and my alcoholism is just a symptom of my disease." So I sit in silence and ask God to guide my thoughts, my actions, my life for the day. I don't want to be in charge anymore. I am too tired, and my leadership skills have proven to be wildly ineffective. I want God to take over, tell me what to do, for I am not self-sufficient.

If I have learned one thing in the program, it is that I am not self-sufficient. I need help. When I rely on myself by taking the director's chair, chaos quickly ensues, like a tornado coming across the plains. And, just like a tornado, I will indiscriminately destroy all relationships, all things in my path.

"Hey, lover, what ya thinking about?"

In days gone by, I would answer this question by saying, "Nothing," but if I answer that way, I will get the same response I used to get, but if nothing changes, nothing changes, so here it goes … :

"I was thinking about how I have been completely selfish and self-centered all my life, and how my destructive thinking has dominated my life for the past forty years."

"That's good," Maria says as she sits up in bed. "That means you are growing."

"Maybe I am," I respond. "I don't know. I don't even think about it or analyze it. Just be. Ask for God's help and guidance and just be."

We dress and head to breakfast and the choices are endless: eggs, bacon, toast, cereals, fruits, egg noodles, lechon, fried pork, chicken, soups, and salads. I don't pay too much attention to what is offered, for I get the same meal every morning—an egg white omelet and fruit. Maria takes full advantage and delights in the various entrees laid out before us, treating the meal more as an experience in which to participate, a garden of pleasures to walk through, a valley filled with treasures from above, so each and every one should be given due attention and consideration .

While Maria ponders the cornucopia laid out before her, I flip through the *Manila Bulletin*, the local paper. I am not really reading—just content to be looking at the captions and a few pictures while I sip my coffee.

It is Friday morning in Manila. We arrived late Sunday night. This strange, foreign, wild, unruly, crowded, dirty, smelly, beautiful, unique, and yet extraordinary place has put her arms around me, and I am comforted. I feel peace, contentment. There is no other place on the planet I want to be other than Malate, Manila, Philippines, in the midst of its gracious and kind people struggling each day to move forward, as they do with smiles on their faces and good will in their hearts. I am at peace.

As I let myself drift in these unknown and elusive waters, I glimpse what the Bible and the Big Book describe as a peace beyond understanding—a new freedom, a new happiness. The only things I want to be selfish for now are these: peace, freedom, happiness, understanding that if my Higher Power bestows these gifts upon me, they are gifts, freeing me to do His will not mine—that is the road I strive to stay on, the only path I want to take.

"Hey, love, you good?" Maria asks.

"Yes, I am," I reply putting down the paper and picking up my coffee.

Maria sits down and tells me about the various foods on her plate as I continue to drift. We eat slowly, drink slowly, and talk slowly, not wanting this moment, this breakfast, or this time to pass.

However, pass it does, as time is unforgiving. When the unforgiving minute betrays us, Maria breaks our slowness and my drifting and says, "So what do you want to do about those bags?"

Those bags—those heavy bags filled with rocks or body parts. Those bags brought Maria and me to tears outside of the BI yesterday. Those bags are what stand between us and true freedom and peace. Well, maybe I am overstating that a bit, but that is how it feels sitting at the table drinking coffee in Malate this Friday morning. I have come to know Manila, the people, the streets, the manner in which life flows, or doesn't flow, and I know that getting these bags shipped to Bangkok is going to take time, money, and patience, all of which I have just about run out.

"Throw them in Manila Bay?" I say as I smile and continue to sip my coffee.

"Funny, and I *do* wish, but this is our last detail and then we are done. Afterwards, we will have the whole day and night to relax and enjoy."

"But I'm a high powered international criminal defense attorney. I don't do luggage," I say as I try to hide my smile behind my coffee cup.

"You do luggage, laundry, omelets, and bathroom floors." Maria sits back in her chair and seems to completely relax for the first time all week. Until now, I had not noticed that this life and death journey seems to have taken a toll on her, too. However, at my core, I am still selfish and self-centered, my worst character defect and possibly the strongest and most prominent of them all.

"How are you doing, love?" I ask.

"Me—I'm good."

"Really, how are you?"

"Good, but tired. I want to get these bags off our hands, and then head to the Baclaran barangay, a barrio in Manila that is well-known for some first-class lechon."

"Go where for what? I knew you must have something planned for today."

"Of course I do. You think I'm coming all the way to Manila to run from one government agency to another? You would be crazy to think that." We laugh.

"Where and what is this that you wish to do?"

"I want to go to Baclaran, which is a district south of Malate. It is supposed to have an outdoor market and lots of lechon, which is a kind of fried pork. Don't even say it, because I know what you are thinking that I'm always doing something around food, and while that may be true, this is different. Going to Baclaran for roasted pig is an experience."

"And you are all about having experiences."

"You know it!"

"Well, Baclaran and lechon it is, after we dump the bags in the bay."

"Ha, ha," she smiles. "I do wish we could dump those freakin' bags in the bay."

We leave the restaurant and go to the registration desk. The man behind the front desk sees us coming and quickly ducks into the small room behind the desk. When he returns, he is in a full-on fight with one of Ron's bags, pulling, yanking, and yelling at it under his breath. He places the bag next to me, smiles, and returns to the small room for Round Two.

He wins round two—but barely. Just as he walked out of the room, the bag shifted and the weight of it nearly took him to the ground. He places the second bag next to the first and smiles with the satisfaction of a mission accomplished.

I don't want to tip him, for I feel like I should be the one receiving money, because now it's MY turn to take the bags off of his hands. While Maria stands out front waiting for a GRAB, I wrestle one bag out the front door and then the next.

"Where are we headed?" I ask.

"The Diamond Hotel," she replies. I look at Maria quizzically, and she continues. "It's a five-star hotel that should know how to ship a suitcase for a guest. I'm sure they do it all the time."

"Brilliant, *Della,* just brilliant!" And it is—brilliant that is. The car pulls up, and I let the driver earn his future tip by putting the bags into the trunk.

"Why are we taking the bags with us?" Maria asks. I pause. I have no idea, because I am not thinking—I am on autopilot. "Yes, let's first see if the hotel can ship the bags or knows where we can get them shipped before we drag them around Manila." *Good point, Della.* The cab driver takes the bags back out of the trunk, and we return them to the front desk to the horror of the front desk manager.

Maria tells the driver to head to the Diamond Hotel, and I sit back in the seat and take in the morning streets of Malate. The street vendors have already unpacked their stalls, and families tend to selling their wares.

When I was a child, my dad left for work in a suit. I would not see or hear from him all day until late at night. When he would return, we would eat dinner, and then go our separate ways before we went to bed to start the process all over again. My dad was and is a loving man—that was just the routine, what the situation called for—my dad did his thing during the day and I did mine.

These families operate under a completely different routine. They go to sleep together, huddled next to each other on the street or packed into a one-room apartment. They wake up together, prepare the family business for the day together, and then remain with each other all day, watching as the family fortune rises and falls, completely dependent on the whims of the people walking past their stall.

Do they stop there for a Coke and a bag of chips, cigarettes, or a water, or do they walk on to the next stall? These momentary decisions of the people walking to work define whether this family will survive and eat for the day or go hungry.

I sit in the back of a GRAB, air conditioner blasting, money in my pockets, and food in my stomach, with nothing to do but head to the Diamond Hotel to see about dropping off some bags and then on to Baclaran for some lechon. Somehow, this stressed me out when I woke up this morning. The car moves down the street, passing vendor after vendor, family after family. I sit in the conditioned air, passively watching out the window, my head resting on the cushion behind it.

The Diamond Hotel is located on the north side of Malate a few blocks south of the United States Embassy. Because of its central location, Maria and I have been passing the hotel all week on our way to meetings with various government officials and as we strolled through the warm nights on our way to dinner. This hotel would have no trouble locating itself on Fifth Avenue in New York, Michigan Avenue in Chicago, or nestled among the other hotels near Victoria Harbor in Kowloon, Hong Kong.

The elegant hotel rises high above Roxas Avenue overlooking Manila Bay. The GRAB driver pulls to the front of the hotel and up the drive leading to the front entrance. A group of armed guards surround the car. One has a bomb-sniffing dog, while the other has a mirror attached to a long pole that he places under the car, looking for explosives attached to the undercarriage.

Do they have a bomb problem at the Diamond Hotel? Maria and I step out of the car. A doorman greets us with a broad smile. We enter the lobby and go from one world to another. Inside we enter not just the first world, but the top, the most elegant and extravagant level of the first world. The lobby is carved in marble and granite. Three massive chandeliers hang from the ceiling, but those are overshadowed by the thirty-foot Christmas tree suspended from the ceiling, draped in crystal ornaments.

We are just feet away from the streets of Malate. The wealth. The poverty. Like a freshwater river flows into the sea, the line between these two is stark and prominent. Gone are the smells of the city, the exhaust, the urine, the wood burning underneath a soup simmering on the side of the road, and are replaced by lavender and lilac Christmas pine and potpourri.

"May I help you?" The man is wearing a Diamond Hotel sport coat, a tie, and matching trousers.

"I sure hope you can," I reply.

"We have two bags that need to be shipped to Bangkok. Do you know of any shipping company that would that?" Maria's question should raise a thirty-foot red flag, but the man does not hesitate.

"Are you a guest of the hotel?" I was waiting for that one.

"No, but we are frequent visitors to Manila and plan to stay at the Diamond Hotel in the future." *Quick thinking, Della.*

"Very good. So you need two bags shipped to Bangkok. I know of a company." He says the company name.

"Yes, we tried that one, but they only take cash. Do you know of a company that accepts credit cards?"

"Hmmm, I am not sure. That is the only company we deal with." And with that I am back in Manila, no longer in the first world, but squarely in the third. This luxury Five Star hotel only deals with a shipping company who deals exclusively in cash. That's crazy. That's insane. That's Manila.

"So, you don't know of any shipping company that will take a credit card?" Maria asks trying to hide her incredulity.

"No ma'am. The only one we use is a cash only business. But let me check with my supervisor—he might know." The man scampers off.

"Can you freakin' believe ... "

"Actually Maria, I would be shocked if it was any different."

"They don't accept credit cards? What do people do, carry around shoe boxes full of cash, in case they have to ship something. I mean—come on, people, get with the program. No wonder Manila is not a tourist destination." Maria looks around. "Who stays here anyway? "

"Businessmen."

"You must be right. No one staying at this hotel is shopping in Baclaran and eating lechon from a street vendor."

"Speaking of tasty reminder, I say we leave Ron's bags where they are and tell Ron to figure it out. I'm sure he can get Chito to find someone to ship his bags to Bangkok."

"Let me call Tia Darlene. The optical factory has a FedEx account. Maybe we can use that. I also think my mom has a FedEx account. Maybe we can just charge it to the account, and we get the bags shipped."

Maria has decided to finish the marathon. However, I have stopped on mile twenty-four, or maybe even mile twenty-five, and with the finish line in sight, I want to jump into a car, get a cool glass of water, and be done with it. I have hit the wall. I am physically unable to assist Ron anymore. Maria moves on, unable to stop until the race is over. I sit. I am done. Ron, it's up to Maria.

Maria informs me of the lack of progress. Her mom no longer has a FedEx account. Her aunt's optical factory's account will not work either. Maria informs me of the reason, but I do not hear it, my mind has shut down. We can get a man out of a Manila prison, but we can't get his bags shipped using a credit card.

This does not surprise me, nothing does anymore. I take Manila as it comes, and part of why we can't ship Ron's bags is the part of Manila that has drawn me close to her—the simplicity—cash only. Maybe that should be on a t-shirt they sell in the airport. "MANILA – CASH ONLY."

That would sum up the city, its people, its culture, its pace, its uniqueness, its stubbornness. Manila is not New York, nor does it try to be. But while that might provide someone like me, a first worlder, times of stress and periods of incredulity. The fact that Manila and its people remain true to who they are and operate as they always have is why Manila in all its beautiful craziness has burrowed its way into my heart and brought me a sense of peace and comfort I have never felt while traveling in another city.

Maria looks around, puts her hands on her hips and says, "Fuck it." And with those two words uttered by my sweet darling Maria, I know the race is over, the marathon complete, or at least for us. Our mission for Ron is over.

# SOMETIMES THE WALK BECOMES A CRAWL

I don't like to walk, let alone crawl. I don't jog—I run. I don't just swim—I swim around Key West. I don't go on a Sunday morning bike ride—I ride sixty miles and then run eight. I don't train for triathlons – it must be an Ironman. I don't get tired from working out, but I blow myself out.

The more extreme the better. I want to feel muscle failure. That happens usually into hour three of my workout. I am beyond tired. My muscles greedily grab oxygen and sugars from wherever they can find them. My heart rate stays at 145 beats per minute for hours.

I cease thinking about anyone and anything around me. My thighs begin to cramp. I start at 5:30 a.m. It is now 8:47a.m. Other people are out on their morning runs taking care of themselves and being healthy. I already swam one mile, biked thirty, and I'm on mile four of my run. It is Saturday morning and I am not in a race, but I look at my watch. I know exactly where I should be. I am running a 7:47 pace, which is not too bad after the swimming and biking. I want to get it down to a 7:30 pace, which will come if I push myself harder, always harder.

I participated in the Swim around Key West. My leg of the race was 4.1 miles long and the water was choppy. While waiting my turn on the boat that followed the first swimmer, I became seasick. My swim began at Mallory Square, where I jumped into the water and began to swim. About two minutes in, I rolled over on my back and puked my guts out into the water. Awesome! I thought to myself. This is going to be really difficult.

*To swim that far with nothing in my stomach,* I thought, *I am really going to have to punish myself,* and punish myself I did. I pushed through the pain, the cramps, and the dehydration. I became hyper-focused on each stroke, arm up, out, in, and pull. Roll from one side to the other. Watch the kicking. Keep it calm and steady. Too much energy expended if not controlled. Forearm cramps. Calf cramps. Foot arch cramps. Push. Push. Push. PUSH!!!

I like to check things off. Get things done. Before I leave work every day, I write a To Do list on a legal pad of all the things I have to do and want to accomplish the next day. As I go through the next day, I check them off one by one.

When I first came to the rooms, I saw the Twelve Steps written on a banner that hangs on the wall. Before the meeting started, I read them. I wondered how long it would take. If I push, I bet I can get through those steps faster than most. I had absolutely no concept of what the Twelve Steps were about. They are not a checklist, going from one to the next, until you reach number twelve and graduate from the program.

The steps are designed to uncover your character defects and the root of your spiritual malady. Alcohol is but a symptom of my disease. The real root of my problem is my thinking, my desire to run my life on self-will. Push, push, PUSH!!! Reading the steps up on the wall didn't teach me a damn thing. I had to get out of my own head.

A sick mind cannot heal a sick mind. I had to listen to others. Take others' experience, strength, and hope and apply it to my program. I had to get connected to my Higher Power, and I can't read my way to that connection. I can't think my way to that connection. I can't PUSH my way to that connection.

As I kept coming back to the rooms and working the steps, I began to realize that my life was unmanageable, because I was trying to live on self-will. I used God as an errand boy: God, please do this for me, please do that for me, please make this happen, and please help me get this or avoid that. I did not live for God's will, but my own, and if God blessed my plan then great! If not, then PUSH! I studied law at St. Edmund Hall in Oxford, England. I matched wits with some of the best legal minds on both sides of the pond, but my life, my inner life, was unmanageable. I needed another type of teacher, and God provided me many of them, if I could only stop, get out of my own way, and LISTEN! rather than PUSH!

Mike says, "I went to prison when I was twenty-seven years old." He sits at the far end of the table on the other side from me. "I killed someone in an accident while driving drunk." Mike wears a light-blue collared-shirt neatly tucked into tan pleated pants. He is balding and his remaining hair is white. He wears glasses and a gold ring on his left pinky. He speaks in a slow Southern drawl, maybe from southern Louisiana. If I had to guess, Mike is eighty years old now.

Before meetings, he sits on the back porch with the regulars and smokes a cigar. Sometimes he stays on the porch after the meeting begins and sits by himself, maybe to finish his cigar, or maybe to be alone with his thoughts and his Higher Power. Mike looks like a retired accountant—not a man who spent time in prison.

"I killed that boy, just sixteen years old, because I had been drinking bourbon all day. I don't even remember the stop sign that the police and witnesses say I ran. At my sentencing, the boy's mother couldn't even look in my direction. I wanted her to look at me, make eye contact, so maybe she could see how sorry I was, and still am all these years later.

"I lost everything when I went to prison, and rightfully so. I had a lot of time to think in prison, more time alone with my thoughts than a man should have. There was the guy from New York, a Yankee, who was always reading this darn book. At first I thought it was the Bible, but after a while I knew it wasn't. One Sunday afternoon I asked the fella, 'What are you reading?' and he said, 'The Big Book.'

"The book didn't look all that big to me. He handed it to me and I saw the cover: *Alcoholics Anonymous*. I asked him why it was taking him so long to finish the book he had been reading that book for damn near a full year. He said it wasn't a book you just finish and put away on the shelf. He said it was his Bible and like the Bible, God had a hand in writing it.

"Well, any book that God wrote surely would be a pretty darn good book, so I asked if I could borrow it someday. Four days later, that man walked up to me in the yard and handed me a copy, and said, 'I'll only give you this if you come to our meetings. We meet Monday, Wednesday, Friday, and Sunday at 12 p.m. in the library.'

"And that's how all this started for me. I learned about my disease in that prison. I learned about my character defects and my spiritual malady, while paying my debt to society, and to that young boy who I killed and his family who would never forgive me for taking their boy from them. I was not a fast learner, but I did learn.

"When I got out of prison, the first thing I did was find an AA meeting and continued my learning right here in these rooms. My life has not been easy since I left prison. Jobs were hard to come by. Other tragedies came knocking at my door. Sometimes my walk became a crawl, but I was determined to keep moving forward. I killed that young boy, and there's nothing I can do about that. For a long time I thought that night had ruined my life, but it didn't. It woke me up. I am a blessed man. I have made my peace with my God. I continue to walk along my path and even crawl along it when I have to. I am blessed to be in these rooms tonight and thankful for each one of you. Thank you for letting me share."

"Thanks, Mike."

No highly acclaimed Oxford professor can teach that lesson. For all those years, I ran and ran and ran, always looking at my watch, faster, faster, faster, but I wasn't going anywhere. Mike taught me that a man can crawl if that man is strong enough to drop to his knees, give himself up, and ask for help. God, please give me the strength to just crawl today.

### Day 5

## Chapter Two

# A Walk About

"SO NOW THAT WE ARE FREE from the bags, what do you really want to do?" Maria asks as we step out of the Diamond Hotel leaving behind the lavender and lilac, the Christmas pine and potpourri, to go from the first world to the third world in seconds.

"Let's just walk and enjoy the streets. Do nothing. No agenda." Walking the streets of Manila is quite different than walking the streets of New York or London. You can window shop in all three cities, but what you encounter in those windows is as divergent as oil and water or hot and cold.

Actually, you don't window shop in Manila at all, you sidewalk shop. Almost everything is being hawked by a vendor on the sidewalks of the city: clothes, hats, shoes, fruits, soups, seafood, cigarettes, magazines, and anything else one might need.

Maria and I walk slowly, holding hands, and it is not until this moment that I realize just how fast we have been moving, from the United States Embassy to the Bureau of Immigration to the National Bureau of Investigation to Camp Bagong, and back again. We have been running, sometimes in place, but running nonetheless, and now we are finished. There is nothing else we can do, for we have set the wheels in motion, and if any obstacles appear, they are beyond our control.

We begin to walk through a neighborhood and Maria takes out her phone and begins to film. "There is no way I can describe this place. I just have to take a video." She narrates as she walks, as we pass Jeepneys, an array of motorcycles with homemade sidecars, food stands, barber shops, starving animals, alleyways where women are washing clothes with water dripping from an open pipe, children without clothes, makeshift homes with cardboard walls, and smiles, always smiles.

I feel at peace on these streets and wonder what it would be like to live here with them, joining this neighborhood where neighbors help neighbors, live next to and on top of each other, with no personal space—a togetherness, a cohesion, a village within this city of two million people.

What would it be like to live here? What would *I* be like? How would these people change me? I see crucifixes hanging from doors and around the necks of women. These people have faith, true faith—not the Norman Rockwell faith of the family skirting off to church with kids in tow, while dad hides behind his Sunday paper—but true belief deep within.

These people have found it here amidst the crumbling sidewalks and uncollected garbage. The closest I have come to such a faith is within the rooms of Alcoholics Anonymous, also in a building that is desperately in need of repair. Is there any correlation between physical decay and inner growth? I smile at this thought.

Maria is still filming. I am not thinking One Day at a Time but rather one *step* at a time. I am at peace, that elusive and slippery state of being, and I'm afraid if I walk too fast, or speak too loudly, or stumble on a crack in the sidewalk, the peace will vanish as quickly as it came. I know that this is not the stable, lasting, inner peace, of which the Bible and the Big Book speak, but it is my peace, and it is within me right now. So I will take it and gently walk with her for as long as I am able.

"Amazing how these people live. I am really not okay with it," Maria says as she continues to film. "I don't know if I should be filming. Am I invading their privacy?" she asks as a young mother tells her daughter to wave at the camera.

"No, I think they're fine with it." We hear a little voice coming from above a barbershop. Maria and I look up. The tiny face of a precious young girl appears inside a tear in some cardboard that is functioning as the wall for her small home. She smiles at Maria. Maria waves. The girl waves back. The girl giggles. Maria laughs, and my peaceful state of being holds on for just a while longer.

We continue to wander, taking in the world as it comes. Four young schoolgirls approach us. We realize that they are not street kids, as they are wearing school uniforms. Maria stops to talk to them. They giggle as she talks. I watch from across the street. Maria gathers the girls together and takes a selfie. Maria asks each child a question, always putting the focus on others.

The girls wear colorful backpacks filled with items all school children have. I am sure Maria is talking to them about their classes, their teachers, their school, and their home life, for Maria has the gift of not focusing on herself.

She has learned to smash and re-smash the Ego. Maybe this comes easy for her? Maybe she has just trained herself or asked her God to guide her way, to be a conduit for His will. I stand on the sidewalk across the street as Maria says her goodbyes. She hugs each child as if saying goodbye to a family friend or a niece and nephew. They giggle, hug, and wave goodbye. Maria crosses the street and walks up to me.

"I just talked to the sweetest group of girls. They go to the Catholic school around the corner." We hold hands and continue our walk about. For the first time since we landed in Manila, we have no agenda, no To Do list to cross off, no agency to head to, no officials to talk to, no documents to get signed or drop off, and no lines to stand in.

We walk where the city takes us, and it takes us down a small alley lined with small residences, tiny third-world condos. Clothes hang from wires. Kids are running about. Most of the men are not wearing shirts—just shorts and flip-flops. Two ladies sit on a bench with large metal pots simmering on the table. Maria stops to talk to them. The three laugh.

Again, I am out of earshot. Maria is taking in all the world, which we busily passed during our mission to free Ron. Maria is stopping to smell the roses, and it does not matter if those roses are street vendors, Catholic schoolgirls, or old ladies sitting on a bench. To Maria they are all roses, each with their own distinctive fragrance offering the world a cacophony of unique smells and aromas.

Maria is beautiful in every way God intended a person to be beautiful. I hold my hands together and offer up a prayer in the only way I know how. At least for today, I feel as it is enough that God does hear my humble thanks. I walk over to Maria, slide my hand into hers, as she says her goodbyes to the ladies on the bench and we continue down the road.

# GOD DIDN'T SAVE ME FROM DROWNING TO KICK MY ASS ON THE BEACH

My mother passed away while I was writing this book. She died on a Monday, April 23 at 1:45 in the afternoon, and exactly four hours later I am sitting in the rooms praying for some experience, strength, and hope from the AA fellowship. The room looks the same as it did yesterday, before my mother died. I'm not sure why I thought it would look different, but it doesn't, so I sit next to Sarah. She puts her arm around me, and says, "I'm sorry to hear about your mother. How is she doing?"

"She passed away a few hours ago."

"Oh, honey, I'm so sorry." Sarah pulls me into her as my mother would when I was a child. "If there is anything I can do, you let me know." Sarah means this. She is not just saying it. I can see it in her face. Hear it in her voice.

AA is a people helping people program. We all suffer from the same disease. We all struggle with the wreckage of the past. We all have surrendered ourselves to the God of our understanding. We have a singleness of purpose—recovery—from alcohol, from our spiritual malady, and from a hopeless state of mind. There are no ulterior motives in the rooms. No one tries to look better than the next sick and suffering person sitting in the chair to the right or to the left.

Sarah is a grandmother, maybe sixty-five years old. She has short white hair, and a lovely Southern drawl. She keeps her arm around me holding me tight. I can tell she knows about loss, about tragedy, and about madness. I am comforted by Sarah—her arm holds me up, mentally, physically, spiritually, and emotionally. God put me by her side, right now, at this moment, after the passing of my mother. God put me in the arms of this woman.

If I ever thought of how I would grieve the death of my mother, it would not have been in the rooms of Alcoholic Anonymous, leaning into the arms of another sick and suffering individual, but here I am, and here I need to be.

Sarah keeps her arm around me. There is nothing unusual about someone putting their arm around another person in the rooms—it happens all the time. Everyone in these rooms has experienced tragedy, inward and outward, and the pain of living like that for so many years does not fade quickly into that good night. It lingers, sometimes just beneath the surface, waiting for a sign of weakness, a chink in the armor, distance from the Higher Power, and then the disease will come in and lie to us and tell us that a drink will relieve the pain, but it is a lie, and we must remain vigilant in our daily effort to remind ourselves of this fact.

The meeting begins. We start with a moment of silence. I ask God to take care of my mother. To make sure she is not scared as she enters through gate, but I know she is not scared. I picture Mom smiling, sitting next to Jesus, excited about her new role as His helper. She has a notepad in her hand, waiting to take instructions. Jesus laughs and puts his arm around her.

He has known my mom since June 26, 1940—her birthday. He has watched her along the way, carried her at times, and walked beside her at others. Jesus kept my mom company as she sat at her small desk in the living room of her home taking notes in the margins of her Bible. She prayed to Him when worry brought her to her knees. Though Jesus has known my mom and stood next to her with every breath she drew on earth, I still picture him laughing as Mom pulls out a pen and pad and sits next to him, not wanting to miss a word of what He has to say.

We follow the moment of silence with the serenity prayer. God, give me the serenity to accept the things I cannot change, the courage to change the things I can, and the wisdom to know the difference. I cannot change what happened at 1:45p.m. My mom died. That is a fact. I must accept it. I must accept it, because it happened, but how will I choose to deal with it?

This is an *As Bill Sees It* meeting. Bill W. is the co-founder of Alcoholics Anonymous. He wrote the Big Book, which was published in 1939 to set out a program of recovery from alcoholism. He did not sign his name to the book. He did not accept royalties from the book. The Big Book is designed to help people recover from a sick and suffering state of mind. Bill W. had the foresight to write a book and create an organization devoid of money, politics, and egos.

The Big Book has been translated into seventy languages. It has sold over thirty million copies. There are AA meetings in over 170 countries around the world, all with a singleness of purpose—to help another sick and suffering alcoholic. There are no dues to join. No one is turned away. There is only one requirement—the desire to stop drinking. Once you stop drinking, to live a way of life free from the spiritual malady that led to obsession over alcohol.

Alcohol is just a symptom of our disease. The real root of the problem is our thinking. Alcohol is not our problem. Being sober is our problem. I didn't know how to deal with life sober, so I drank. Now I don't drink, so I need to reach for something other than alcohol when life smacks me in the gut.

*As Bill Sees It* is a collection of Bill W.'s writings on many topics, and today we are going to read from the book and offer experience, strength, and hope to others. I sit back into my chair.

Jan is the first to share. She is crying. She "went out" last night. "Going out" means relapsing. "I'm so sick and fucking tired of myself," she says holding a tissue to her nose. Jan is thin, too thin and likely also suffers from an eating disorder (just another form of control meant to try and bury the spiritual maladies we all live with).

"I was on my way home, and for some reason, and I really don't know the reason, I pulled into the liquor store, bought a pint of vodka, drove back to my house, closed the shades, and proceeded to drink the whole damn thing. I don't even know why. I am just tired. Tired of having to smash my damn Ego every morning. Tired of having to make amends for all of the stupid shit I have done and continue to do. Tired of begging God to come into my life and remove the pain. I needed it all to go away I guess, even if just for a few minutes.

But it doesn't work anymore. Alcohol just doesn't work. You guys have ruined my drinking career." A couple people in the room chuckle, not because what she said is funny, but because what she said is dead honest truth. The fellowship of AA will ruin your drinking career, for after spending time in the rooms, you will never be able to comfortably enjoy a drink again—and that is a good thing.

She says, "I just sat there and drank and cried. So pathetic." Jan looks into her hands as if looking for them to help her in some way. "I don't know why I am having such a hard time with this. My life sucks when I drink, but I continue to drink. I think I am punishing myself for not being able to live a better life. A more spiritual life. A life without me as the focus. I just want peace."

Jan looks up and scans the room, taking in each one of us. "I've had the big job. I excelled at my job. I made a shit ton of money but was never happy. I was running and going nowhere. I don't care about any of that stuff anymore. I just want peace and serenity. I want to get up in the morning and not cry. Simple really. So simple, but the hardest thing I have ever tried to do. I'm not saying I'm suicidal. At least, I don't think I am. I don't even know what I am saying. I'm rambling."

Jan looks back down at her hands, which are folded in her lap. "I want what the tenth step promises to come true in my life. I want to do God's will for my life, but this can't be it. I can't find it. I'm rambling. I'm sorry. I will shut up now. I'm glad I'm here and I love you guys."

"Thanks Jan," the room says collectively.

Rick says to Jan, "Just a few minutes ago you made the best decision you will make all day. You walked back into these rooms. Just keep coming back. The miracle will happen. The promises will come true," and everyone in the rooms nods in agreement. Then the room goes silent. We can all identify with Jan. We are all Jan.

The topic for the meeting is Acceptance. If I am to do God's will in my life, I must find acceptance. Marie starts the reading. I don't listen. I think about Mom. She is gone. Can I accept that? I know I must, but can I? Can I accept that one day too, I will die? What is all the toil for? Ecclesiastes comes to mind—meaningless. All is meaningless. There is nothing new under the sun. Everything that is happening has happened before and will happen again. A mother dies. A son cries. It is happening right now, today, and will happen tomorrow, many times over, and a hundred years from now, and hundreds of years after that. I have wasted so many days like Jan has, drinking with the curtains shut. Even if I was drinking at a bar on the beach without a cloud in the sky, I was always drinking with the curtains shut.

"My name's Mark, I'm an alcoholic."

"Hey, Mark," the group replies.

"Last week I picked up my fifth DUI. I had twelve years sober, and I guess I just wanted to do it one more time."

The room is silent. "I'm ashamed. I'm embarrassed. My wife is destroyed. The memories of all those bad times, times I spent putting a good deal of distance between us, all came flooding back in. Twelve years of quality sobriety are gone. I didn't just drink that night. I have been drinking every night since. Today is my first day of sobriety."

Mark is in his mid-fifties. He is balding, wears Hawaiian shirts and flip flops, and speaks in almost a whisper. I look at him. The pain is etched in deep lines on his face. I have seen that face smile many times. Mark and I have become friends in the rooms. He is not smiling today. He is adrift in a familiar sea of despair. He is in the only room in the world where he can tell his story of relapse, of failure, and not be judged.

He says, "I don't know what to do with myself." His hands are folded in his lap. He stares into them. "Acceptance. Good topic for me today. How do I move forward if I can't accept myself? Who I am? I'm literally paralyzed with fear. After twelve years, I just picked up, and I don't even know why. I can't accept that, but it happened. My wife can't accept that. My kids can't accept that. My boss can't accept that. Maybe God can, but I'm not sure how that helps me right now. I need something tangible. I'm afraid for my life. I don't want to live right now. I don't want to die either. I want someone else to make that decision for me."

Mark stops talking. In the rooms, there is no cross talk. No one is going to say, "That's okay Mark. You are doing the right thing by being here. Remember all the good things you did in the past twelve years of sobriety. You will get there again." No one says that. No one says anything. I know why Mark came back to the rooms, because he knows that we, the other drunks in the room, accept him. That might not be much, but it's all he has right now. It's all many of us sitting around this table have right now. We can accept Mark, because we know Mark, we understand Mark, we are Mark.

Mark continues, "I don't know what it's going to look like this time. I just threw away a whole bunch of trust with my family that took me years to get back. Gone in an instant. How do I accept that? How do they? I know one thing for certain. There is no depth to my selfish and self-centeredness. I couldn't even look at myself in the mirror this morning. Literally. I brushed my teeth in the dark, disgusted at what I would see if I flipped that light switch on."

Mark looks into his lap for answers that are not there. "I also feel like I let all of you down." He looks up and slowly scans the room. "But then again, I know I haven't let you down. I relapsed. I screwed up. This is the only room in the world where I can come and feel loved right now. Feel understood. I love everyone in this room. I truly do. Best decision I made today was to come here and sit among you guys, and I will be here tomorrow, God willing. Thank you for letting me share that."

"Thanks, Mark," the room responds.

The meeting continues. Marie asks for a reader. Joel reads. My mind wanders again. I cannot stay focused. My mother passed away just a few hours ago, and I am sitting in an AA meeting. My mom never got to know about my relationship with AA. My decision to surrender and step into these rooms came too late in her life. She would love it here. She would be fascinated by the fellowship. My mom was a very devout woman and had a close relationship with God and Jesus. She would be fascinated by the A.A. fellowship. How people from every race, age, socioeconomic background all meet around this table, surrender themselves to a God of their understanding, work on their spiritual maladies, and support one another through the most difficult times in life. The fellowship offers experience, strength and hope to one another. That is it. My mom would have loved reading the Big Book with its focus on surrendering the Ego and one's life to the care of God as you understand him. She would like the metaphor that once a person comes into AA, the person works for a new employer—God. She would have recognized the struggle to cease fighting anyone and anything, including ourselves. She would have been able to find real acceptance, the topic of today's meeting. She accepted everything that came her way with God's grace and humility. I am in this room trying to learn how to do this.

"Are there any burning desires?" This means that the meeting is coming to a close and does anyone have something quick to share. The room is silent.

"Okay, we have a great way of closing." We all stand up, clasps hands, made a big circle, and Marie asks, "Bill, will you take us out?" I hold onto Sara's hand to my left and Paul's hand on my right. I take a deep breath.

"Who keeps us sober?" I ask.

"Our Father, who art in Heaven, hallowed by thy name ... " the room begins in unison.

We say the Lord's Prayer, the prayer Jesus taught his disciples to say from the Sermon on the Mount. We are one voice, one fellowship. I have said this prayer so many times in my life, but now, in the rooms, I let its meaning filter through me.

"Thy will be done, on earth as it is in Heaven … "

I want the prayer to last, the circle we have created to stay unbroken for just a little longer. I don't know if I can accept life on life's terms right now. I need the shelter of these rooms.

"And lead us not into temptation, but deliver us from evil … "

I hold on tight.

"For thine is the Kingdom, the power, and the glory, forever and ever. Amen."

The fellowship squeezes hands and chants. "Keep coming back, it works if you work it!"

The meeting is over. Sara puts her arms around me.

"I'm so sorry honey." I lean into her. Tears well up at the back of my eyes. I don't care if they come. Tears often come to those who enter these rooms. Tears are part of recovery. Part of feeling the full force of the present, dealing with the past, and letting go of all worry about tomorrow. Tomorrow will have enough trouble of its own. Jesus said that, and so did Bill W. The tears don't come.

Sara releases her hug. I am on my own. Acceptance. My mom is gone. What does acceptance look like, feel like? I linger in the rooms. Carlos puts his hand on my shoulder.

"What's up, bro?" He wears a t-shirt covered in paint and dirt. His forearms are powerful, veins lining them like highways on a map. He is excited about his sobriety. He has strung together eight months. Longest period since he was twelve years old. He sticks close to God. Checking in throughout the day. Asking for guidance, wisdom, and strength. Carlos has been in prison and looks like he had no trouble taking care of himself. He is powerful, yet in these rooms, in his shares to the group, he embraces and celebrates his weakness, and he thanks God for the gift of humility.

"Not so good today. My mom passed away a few hours ago." In the rooms, there are no bullshit responses. "How are you?" "Fine."

That's how I respond outside these rooms no matter what is going on in my life. "Fine." Is anyone on the planet actually "fine?"

"Oh, man." Carlos gives me a full body hug, not a half hug with just the arm around the shoulder. He takes me into his chest and holds me tight. This is not an uncommon occurrence in the rooms, people hugging people. It is actually the norm. Hugging happens all the time, before and after every meeting. We hug to celebrate. We hug to commiserate. We hug in understanding. We hug in acceptance. Men hug women. Women hug men. Women hug women. Men hug men. Carlos releases me.

"Anything I can do for you?" Carlos means it. I have only known him for a few months, but I know he would do anything for me. He lost his driver's license to multiple DUIs and drug charges. He rides his bike to the rooms. He wakes up at three in the morning and starts his long day in prayer, and if I asked him to bring me food, he would tell his boss he needed some time off from work. He would ride his bike to the grocery store, spend what little money he had, ride his bike to my place, and bring me dinner.

"You just did, brother," I respond. He smiles. The room is thinning out. I linger, not sure how I will feel when I step out into the world. The members of the fellowship are spilling out into the world, back into their lives, to face their troubles and triumphs. The setting sun hits my face with a gentle warmness. The sun has not changed. It will not change today. It will not change tomorrow. There is nothing new under the sun. People live. People die. The sun shines on.

## Day 5

## Chapter Three

# The Great Escape

MARIA NOTICES THEM FIRST. "See those ladies sitting on the ground in the park?"

I look over. "I do," I say.

She continues, "Most of them have babies in their laps. I love Manila, but there is so much sadness here. So much poverty."

About six or seven women, all young and all filthy, are all quietly sitting in a dirt patch in a park resting, or waiting, or praying, or sitting idly as the minutes pass into hours, then days, then weeks, months, and years. These women have nothing, materially speaking. I have learned that the riches in one's heart can never be judged from afar, but only after engaging, speaking to, and experiencing another person.

One young mother catches my eye. She is wearing a t-shirt and shorts. She is pretty, but her features lay hidden beneath worry and dirt. Her child, just an infant, sits in her lap. Our eyes meet. I smile. She smiles. I nod for her to come to me and she does.

As she walks towards me, I pull out a $500 peso note, about eight US dollars. She approaches, holding her child in her arms. What life does that child have ahead of her? Does she even have a chance? Will she go to school? Play sports? Laugh with friends? Learn to read? The child in her arms is as filthy as is her mother. I fold the bill and place it into the mother's outstretched hand. She was expecting my gift. Our hands lightly touch. She mouths, "Thank you." I smile. She turns, and so do I.

I see it on Maria's face, before she says the words.

"Oh no. We have to get out of here."

I turn and see the other mothers with their children in hand, walking very quickly towards me. I reach into my wallet and pull out five $500 pesos notes. A mother comes up to me, holding her child in one hand, placing her fingers in her mouth with the other, indicating she is hungry.

I place a bill in her hand. Then another mother excitedly comes up. I turn and see that Maria is quickly walking ahead of me. I place a bill in this young woman's hand and quicken my step. I feel a tug on my shirt. I turn, and a woman no older than eighteen is holding a precious child. My heart aches. I place a $500 bill in her hand.

*The Great Escape*

At that moment, I see dozens of women, all with kids in tow, running towards me. Where all these women came from, I have no idea. It is if the mothers who were sitting in the park sent out some inaudible beacon, a sophisticated sonar, alerting all others in the area to come quickly.

I turn towards Maria. I immediately realize the depth and breadth of my mistake.

"Billy, we must get out of here quickly." I rush towards Maria, and we begin to half jog up the sidewalk. When I look over my shoulder, dozens of women and a few men are running along the sidewalk towards us.

One lady is much faster than the rest. She reaches me. I know I shouldn't, but I have one $500 bill left, so I place it in her hand. Her shriek is loud and that sets off a full-on frenzy.

The neighborhood seems to empty onto the sidewalk. The woman's shriek signals everyone within earshot to come quickly, a crazy blonde-headed American man is passing out $500 bank notes.

Her shriek works. The entire neighborhood is now giving Maria and me chase. I am out of money. Maria stops at a street crossing. The traffic is horrendous. I see fear in Maria's eyes, and I know she sees fear in mine. Woman and men are yelling at us as they struggle to catch up. The women are holding their infants above their heads, as if trying to show me that they too have hungry children to feed.

Maria steps off the curb and into the traffic before the light changes for us. She has made the calculation that stepping out into the chaotic traffic is safer than waiting for these desperate people to catch up to us. I follow Maria into the street, concluding that her risk calculation is correct. We safely cross, but so do a couple of the women. One tugs at my shirt.

"Please," she pleads holding her baby in one hand, continuing to tug my shirt with the other. Her child is filthy, and underneath the layers of dirt and grime, I see that the child suffers from a skin disease. Red bumps and blotches discolor the child's face. I want to look more closely, but I continue to walk. I see that a number of women and men are beginning to make their way through the traffic and to our side of the street.

"I'm sorry, but I can't help everyone," I say as I pull her hand from my shirt.

"Please, sir." She grabs my shirt again. Her voice cracks. I have never been face-to-face with true desperation before, but I am sure this is what it looks, sounds, and feels like. This woman ran across eight lanes (of what cannot even be considered lanes) of traffic, putting herself and her child at risk in the hope and desperate prayer that this blonde man from America will also give her eight US dollars.

How many times have I paid more than eight dollars for a gin and tonic at some bar late at night, pulling cash out of my wallet without the slightest thought of the price—just wanting to pour more liquor into my already alcohol-soaked body? Countless times. All wasteful times. Completely unnecessary each time. And here this woman stands at my side. Is that pain in her eyes? I have never really seen the emotion so starkly. Books and movies cannot portray it. She tugs again.

"I can't." I pull her hand from my shirt.

But I can. If I really wanted to, I can. I know that, so I guess what I am saying to this woman is that I won't. Since all the cash is gone from my wallet, I won't help you, but I certainly can. Helping her would require much more than money, but time and effort, and I am unwilling to give those items to anyone. I keep them selfishly locked up for myself.

"Let's go to the hotel at the end of the block," I yell to Maria who is about ten yards ahead of me. I pick up my pace, leaving the woman behind. I look over my shoulder. I see a stream of street women crossing the street with children in their arms and young kids running by their sides. They are coming after me, the blonde American who is handing out money.

Maria reaches the front door of the hotel first. The bellman outside holds the door for her and she races in. I follow closely behind. The bellman quickly closes the door behind me, as if we have rehearsed this escape sequence before. A man behind the front desk comes around to greet us. He looks beyond me at the number of street women gathering at the front door.

"Come with me." He asks no questions—only offers a solution. He takes Maria and me into a room just off of the main lobby where guests can wait while their rooms are being readied for occupancy. "I will keep you informed. Just stay here for now."

Maria and I look at each other. How does he know what is going on? Has this happened before? Does he often have a beautiful brown-haired American woman run into the hotel followed by a blonde-headed man, who is being chased by half of the homeless mothers in Manila?

"So I guess this is the room where they put all the people running for lives. Nice." Maria laughs. So do I.

"That was crazy," Maria adds. "I mean, I don't know if you saw it, but after you handed that first lady the money, she turned around and waved it to her friends. One of the ladies jumped up. I thought she was throwing a towel over her shoulder, but it was her child. I have never seen anything like that."

"You haven't? Happens to me all the time on vacation."

"Ha, ha," she laughs. She looks around the room and then asks, "How much were you handing out?"

"$500, so about eight US dollars."

"You would have thought you were handing out thousand dollar bills. All that over eight dollars. That's so sad, so terribly sad." Maria's voice cracks as tears push to the back of her eyes, a few making their way around the sides and down her cheek.

Maria is right. This is not a frightening, or an exotic, or funny, or even an adventurous tale. It is a tale of sadness, gripping poverty, and the fight to stay alive. What just happened? These women put their lives and the lives of their children at risk by running into traffic after a stranger in the hope, the desperate hope, that this stranger might ease the pain, even just for one day.

I sit in the hotel. Maria and I will walk the streets later, stop into a bar for a drink, pick out a nice restaurant before our last night in Manila, fly home, being served food and drink all the way back to Tampa as we comfortably watch movies and read books.

Then we will rejoin our lives in South Tampa, taking the kids to soccer, hockey, gymnastics, dance classes, field trips, cub scouts, and movies. I will wake up some mornings grumpy, complaining about all the work I have to do, the hearings, the motions, the trials, but I do not have trials—not real trials, not the kind of trials that these women face on a daily, or even hourly, basis.

They face the ultimate trial—trying to raise children on the streets of Manila with no money, no education, no job, and no hope. Yet they press on, so I suppose there is some hope, some glimmer of a better day, a better tomorrow—always tomorrow, a day that never comes. A fleeting hope that vanishes like the blonde-headed American did behind the doors of a hotel.

"How long do we have to wait?" Maria asks.

"I have no idea."

"That was crazy. I mean crazy. I can't even believe what just happened. After you handed that first lady the money, she turned around and showed it to the others, and you were facing me so you didn't see, but it was unbelievable. All of these mothers began running. Running after you. It was like a scene out of a zombie movie, but even crazier than a movie. I am still in shock." Maria puts her hands to her face and takes some deep breaths. "How much were you giving out again?"

"$500 pesos. Eight US dollars."

"Unbelievable. Oh my God, the poverty here is so crushing. So sad. Those women risked their lives and the lives of their children. Did you see them run into the street after you? I mean run right into traffic with an infant in their arms. That is crazy desperate. I can't imagine. I have no idea."

Maria leans back into the chair. We sit in silence, letting what just happened wash over us, allowing it to slowly sink in. Those women are on a life and death mission every day of their lives, every minute of every day. My life and death mission lies within my mind. My mind is my only true danger in life—not my surroundings.

I am surrounded by loved ones and comfort, yet I continually try to sabotage myself, my life, and my relationships with my mind, creating an unnatural panic and unease where there is no reason. I desperately pray to my Higher Power to take control of my thinking, because my thinking is my greatest and only real problem. I am a danger to myself. The enemy within.

I can sit in my comfortable townhouse with a refrigerator filled with food, money in the bank, a car in the driveway, loved ones a call away, books on my shelf, the Bible on my desk, dozens of AA meetings within fifteen minutes of my house, and a fellowship of men and women ready to offer me experience, strength, and hope, and I can think all of these blessings.

In my mind, I am walking through the valley of the shadow of death, and I fear everything and everyone. These women live in that valley. It is not a creation of their mind. How do they survive one day to the next? Do they have a relationship with their Higher Power? Do they give thanks for all they have?

How can they? I couldn't. I am not that strong. I could sit at a table of riches in the Hall of Mirrors in the Palace of Versailles and still think I was lacking of something.

The man from behind the front desk opens the door and peers in. "We are trying to arrange for a car," he says.

"They are still outside the hotel?" I ask.

"Yes, sir. It is not safe now. You must wait here. We are arranging transportation for you to leave the hotel."

Did he just say that it is not safe? Arranging transportation for me to leave the hotel? I sit back in my chair and look at Maria. I see the shock on her face. I am so naive, so sheltered. I thought handing out eight dollars would be a nice gesture.

Now I sit hidden in a hotel, waiting for transportation to sneak me out, away from the crowd of desperate women, who are gravely pained by my gesture, rather than helped by it. I am not coming out to even tell them that I am not going to give them any money. The blonde American is going to stay hidden, out of sight, a phantom, a ghost, an illusion. There will be no five hundred dollar bills for them. They will be cruelly turned away, their hopes vanquished. They will return to the park. The blonde American will return to his hotel room. Their lives will not intersect again. I did not help. I hurt. I did not ease pain. I caused it.

"Okay, we have transportation for you." The man sticks only his head into the room. He motions for Maria and me to come with him. We follow. He opens up the back door and we see a man sitting on a motorcycle with a homemade sidecar. "Please, this way." The man motions for Maria and me to get into the sidecar.

"Thank you, so much," Maria says as she gives the man from the hotel a hug.

"Yes, you have been amazingly kind," I add. "I would give you a tip, but I am out of money." He laughs.

I never told the man from the hotel what was happening. He just knew. Why else would two Americans be running from a neighborhood of street women? This man could have turned us away, not wanting a gang of desperate homeless women pushing at the front doors of his hotel, but he didn't. He gave us shelter from the storm I created. He provided kindness, understanding, patience, and a willingness to do for others at no benefit to himself. He asked for nothing. Received nothing.

But maybe this is where I am wrong? Maybe this is where I miss the point that the program and the Bible have been trying to teach me, because I am too thick-headed to understand. Maybe in the giving of himself, he receives. A simple concept, yet virtually impossible to grasp, because I can't think my way to an understanding of this concept. It is not an analytical problem to be solved. I must surrender myself and feel this concept, live this concept, breathe it in and out, rely on it without hesitation at all times in all situations.

Maria and I get into the covered sidecar. The hotel man says something to the driver in Tagalog, and then we are off. The man drives slowly out a side entrance of the hotel. He turns down an alley, crosses a street, and continues down another alley, until we pull into the parking lot of another hotel. He drives through that parking lot, down a third alley, as he continues to twist our way from the chaos I created.

"What are Billy Sansone and Maria Giglio doing right now?" Maria asks.

"They are in Manila in a motorcycle sidecar, driving through alleys to escape a throng of homeless women and their children, after having gotten a man out of a Manila prison. Why do you ask?"

We laugh. Though the laugh is nervous, and the weight of what happened still presses upon us, I begin to relax as we move through the back alleys of Manila. How does this man even know where we are going? Did the man at the hotel tell him? Did Maria? As in so many other times in my life, I am being moved through life, out of danger, by the kindness and strength of others.

## Day 5
## Chapter Four

# And Let There Be Light

"SO WHERE ARE WE GOING to eat on our last night?" I ask. Such a trivial question considering what just took place, but I ask it, because I am thinking it, and we have to eat, and it is our last night, and life does not stop.

"There is a Korean place not too far from Adriadico that is highly recommended. We can go there." Maria and I have been in Manila for only five days, but she speaks as if she knows these strange and chaotic streets, because she does. We have logged miles, going from one agency to the other on our life and death errand.

I sit on the bed, already showered, waiting for Maria to dry her hair and put on her makeup before we head out. I shaved, put on one of my favorite shirts, combed my hair, and now I sit on the edge of this soft and inviting bed.

But the faces of those mothers come back to haunt me. I can see the desperation in their faces as they grabbed at my shirt, pleading at me with their eyes. They are so young yet aging quickly under the weight of a world that has forgotten them, if that world ever even knew who they were to begin with.

Do these women even exist? Do their children exist? If one dies, is there a record of their death? Is there a record of their birth, their life? Or were they born on the streets in a back alley, just like the children they are holding in their arms. Does anyone know that these women are sitting in a park with children in their laps suffering, suffering from unimaginable poverty? Hunger? Where do they go to the bathroom? Where do they change their babies' diapers? Do they have diapers? Do they sing lullabies to their children when they lay them down at night? Where do they lay them down? On a piece of cardboard? Do they brush their teeth at night, wash their face, "get ready" for bed?

And here I sit on the edge of a bed in an air-conditioned room waiting for the love of my life to finish getting ready. Then we will go out and dine wherever we want and come back to this bed, make love, and fall quietly asleep in each other's arms.

What did I do today? What was I thinking? I mean, what are five hundred pesos really going to do? Ease their pain for a few days? I guess that is something, but not much. These women, these children, need services, clean clothes for themselves and their children, toothpaste, toothbrushes, diapers, baby food, medicines, education, and a bed to sleep in. I did no great deed. In total, I handed out less money than I would spend on one night out in Tampa.

Then I ran from these women, ran from their problems and those of their children, ran from their existence, because acknowledging their existence is too much—because if I acknowledge their existence, how could I run? If I did run, then what kind of a person am I?

I ran and hid in a hotel waiting room, until I was whisked away in a sidecar down the back alleys of Manila, away from these women and their children and their poverty, their problems, their pain.

And here I sit on the edge of this bed. I will go out tonight and try to forget, forget their faces, forget their little ones bouncing up and down on their sides as they ran into the street trying to catch up to me, the blonde-headed American handing out pain relief. I will try to forget, because by forgetting, I can protect my world and the bubble in which I live. If I remember, a pin prick is inserted into my bubble, and it will slowly deflate, until I take some action to repair it.

"Love, love, you ready?" Maria asks from the bathroom.

"Yes, Mir," but ready for what I am not yet certain.

"I think the Korean restaurant is near Adriadico Circle," Maria says as we walk the streets on our last night in Manila. I begin to miss Manila even though I am walking in the heart of the city, like a person begins missing a loved one the night before leaving on a long business trip.

I walk slowly, holding Maria's hand. I am not in a hurry to get anywhere. I look down at my feet. They are on a cracked sidewalk in Manila, Philippines. They are exactly where they need to be, and so I am. I am not looking to get somewhere, into the future, thinking about tomorrow, or the next item on life's to do list. I am here. My feet are where they are supposed to be and so am I. Maria and I walk holding hands. I am content, happy, and in love. Then I see it.

"We are eating there," I say pointing to a restaurant I see on the other side of the street. It is an open-air place filled with locals. We approach. The tables spill out onto the sidewalk. The tables are plastic and so are the chairs. It is Friday night, and this is clearly a local place to decompress after a full week, and that's what is happening. Young and old Filipinos are laughing, smoking, eating, drinking, talking, and relaxing in the warm Manila air. There is no entrance to the restaurant. The street blends into the sidewalk, the sidewalk melding into the restaurant, a continuum of sorts. Yes, this is the place.

"Do we wait to be seated?" I ask, and Maria gives the answer I already know.

"No. I think we just sit down." Maria and I weave through some tables and find a seat at a blue green plastic table. We sit and I smile.

"What you thinking about, baby?" Maria asks.

"Nothing, just happy and content. I love it here. I love Manila. I'm not sure what it is about this dirty, smelly, lovely place."

"I know. I feel the same way."

"Five days ago, I thought you were going to have a panic attack."

"I know. I couldn't take it. The smells, the exhaust, the heat, and the poverty. I didn't think I could make it here."

"And now?"

Maria smiles. "I love it like you do. Well, maybe not as much as you do, but I still love it."

"What do you mean not as much as I do?"

"I can see it in your eyes. I can see it in the way you walk the streets. You are comfortable here. You feel at home here. You love it here."

"Do you think we could … "

"No, I don't think we can move here."

"How did you know that's what I was going to ask?"

"Because I know you, Billy Sansone. I know that Billy Sansone is trying to figure out a way, some way, to move to Manila, but sorry, sweet love, it's just not going to work."

"But … "

"No buts, baby. We can't move to Manila. It's too far from our kids."

I look down into my lap. Maria does know me. I do want to move here, though I know I can't, so I sit back. No need to think about a tomorrow that will never come, for I am here tonight. We are at Erra's, a ramen noddle restaurant in central Manila. It is not listed in Zagats. There are no stars next to its name. The chairs are plastic and the floor is bare concrete. The ceiling shows the metal support beams that hold up the tin roof, and the tables are filled with families, sweethearts, and friends gathered together to break bread.

I look around. "This is so much better than a top-rated Korean restaurant."

"I agree. This is perfect. Absolutely perfect." Our waiter comes up and I let Maria order. Maria orders our food, a Red Horse Filipino lager for her, and a water for me. Our drinks come. Maria proposes a toast.

"We did it baby. We came here to get Ron out, and we got that shit done. To you and me, baby." We clink glasses. The waiter brings out the food and places it between Maria and me to share.

"What are these?" I point to the plate next to the noodles.

"I think they are marigolds."

"Is that usual? I mean to eat marigolds?"

"No, I have never eaten marigolds before, but I think they are the only greens on the menu." So Maria and I settle into our meal of noodles and marigolds and everything is right with my world.

Halfway through dinner, I head to the restroom. It is located at the back of the restaurant. I walk down a narrow corridor that leads to a door that says, "Ladies." Just to the right is a urinal with yellow sign taped to the side of it that reads, "Men." No door, just a urinal sitting at the end of the corridor next to the door that says Ladies.

There is a cage next to the urinal with a chicken in it. I can't remember if I saw chicken on the menu, but if we decide on more food, I think I will stay with the noodles and marigolds and leave this bird in the bathroom alone. The floor is exposed concrete, and it is cracking.

I use the bathroom hoping no one else comes down the corridor, and then turn to wash my hands. The sink is old and stained. There is no soap, so I run my hands under the water and dry them on my shirt. There are no towels, or for that matter, toilet paper for men. There is no toilet for men. Just the urinal with the yellow sign taped to the side of it.

I walked back down the corridor filled with empty crates, bicycles and other boxes. I realize that the entire restaurant is open air, and the tin roof is almost like the roof of a very large porch. Maria has finished eating. I sit next to her.

"Isn't this place perfect? I mean absolutely perfect." I ask.

"It is." She looks to the right, and then to the left. "It really is." Not many people I know would say that this restaurant is perfect, but Maria does, and she means it.

I want life to PAUSE. We go back to Tampa tomorrow, and I am not ready. It's not that I am not ready to be in Tampa. I love Tampa. It is that I am not ready to leave Manila. I am not ready to leave the chaotic streets, the traffic, the street vendors, and the unexplainable pull this place has on me.

Manila is not a vacation destination, but I feel more at peace, more at ease than any other vacation I have even been on, even through all the trials, agencies, and the waiting of the past week.

Thinking back, I loved every second of it, and now I sit on the edge of its passing, and I want to hold on, as a child does to Christmas vacation, hoping beyond hope that when I open my eyes tomorrow, it will be Christmas morning again—but it won't be.

I look at my phone. Two messages appear. One from Chito and another from Ron.

Chito: "Nice pic. The Dream Team. Thanks, Bill."

Ron: "I'm on the plane. Thanks again for making all this happen. Special thanks to Maria who is very much an Angel. I'll write you soon and let you know how I'm … "

I close my eyes and bow my head. We did it. Unbelievable. Ron is on a plane. He is out of that shithole. Before we left for

*And Let There Be Light. We Did It!*

dinner, I sent Chito a picture of the three of us waiting outside an office at the BI.

When we arrived in Manila, I had only two items on my agenda. Meet Chito at the Bayleaf Hotel at 2 p.m. on Monday, and at some point, go to the United States Embassy and pitch a fit. Now, Ron is on a plane. He is free! Holy Shit!! We did it!!!

"What's going on, love love?" I hand Maria the phone without saying a word. She reads the text messages. She looks up at me. Her eyes are sweet, tender.

"Congratulations, Billy Sansone, you did it. No one, and I mean *no one* would do for a client what you just did for Ron. You flew 9,000 miles across the world to help him. Who does that? You paid for this trip yourself. Really? What lawyer would do that? You saved his life."

"What about you? You didn't even know Ron."

"I only came because I don't like to leave your side. It had nothing to do with Ron." I laugh. "It's the truth," Maria adds.

"Can you believe it? Ron is on a plane," I say.

"No. I really can't. I can't believe it. It is truly unbelievable."

"How will we tell our friends, our family, what happened this week?"

"We can't. Not really. It's too much." Maria looks around the restaurant and then out into the street as motorcycles, Jeepneys, and people passing by. "You can't describe this place. You just have to be here. I mean from the Embassy to BI to BI Camp Bagong to Ron's suitcases to Jodi to Homer to all the waiting, all the travelling back and forth across this city. We didn't even get here until early Monday morning, and it is Friday night, and Ron is out. On a plane. Free from that horrible place."

Maria smiles and reaches across the table and grabs my hands. "No, we won't be able to explain it to anyone. It's too unbelievable. I can't believe it myself, and I am sitting at an open air restaurant in

Manila with you, having done what we did, and I still don't believe it."

She sits back in her chair. "Seems like we have been here a month, and we have been here for only five days."

"So when we came, you didn't think we were going to get Ron out?"

"Hell, no. Not a chance. Did you?"

"I wasn't sure. I didn't want to think too hard about it."

"But you did do it. Ron is a free man. He would have died in that jail if you had not come."

"If *we* had not come."

"Yes, but I never would have come. You are the one who said we are going to Manila to get a client out of jail. That's crazy. Who does that for a client?"

"We do, *Della*, we do." All is right with the world, for at least this moment at Erras, sitting across the green plastic table from the love of my life, knowing Ron is on a plane likely drinking a glass of well-deserved red wine.

And God said, "Let there be light," and I see the light. For once, I see God's light, a peace that passes my limited and fragile understanding. The world is spinning, but for once I am not, I am firmly seated in this chair.

Step Twelve says, "Having had a spiritual awakening as a result of these steps ... " Is that what this is, a spiritual awakening? Am I going to screw it up by thinking about it, over-thinking about it, turning it around, looking at it from all angles, looking for some flaw, or some reason to say, "Yup, I knew it. Life cannot be that good. It cannot be that simple. I just knew it." Not tonight."

We slowly finish our food and linger over our drinks until Maria finally says, "Let's go home, Bill Bill." And with that we slip out of the restaurant and onto the streets. We hold hands in silence. We pass families bundled up on the sidewalk for the night. Maria does not say anything, but I know she is crying inside if the tears have not pushed their way out.

We come to the Malate church, and I pause. I look up at the magnificent structure as if to say goodbye—and it is goodbye, as we leave in the morning, but I want her to know that I will remember her, and I will be back. Maria does not ask me what I am doing or thinking. She knows. She gently holds my hand and gives me the time I need, not caring whether it is a long or short goodbye. We continue down the street towards our hotel, two lovers in love.

"The first morning we were here, I didn't think you were going to make it," I say breaking our silence.

"I didn't either. Seems like so long ago. I couldn't take this city. It was too much. Too overwhelming. The people, the smells, even the street food. I couldn't take it."

"And now?"

"I love this place and the people. I still hate the smells, but they don't bother me."

"So you really don't think we could move here?"

"NO!" Maria laughs.

"I mean, the kids could come to visit for the entire summer." We laugh and Maria holds me tight. The life and death errand is over, even if just for today. We only have a daily reprieve, and I am learning to live at peace with that.

I am beginning to see the way out, a way out of myself. I am my own worst enemy, and if I dwell within myself, a darkness comes over me. I went in through the doors of alcoholics anonymous, because it was the last house on the block, but the only one with a light in the window. If I didn't make that step, never crossed that threshold into a new life, I would not be walking down the streets of Manila holding Maria's hand.

I don't know where I would be, but I would not be here. And God said, "Let there be light." I never thought about what this meant,

meant for me in my life, in my recovery, and in my relationship with others and with God. Now I do, and I am beginning to see there is a light. I can see it now, and I ask for help, humbly ask for help to stay on the path.

"What's wrong, lover?" Maria asks as she puts her arm around me.

"Nothing, love. Right at this moment, not a damn thing."

# Closing Statement

## Manila – Six Months Later

# The Blacklist

MARIA AND I RETURNED TO MANILA six months later to get Ron off the country's blacklist. Because the Filipino government arrested Ron at the behest of the United States on a warrant for a sex offender charged with the possession of child pornography, Ron was placed on the Philippines' blacklist, never to return to the country once he was escorted from the jail to the airport and placed on a plane. The country deemed him an undesirable.

"What about my house? What about all of my belongings? I have two pre-paid credit cards with over $20,000 on them sitting in my desk drawer. What do I do about them? What about my girlfriend and our child? What about … "

"I'm not sure what to tell you, Ron." But I was sure. I did know what to tell Ron, I just didn't know how to tell him, because if I did, I knew what would follow. I knew that the only way to get Ron off the country's blacklist was to return to Manila, return to the Bureau of Immigration, return to Homer, Jody, to the heat, the cars, the Jeepneys, motorcycles, exhaust, smells, food, and of course, the crushing poverty.

Ron would only get off the blacklist if Maria and I again travelled nine thousand miles again to stand in endless lines and pitch a fit when and wherever necessary. That was how we got Ron out of jail.

To say his release was secured by my legal acumen and international diplomatic negotiating skills would be telling you a story developed, honed, and crafted by my Ego—a story that is not true, but one I would believe and in telling you, I would want you to believe it, too.

But we got Ron out of jail by standing in lines, refusing to give up, and pitching fits at opportune moments.

Our return to Manila was not precipitated by Ron's call that night, as he sat in a hotel room in Cambodia begging for my assistance. Maria and I decided to return to Manila for the children—the street children. Those precious dirty faces we saw as we walked from one government agency to the next, lining the sidewalk with smiles on their faces, and a love I could feel emanating from their hearts. We returned to Manila for them, hoping to do something to alleviate their suffering, to better understand their joyless plight, and to bring light to an insidious darkness.

Kilos Bayanihan (KB) means a good gesture in Tagalog and is also the name of a charity run by Alan Nielwand, who lives in Las Vegas. I found Alan and his charity on the Internet one night looking for a way to contribute to the street kids of Manila. I sent Alan an email informing him I was interested in his work, and he promptly got back to me. We talked and quickly forged a bond that has woven into a friendship. It is a friendship that centers around the desire to literally lift these Filipino children out of the garbage.

I quickly realized that Kilos Bayanihan, or KB, was a true labor of love for Alan, for he labored, and he labored mightily, and he loved—loved the street kids of Malate and Tongo, and all the slums in and around Manila. While Alan's charity is small, I could see that it was doing amazing work. Alan had put together a number of dedicated volunteers who would bring food, education, and love to the streets of Manila. I wanted to be a part of that love.

"Maria and I are heading back to Manila in June. Do you think we could work with your volunteers and help the kids?"

"Of course, you can. I will set it up." Alan did and we did. Maria and my experience working with KB for the Manila street kids could be a separate book, a book filled with love, prayer, heartache, frustration, tenderness, and tears. Here is a bit of what we saw:

At first Maria called him "Lover." Only the kids whose parents signed them up could be a part of the KB project that morning in Malate square, for there had to be some type of order to the day. KB not only feeds, but tries to offer instruction to the kids. "Lover" did not have a KB nametag, so he could not participate.

However, Lover found a place in Maria's heart and tugged on it, so Maria made him a name tag. She wrote "Lover" on his tag, for that was what he was and that is what he exuded. Lover, whose name we later determined was JemJem, was about six years old. His clothes were filthy, his skin was filthy, and his teeth were rotting out of his mouth, but he carried God's love in this heart. Maria felt that love and was drawn to its warmth and power, as she put Lover under her arm that day.

In Malate Square, Maria and I fed the street children. We also tried to give some educational instruction, but Maria was much more successful than me.

All of the children, were well-behaved, respectful, and polite. They might not have food, clothes, or a roof over their heads, but these children do have manners, respect, and smiles—maybe that was the only thing their parents could offer them.

Maria bonded with the street kids of Malate that day. We were hugged and gave hugs. The children adored Maria, and we returned to Malate while we were trying to get Ron off the blacklist.; During our week in Manila, we passed out clothes and took a couple of the kids to their first restaurant. The day before we returned to Tampa, Maria and I went to Malate to say goodbye to the kids, Even before Maria crossed the street, the kids came running.

"You are the Pied Piper of Malate," I joked, but the joke was based on truth, and the kids hung on to her, laughing and jumping with excitement just to be in her presence. Maria said her goodbyes, while I stood nearby and watched. A happy sadness filled the square. Maria did not want to leave these kids—leave them to what? What future do they have? What can we do? The children took turns holding Maria's hand. These kids are desperate for so many necessities—love and affection are just two of them.

The young girl came up to my side saying, "I will miss you, too, Mr. Billy." . She smiled and slid her hand into mine. My heart melted and then broke.

*Maria, the pied piper of Manila.*

North Manila Cemetery is also home to many of Manila's street children. The cemetery is a sprawling place that has become its own city of sorts, or at least a neighborhood. Maria and I met our contact with KB, and when all of the other volunteers for the day arrived, we proceeded to the cemetery. I had not asked why we were going there, but I just thought it must be the meeting place for the day, like Malate square was on the day before.

As Maria and I walked deep into the cemetery along its windy paths, Maria noticed them first and asked, "Are those street signs?" They were hung on makeshift poles for makeshift street signs.

"Why would those be street signs?" The answer came only moments later.

"I think people live here," Maria said. A look of bewildered realization and shock descended upon her face. "I think the families and the kids we are servicing today live in this cemetery."

I looked closely into the crypts as we continued to walk. Inside some of the stone structures I could see chairs, clothes hanging in the corner, cups on top of the crumbling granite coffins, and then I saw people. At first, it was just two men playing cards at a plastic table, but as we continued deeper into the cemetery, I saw women with children beside them.

These families do not live on the street, but in this cemetery. The abandoned crypts had become their shelter and the cemetery their neighborhood. I closed my eyes, not knowing what to think. My mind was not being able to process or comprehend what I knew to be true. These families with these children actually live in this cemetery.

We came to a clearing next to a large crumbling mausoleum. The grass was long and unkempt. Trash, some old and some new, lay about. Then they started to come, from where I am not sure. How they knew we had arrived is also unknown, but they did.

At first, I saw the children running towards us with smiles on their faces, as if arriving at a local park on a Saturday morning. Next came the parents, who also had smiles on their faces. These children, the children of North Manila Cemetery, are the same as the street children of Malate, without any material possessions, but possessing what I can only describe as an energy, a force, a power of life I had never experienced before.

Most of the children spoke English, and they translated what I was saying to the other children who only spoke Tagalog. I don't have any recollection of what I said that day. Although I'm sure it wasn't important, I clearly remember, and will never forgot, how the children sat silently on the crumbling wall behind the mausoleum and silently listened to me, as if I were their teacher and their final grade depended on their attention. I was not their teacher and they were not in school, but there they sat on that wall silently listening to me, a blonde-headed stranger from a strange land.

I looked over at Maria. She had her own group of kids. As with me, they were silent, paying attention, and listening to every word she said, this foreign woman from a foreign land.

I remember thinking that Maria is much more equipped to give this lesson to the kids than I am, and we should combine our groups so these kids do not miss out on listening to a real teacher, not some criminal defense attorney windbag. However, this windbag spoke on and the kids listened.

I remember the smiles and laughter from both the windbag and the children. I found a peace that passes all understanding sitting with those kids in the North Manila Cemetery, the highest form of love, tranquility of mind and spirit—a state I have never reached, but have been searching for all my life.

Standing in that cemetery I was in the present moment. There was no other time, no other issues, no other concerns pressing in. My clients and their problems were tucked safely away in Tampa. My mind was not rethinking about yesterday and fretting about tomorrow. I was in the space of the now, a place alien and elusive for me.

In my forty-six years on earth, I had only occasionally stepped foot upon this road. My mind operates in a perpetual state of dis-ease, which is the root of my disease. I suffer from a hopeless state of mind, but in that space with those kids lined up on that wall in that cemetery next to that crumbling mausoleum, I found a hope that no amount of money, no accolades or awards, no jury trial victories, and no amount of material possessions or anything of this world could give me. The peace came from within, so I know I need not search for it.

As I write these words, I am transported back to that space, to that time, and I don't want to leave, but continue on with another paragraph, some other detail that I might have forgotten to tell, anything to stay here, in the place I am trying to find on the road upon which I am praying to travel. I am not in the North Manila Cemetery. I am sitting at Maria's kitchen table. The world is loud, banging at the outside, trying to get in.

Maria and I were successful in getting Ron removed from the blacklist, although we didn't get the formal letter authorizing his removal until months after we had returned to Tampa. Though we were never certain about the outcome, we were certain of the process.

We first made our way to the BI. "Ron must be a very good client," Homer said as Jodie showed us into his office. Maria and I filed the formal petition for Ron's removal from the blacklist with the Commissioner, gave a copy to Homer, and stood in line at window number 23 to pay the fees necessary to have his paperwork processed. We would not leave until we were informed that everything we needed to file to have Ron removed from the blacklist had been completed. Maria tried to push the Commissioner of the Bureau of Immigration to decide before we left the country. (However, not even Della Street herself could pull that one off.)

In between meetings, standing in lines, and waiting for official word about our petition, Maria and I returned to our Starbucks across the street from the BI in Intramuros. We sat outside at a table and drank coffee planning our next steps for Ron and also with our service work for KB. Manila had become a familiar place. The heat, exhaust, smells, cars, busses, Jeepneys, motorcycles, food, and the people are all part of a collective whole of this magical city. I use the word magical because I don't understand its power, but I don't have to. Some things cannot be understood, and that is okay for me now.

"Constant vigilance is the price of recovery." An eighty-one-year-old man with fifty-three years of sobriety told me this as we sailed on a cruise ship just off the coast of Cuba. We were the only two people in the meeting on the ship that Friday morning. I am a child, just beginning my journey, and constant vigilance is the only thing that will keep me in the middle of the boat on the right path. I will continue to try to abandon myself to God, admit my faults to Him and to another human being, seek to clear away the wreckage of my past, and give freely of what I find.

May the God of your understanding bless and keep you until then.

All money earned by the purchase of this book will benefit the
Daniel J. Cavallaro Foundation

## djc-foundation.org

### The Daniel J. Cavallaro Foundation Mission

In his short but impactful life, Daniel Cavallaro faced all adversity and obstacles with strength and perseverance. From the classroom to the hockey rink to the mixed marital arts ring, Daniel worked tirelessly to achieve his goals in life. Daniel lived his life by Gospel teaching, "I can do all things through Christ who strengthens me." Philippians 4:13. To all those who knew and loved him, Daniel was a bright light gone too soon from this world.

The Daniel J. Cavallaro Foundation's mission is to pass along Daniel's gift of strength and perseverance to underprivileged youths by helping them attain their goals, whether in the classroom, on a sporting field, in a culinary academy, or in a trade school. One hundred percent of the monies donated to the Foundation will go directly to assist underprivileged youths overcome the obstacles before them so their light might shine upon the world.

Daniel would be proud of his Foundation, and he will always be its guiding light.

### Thank you for your support, Maria and Bill Sansone

Bill Sansone is a former prosecutor, current criminal defense attorney, and an open water swimmer.

Maria Sansone is an elementary school teacher, yoga enthusiast, and President of the Daniel J. Cavallaro Foundation.

Printed in the USA
CPSIA information can be obtained
at www.ICGtesting.com
CBHW031349140724
11411CB00014B/437